LEADERSHIP PERSPECTIVES

WITHDRÁWN

NURSULTAN NAZARBAYEV

PERSONAL ESSAYS, SPEECHES,
ARTICLES AND INSIGHTS

LEADERSHIP PERSPECTIVES

FIRST

"It is vitally important that states and societies join forces to tackle the problems of poverty, famine, epidemics, unemployment, and the battle against the aftermath of natural disasters and man-made disasters. This must form part of the new architecture for a secure and harmonious world."

— Nursultan Nazarbayev
President of the Republic of Kazakhstan

"As it develops, Kazakhstan is becoming an increasingly significant regional actor. It has aspirations to serve on the UN Security Council, deepen its relationship with the EU, and has recently gained membership of the WTO. Its ultimate goal is to become one of the thirty most developed countries in the world by 2050. I believe that Britain and Kazakhstan can, by working together on new and more ambitious joint projects in the future, help each other to succeed in the global race."

— Rt Hon David Cameron MP
Prime Minister of the United Kingdom of Great Britain and Northern Ireland

The publishers wish to acknowledge
the assistance and support of
Shell in the preparation of this book

Royal Dutch Shell plc
Carel van Byland 30, The Hague, 2596 HR, Netherlands
Tel: +31 70 377 3944 Fax: +31 70 377 6790
Web: www.shell.com.kz

ABOUT THE AUTHOR

Nursultan Nazarbayev has a unique vantage point. In 1991, following the break-up of the Soviet Union, Nursultan Nazarbayev, became the first President of an independent Kazakhstan. The country faced difficult times and through determined leadership he has transformed Kazakhstan into one of the fastest developing and most dynamic states in Eurasia. Nursultan Nazarbayev has also instigated many international initiatives with the aim of maintaining global security, promoting economic development and encouraging inter-faith harmony. It was President Nursultan Nazarbayev who took the decision in 1991 to renounce the world's fourth largest nuclear arsenal, enabling Kazakhstan and the entire Central Asian region to become free of nuclear weapons.

President Nazarbayev was re-elected to a fifth term as President of Kazakhstan on 26th April, 2015.

CONTENTS

LIST OF PHOTOGRAPHIC PLATES

INTRODUCTION

I first visited Kazakhstan shortly after independence and have had a chance to witness the country's many significant changes and achievements over the past twenty or so years. Kazakhstan's transformation has been extraordinary – steering a careful course from a command economy to an open market-led economic structure. Kazakhstan's forthcoming 25th Anniversary of Independence is an important milestone in the country's development.

President Nursultan Nazarbayev has been the architect of his country's success – overseeing dramatic improvements in the living standards of the people of Kazakhstan, wisely establishing stable international relationships and creating the conditions for significant economic growth. Kazakhstan has attracted USD 208 billion of foreign investment since 2005 and recently gained WTO membership. With its strategic geographic location and dominant position in Central Asia, Kazakhstan now plays an important international role, helping to maintain stability in the region and offering significant investment opportunities.

This book provides a fascinating insight into the thinking, political ideology and philosophy of Kazakhstan's long-standing President. *Leadership Perspectives* explains Nursultan Nazarbayev's vision for the planet, placing the current geopolitical situation in its historical, political, economic, religious and philosophical context. This collection of speeches represents Nursultan Nazarbayev's plan for global harmony and Kazakhstan's place in the new world order.

The preparation of this book is the culmination of work by specialist editors and translators. I would particularly like to thank H.E. Mr Erzhan Kazykhanov, Kazakhstan's distinguished Ambassador to London, for his vital contribution in bringing this important work to fruition. I would also like to thank Lord Richards, Lord Robertson and Lord Cormack for their thoughtful and personal forewords.

Following his re-election, Nursultan Nazarbayev, was inaugurated for a fifth term as President on April 29th 2015, at a special ceremony at the Palace of Independence in Astana. This re-election, and Kazakhstan's dramatic transformation since independence, marks out President Nursultan Nazarbayev as the greatest nation builder to emerge from the post-Soviet era in Central Asia. This book seeks to provide greater understanding of the leadership perspectives of a remarkable national leader.

Rupert Goodman DL
Chairman, British Kazakh Society
Chairman, FIRST

MESSAGE

I am delighted to extend my sincere congratulations on the occasion of the 25th anniversary of the Republic of Kazakhstan. Since independence, under the leadership of President Nazarbayev, the Republic of Kazakhstan has developed rapidly. Today, Kazakhstan is a country distinguished by its strong sense of national identity, its vibrant economy and its success in achieving both multi-ethnic harmony and political stability.

The people of Kazakhstan can be justly proud of their country's many significant achievements in the past 25 years. Internationally, Kazakhstan has grown to become a recognised regional leader in Central Asia – a country which contributes significantly to regional stability in an often volatile part of the world. The Republic's contributions in the field of nuclear non-proliferation, led by President Nazarbayev himself, have been widely acknowledged for the benefits they have brought to international peace and security. Kazakhstan's recent accession to the World Trade Organisation in 2015 is also a very important accomplishment, and recognition of the Republic's further integration into the global economy.

Nationally, the government's proactive policies to encourage diversity and understanding have led to a degree of multi-ethnic harmony and inter-religious tolerance that has become a hallmark of Kazakhstani society. The new capital city of Astana, rightly hailed as the city of the future, epitomises the diversity and tolerance of Kazakhstan's people. Over the past decade, Kazakhstan's economic growth has been one of the highest in the world, and its record of economic development and improved welfare of its citizens is an example to its peers. The government's efforts to improve the business environment and establish a benign and welcoming investment climate has helped to attract significant foreign investment across the economy.

Shell, for its part, began its business operations in Kazakhstan in 1992. Today the company is one of the largest foreign investors in the country, with interests in three major projects. Shell is proud to be a strategic partner of the Republic of Kazakhstan and is committed to developing and nurturing that co-operation long into the future. Shell hopes to continue investing in the country, and working together with the Government of Kazakhstan for the benefit of the Republic and its people, for many decades to come.

Like all strong nations, Kazakhstan is not resting on its past achievements but is continually looking to the future. President Nazarbayev's vision for the country's future is vividly outlined in the Strategy 2050 – and I would like to wish the people of Kazakhstan every success in implementing these plans, for the benefit of all the people of this great country.

Ben Van Beurden
Chief Executive Officer
Royal Dutch Shell plc

PREFACE

The location of Khazakhstan and therefore its geo-strategic significance cannot be underestimated. Its physical size and its wealth of natural resources means that carries great weight and influence in both Central Asia and to the wider world.

Nursultan Nazarbayev has been President of this significant country since its independence and its separation from the Soviet Union. As Secretary General of NATO I met him on a number of occasions both in Astana and in meetings of the Euro Atlantic Partnership Council which I chaired. His country played a full part in the Partnership for Peace – NATO's outreach body to the countries to the East.

The writings of President Nazarbayev are therefore of great interest to all who study and trade with his country. How Kazakhstan has made the journey from the USSR to today will fascinate and educate those who do business, and want to do business, with this important nation.

Rt Hon The Lord Robertson of Port Ellen KT GCMG HonFRSE PC,
Secretary General of NATO 1999-2003,
UK Secretary of State for Defence 1997-1999

PROLOGUE

Few national leaders have expounded their beliefs and aspirations for their country as clearly and compellingly as President Nazarbayev. We at FIRST are delighted to be producing this landmark publication to mark his Official Visit to the United Kingdom, for we are very conscious of the importance of continuing to develop the commercial and cultural ties between Kazakhstan and the United Kingdom.

When we published the official report to mark Prime Minister David Cameron's visit to Kazakhstan in 2013 he stressed, in his introductory message, that Kazakhstan stood out as a country ripe with commercial opportunities. In the years since then many of those opportunities have been developed and as Kazakhstan approaches its 25th anniversary as an independent nation we need together to seek out new opportunities that will be of mutual benefit and in the process further strengthen the ties between us.

The vision and determination of President Nazarbayev shines out in these pages and I know that everyone who recognises the importance of British Kazakhstan relations will welcome this volume as much as Lord Hurd of Westwell and I do. May this book mark the beginning of a wider and better understanding between our nations and further a friendship that is already a strong and binding one.

Lord Cormack FSA DL

FOREWORD

I have dedicated most of my working life to designing and implementing strategy to protect the United Kingdom's people, interests and friends. When I look at Kazakhstan under the leadership of Nursultan Nazarbayev, I see a country that has really strived to get its strategy right.

Of course, Kazakhstan is blessed with ample natural resources that will help to make it one of the most developed countries in the world. What makes Kazakhstan stand out is its adherence to a clear, well-thought out strategic idea that has remained constant throughout much of the twenty-five years since its independence.

This strategy is based on engagement with all regional states and creating an environment that is friendly to foreign direct investment. This is coupled with the promotion of ethnic and sectarian harmony at home that has allowed Kazakhstan to avoid ethnic implosion and civil war seen elsewhere in the region. Through careful management, it has also avoided the worst of the radicalisation and violent extremism that has become such a feature in many of our societies in the past ten years.

As a result, Kazakhstan is a beacon of stability in Central Asia. Such stability encourages a virtuous circle by attracting more external investment which, under wise leadership, helps to underpin greater security that itself attracts greater investment. Kazakhstan's success story over the past twenty-five years has been unique: from an agricultural Soviet Republic to one of the world's fastest developing industrial powers. It is an exciting time for Kazakhstan and her many friends.

Today, much of the bilateral British-Kazakhstan relationship is focused on trade and investment. This is right and proper: over 600 British companies are active in Kazakhstan today. In 2013, David Cameron became the first British Prime Minister ever to visit Kazakhstan, promoting these links. Such engagement benefits both our counties and boosts both our economies; and a strong economy is the most important contribution to a nation's security.

But we should not forget that, recently, Kazakhstan has played a major role in supporting the United Kingdom's and NATO's military operations. Kazakhstan has been our staunchest Central Asian ally. It enabled the resupply of NATO's International Security Assistance Force in Afghanistan from the north, rather than being reliant on the vulnerable road supply route through Pakistan. Without Kazakhstan's active help, the United Kingdom would have found it very difficult to withdraw our military forces from Afghanistan in 2014. Even today, Kazakhstan supports the West's post-withdrawal strategy, promoting regional engagement and development inside Afghanistan.

So, our two countries are tied by mutual interest and a genuine shared sense of doing the right thing. These values underpin our national strategies that have so much in common. In Kazakhstan, these values and the successful national strategy they produce are the result of President Nazarbayev's philosophy and vision; not just for Kazakhstan but also globally. This is what I believe makes this book so interesting and valuable: I commend it to you.

Lord Richards of Herstmonceux GCB CBE DSO DL
Chief of the Defence Staff 2010-2013

ONE

INTERNATIONAL RELATIONS

Each year, H.E. Nursultan Nazarbayev, President of Kazakhstan, meets the heads of foreign diplomatic missions accredited to Kazakhstan. At the meeting, held in 2012 the Head of State outlined the strategically important tasks and key priorities of Kazakhstan's foreign policy.

This year marks the 20th Anniversary of our accession to the United Nations as well as the 20th anniversary of the establishment of diplomatic relations with China, Britain and France. February marked the same anniversary in relation to Germany and March to Turkey. This continues every month of this year with regard to all those countries with which we currently have a relationship. In May, we celebrate the 20th anniversary of my first official visit to the United States as head of state. Also in May is the anniversary of the "major" Treaty of Friendship, Cooperation and Mutual Assistance with the Russian Federation.

As you know, we have exchanged congratulatory messages with the heads of a number of states on the occasion of the anniversary of our relationship with them. We have many more exchanges ahead of us. Today I congratulate all those present in the jubilee year of our bilateral relations with each of them.

In July, we will celebrate the 20th anniversary of the establishment of the professional diplomatic service in Kazakhstan. I would like to state that the support and experience of the many foreign diplomats who have worked in Kazakhstan for the past two decades, as part of their countries' diplomatic missions, has played a major role in the formation and development of our own service.

In the course of two decades, Kazakhstan has built constructive relationships with our closest neighbours and all those countries interested in developing cooperation with our country. I wish to thank all the ambassadors and heads of foreign diplomatic missions, and all the diplomats, for the contribution they are making to the strengthening of bilateral relations between us.

Much progress has been achieved in the 20 years since our country became independent. This is underlined by looking at the results of Kazakhstan's path towards our 20th anniversary of independence celebrations. The 2011 anniversary further confirmed the dynamic rate of economic growth in Kazakhstan, despite the continuing global economic crisis. GDP grew by 7.5 per cent and GDP per capita has passed USD 11,000. We are proud of these indicators as the figures have grown sixteen-fold during the years of independence. We started with USD 700 per head.

Within two years, about 400 new production facilities have been built for the industrial and innovative development of the country. In the industrial sector, 90,000 new jobs have been created. Sixty new businesses have already reached their target capacity and have manufactured products worth USD 2 billion. We all know what has been happening around the world, yet the unemployment rate in Kazakhstan has been falling.

A good start has been made on innovative development. Expenditure on technological innovation in industry has increased eightfold and reached KZT 220 billion. Labour productivity in the manufacturing sector as a whole has risen by 20 per cent. This industry is our primary focus.

Large-scale transformation is continuing in the agricultural sector. The state is supporting agriculture and today Kazakhstan is self-sufficient for two thirds of our quality products and raw materials. We will achieve 100 per cent security in all foodstuffs in the next few years. We are expanding our agricultural export opportunities to global markets especially in corn and meat products.

Kazakhstan's foreign trade turnover in 2011 amounted to USD 126 billion. By comparison with 2010, it grew by 40 per cent. Exports of Kazakhstan's products to world markets totalled USD 88 billion. Of these, more than USD 21 billion was in non-primary goods. This is a first for our economy. Last year, Kazakhstan's economy attracted USD 18 billion of direct foreign investment. This is a good omen for our country. The country's total foreign exchange reserves amount to USD 82 billion, including a National Fund of USD 47 billion, which means that the foreign exchange reserves now account for more than 40 per cent of GDP.

We are continuing to implement the Strategy "Kazakhstan-2030", which the country has been developing effectively for half a decade. This is clearly shown by the results of the last parliamentary elections. Elections have become a new step forward for our young democracy and the Majilis now houses three political parties. Generally speaking, Kazakhstan is becoming a mature country.

In my address to the nation, I put forward a programme of social and economic modernisation, which is very important at this time. We are simultaneously addressing two interrelated objectives. The first is to develop the economy, industry and agriculture. I have already announced some new industrial projects and we are actively planning to develop the electricity sector which will be necessary to aid industry's development. We are commencing construction of the Balkhash thermal power plant and completing the construction of the Moinak hydroelectric plant, to assist this.

Our plans also include improving gas supplies across the country by the construction of a network of internal pipelines. We are planning to develop the gas and chemicals industry and oil refining facilities. In the next few years, the Kazakhstan section of the "Western Europe – Western China" highway will be completed (2,700 km.) In Central Kazakhstan, construction of the 1,200km "Zhezkazgan-Beineu" railway is commencing. There will also be the 200 km Arkalyk-Shubarkol branch line. This will ensure that we have the necessary infrastructure in the country's developing regions and make Kazakhstan a transit state.

These and many other projects represent excellent opportunities for foreign investors, whom we constantly encourage to work with us. A particularly important aspect of our plans is the promotion of a favourable investment climate in the country and in this regard we have outlined the development of "electronic government", strengthening the fight against corruption and reducing administrative barriers to business.

We believe that our large-scale economic initiatives, including infrastructure projects, will be of interest to foreign businesses that wish to work in partnership with us on mutually beneficial terms. I invite all countries to cooperate with Kazakhstan. We are ready to cooperate in the field of public-private enterprise, with foreign businesses, the Government and our pension funds all working together.

The second strategic objective is to modernise social structures and to raise the level of welfare of our people. Creating the best living conditions for Kazakhstanis will also guarantee high rates of economic growth and help to preserve the stability of the country. This will be the primary objective of our domestic policies in the decades to come.

I believe that our plans to roll out a large-scale programme of employment, housing, regional development, education and health will also be of interest to many of our foreign partners. Parliament is currently considering the issue of how to fund these projects. I reviewed the projects yesterday. They are all fully-funded, and we will start work this spring.

Kazakhstan is a young state. Our great strength lies in the fact that the relations between Kazakhstan and other countries are developing on a "clean slate". There are virtually no significant problems that we have inherited from the depths of the past that cannot be resolved through constructive dialogue, mutual understanding and broad cooperation.

In 20 years, we have been able to resolve the issue of state borders with all our neighbouring countries. Our external borders are of good neighbourliness and cooperation. Thanks to our efforts with all the countries in the region of Central Asia, Kazakhstan and the other post-Soviet states have managed to establish a clear modern system of international relations in all strategic areas.

First of all, our region is a nuclear weapon-free zone. This status is enshrined in the Treaty of Semipalatinsk. We intend to strengthen the regional nuclear-free regime and pass on our experience of it to other regional communities in the modern world. Secondly, Central Asia has massive potential to become one of the global centres of energy production. We see the future of the region in the development of oil and gas pipelines, exporting our hydrocarbon resources to Europe and Asia. One promising possibility is to strengthen the hydroelectric potential of Central Asia. We call upon our neighbours to join forces with us to solve all outstanding water management issues on the principles of mutual understanding and equality.

Kazakhstan, as the holder of significant uranium reserves, is planning to develop peaceful nuclear energy. This is in the interests of our country and of all the countries in our region, as well as all those of our external partners who are interested in developing cooperation.

Thirdly, Kazakhstan has been a consistent supporter of Central Asian integration. Our proposals have been put to all our neighbours. Through integration we perceive extensive opportunities for the implementation of joint large-scale investment projects. In my opinion, it would be sensible to consider the creation of a regional free trade zone and to take concerted action in the field of cross-border labour migration. It is also necessary to create and develop a unified Central Asian network of railways and roads. The states in our region could work appropriately on the creation of a unified food-production pool for the region given that we have sufficient energy and food resources.

Fourthly, we see a huge opportunity for the region to be an outpost of the collective global community in the fight against international terrorism and extremism, illegal migration, drug trafficking and other modern-day challenges. In this regard, Kazakhstan welcomes the activities of the specialist offices of the UN, OSCE (Organisation for Security and Co-operation in Europe) and other international organisations. Kazakhstan sees its mission in the region as consistently strengthening the system of regional security and stability.

We are ready to intensify our cooperation on all issues and problems of regional security, including within the framework of the CSTO (Collective Security Treaty Organisation), SCO (Shanghai Cooperation Organisation), CICA (Conference on Interaction and Confidence Building Measures in Asia), as well as partnership programmes with NATO and other international organisations.

I would like in particular to focus on the important points related to Kazakhstan's participation in the global macro-regional and international structures. Firstly, this year is the anniversary of the process of interaction and confidence building measures in Asia. CICA was one of independent Kazakhstan's first foreign policy initiatives, which I announced 20 years ago from the rostrum of the 47th session of the UN General Assembly and successfully implemented.

We are very pleased with how this process has been developing over two decades. In effect CICA has reached such a level of interaction that it is now leading the transition to a more efficient form of participation in the system of modern international relations in Eurasia and the wider world. We are talking about the prospect of creating a fully-fledged new international Organisation for Interaction and Confidence Building Measures in Asia – OVMDA. It is in this context that all the members of CICA must work together in the next few years.

Secondly, I, as President of the country which hosted the historic OSCE summit in December 2010, cannot but worry about the lack of dynamism in the implementation of the Astana Declaration. The good ship "OSCE" is still listing towards the humanitarian dimension. Once again, we are witnessing non-productive attempts to use schemes such as the despatch of observers to national elections to enable one group of countries to put pressure on another. If things continue in this vein, we will be forced to reject such missions in the future for all elections. That is not just my opinion, it is voiced throughout the CIS.

You can hear amazing claims nowadays backed with inexplicable logic. For example, many members of the mission, prior to the elections, commented positively on the organisation of the electoral process. And then suddenly we start hearing the same old line being repeated about some mythical non-compliance with some supposed standards, created by goodness knows whom or indeed completely invented.

We know perfectly well that they come with a prepared text, which is ready even before the election and is read out verbatim after the elections. This drags us back into the past and undermines the importance of the OSCE as an institution of mutual trust.

At the same time, the OSCE has not become a platform for identifying ways out of the economic "stupor" in which all the member states of the organisation find themselves, and which is also bringing more and more countries into its orbit of responsibility. Anyone can see the flaws in the global monetary system. They threaten a relapse of the global crisis, even worse than two years ago. However, issues of economic security remain outside the OSCE's priorities.

The military dimension of the OSCE is in stagnation. The "Corfu process" has stalled. The proposal made by Kazakhstan and other member states for an expansion of the security priorities within the Organisation has still to be implemented. I hope that my position and my concerns will be brought to the attention of all governments and the managers of international organisations.

Thirdly, global participation is to be the essence of our foreign policy strategy in the decades ahead. Kazakhstan has always been and will remain a worthy, proactive player in regional and world politics. We have closed the Semipalatinsk nuclear test site and renounced the possession of nuclear weapons and we urge all countries to adopt the Universal Declaration of a nuclear-free world. Our participation in the global movement to ban nuclear weapons is deliberate and principled.

Kazakhstan has been and remains committed to the idea of inter-religious and intercultural dialogue. Its significance in the modern world can only increase.

Fourthly, Kazakhstan has always seen it as important to move in line with the main trends of development throughout the world. Our foreign policy has never suffered from geopolitical naivety. Therefore, given the process of regionalisation of the world economy and politics in the 21st century, we are deepening Eurasian integration. Kazakhstan, Belarus and Russia have formed a Single Economic Space. Once again I would like to emphasise that this is an economic union.

We are moving consistently towards the creation of a Eurasian Economic Union. This is an important factor in regional stability, to improve the competitiveness of our economies and ensure that they make a technological breakthrough. One and a half years of work on the basis of these agreements has in practice yielded benefits for all the states in this union.

Fifthly, today, the global architecture has been set in motion. It is expressed by many predictions, which, in my opinion, have sometimes exaggerated and demonised the global situation. If you study history carefully, you will see that the world has never been easy.

In my opinion, a feature of the current situation is that humanity is entering a new qualitative state. The essence of this transition is the expansion of the global scope of the information society. Information technology and the possibilities it brings are spurring progress in almost all countries. However, it is impossible not to see that the methods of "adapted modernisation", especially when it comes to issues of "external stimulation" of unprepared political change in some societies, are not helpful. This is proven by recent history.

We sometimes forget the wise words of one of the greatest diplomats ever, M. Talleyrand, who said: *"You can rely on a bayonet, but you cannot sit on it."* So I believe that this political practice has no future in the 21st century.

Sixth. The Global Information Society, which our world is becoming, requires new approaches in international relations. First of all, we need order in the procedure for global decision-making. The reality is that neither the G8 nor the G20 is any longer sufficient. So I have suggested a new format, G-Global – a wider platform for finding solutions to the current problems of the global financial system and a UN integrated anti-crisis pact. G-Global is an invitation to cooperation and collaboration between all states, intergovernmental and non-governmental players in world politics and also certain politicians, public figures, experts and scholars. G-Global is both a virtual form (via the Internet) and a real form of dialogue. Our website on the subject has become one of the most visited. Seventh. World politics must be based on new global principles. For the 21st century, these are constructive multipolarity and transparency, trust and political tolerance, prioritising the evolutionary forms of global development. These should be enshrined in the basic documents of the United Nations and the entire system of international law. As diplomats like to say, the strongest substance in international relations is always paper.

At the same time, it is important for all states to realise their shared responsibility for the fate of their region and the world as a whole. It is necessary to work more closely across a whole cluster of issues regarding sustainable development.

In addition, I have proposed the adoption of a global energy strategy. Experts estimate that in the next twenty years, mankind's electricity requirements will rise by 40 per cent. At the same time, more than 1.5 billion people are living without electricity.

These are our approaches to the current and future development of our country, the Central Asian region and the world.

Speech at the meeting with the heads of foreign
diplomatic missions accredited to Kazakhstan
Astana, 2nd March 2012.

TWO

GLOBAL NUCLEAR SECURITY

During the early days of independence, Kazakhstan made an historic contribution to strengthening peace and international safety by willingly abandoning its arsenal of nuclear weapons and closing the Semipalatinsk nuclear test site.
In this speech, the President of Kazakhstan summarises developments in nuclear disarmament and the current progress in strengthening the nuclear non-proliferation regime, following the first anti-nuclear summit held in Washington, October 2010. He also outlines the concrete steps taken by Kazakhstan to enforce global nuclear safety.

The last two years have witnessed significant events in global nuclear security.

Firstly, in 2011 the NPT (Non-Proliferation Treaty) Review Conference was held. Secondly, in the past two years the world has eliminated large quantities of highly enriched uranium and more than thirty countries have adopted national obligations on nuclear security. Thirdly, in 2010 the Conference of the Global Initiative to Combat Nuclear Terrorism was held successfully in Astana.

Twenty years have passed since the voluntary closure, by my Decree, of the world's largest test site at Semipalatinsk.

Within the framework of long-term cooperation to enhance physical security, Kazakhstan, Russia and the United States have demonstrated a model partnership based on mutual trust.

At the national level we have implemented an unprecedented initiative for transporting 210 tonnes of spent nuclear fuel to a safe storage facility. We will continue to work on the conversion of the reactor to low-enriched fuel and on the creation of a regional training centre for nuclear security.

In conjunction with the IAEA (International Atomic Energy Agency), we have created a unique automated system for accounting, control and physical protection of natural uranium. Kazakhstan has also joined the Global Partnership of the G8 countries against the proliferation of weapons of mass destruction. We have ratified amendments to the Convention on the Physical Protection of Nuclear Material and urge others to take steps towards the early ratification of the amendments so that they can take effect by 2014.

Seventy years ago, the world's first nuclear reactor was built at the University of Chicago. The history of nuclear power plants is punctuated by sixty different accidents. The most recent – at the Fukushima Nuclear Power Plant – showed that nuclear power should be developed only when there is an absolute guarantee of safety and on the basis of three main principles.

First – universality. There is a need for consolidation and codifying of the international legal experience accumulated in the development of peaceful nuclear energy. The goal should be the adoption of legally binding nuclear security standards.

Second – transparency and efficiency. Along with full and prompt notification of incidents at nuclear facilities the development of clear mechanisms for rapid responses to emergencies is required.

Third – equality and trust. All states must be given equal access rights to peaceful nuclear technology, as well as the use of the guaranteed reserves held by the International Nuclear Fuel Bank. We are currently working with the IAEA to ensure that the establishment of such a bank in Kazakhstan becomes a practical possibility.

This is our specific contribution to strengthening non-proliferation and nuclear disarmament.

Kazakhstan proposes that a summit on nuclear security be held every two years. We are ready to hold one of these summits in Astana in the future.

Kazakhstan welcomes the implementation of the Strategic Arms Reduction Treaty (START) between the US and Russia and supports the new nuclear strategy adopted by President Barack Obama regarding the non-use of nuclear weapons against states which comply with the provisions of the NPT.

I urge all nuclear-weapon states to demonstrate the same goodwill.

Unfortunately, the erosion of the NPT regime has become a reality, and the uncontrolled expansion of the nuclear-armed states remains one of the most serious threats of the 21st century.

Some states regard the possession of nuclear weapons as a safety factor. Based on the experience of my country, which voluntarily renounced the world's fourth largest nuclear arsenal, I can say this: real security comes from sustainable socio-economic development.

To this end, I propose a discussion on the application of the most stringent international measures, going as far as isolating and boycotting any country which becomes the first to use nuclear weapons.

At the same time, the nuclear powers must afford states which renounce the possession of nuclear weapons security guarantees backed by the United Nations. I believe that the adoption of the Universal Declaration on a nuclear-free world would be an important step towards a Nuclear Weapons Convention.

Speech at the II Global Summit on Nuclear Security
Seoul, South Korea, 27ᵗʰ March 2012

THREE

STABILITY, UNITY, MODERNISATION

The Assembly of the People of Kazakhstan was created on 1st March 1995 at the initiative of President Nursultan Nazarbayev. Its major role is to develop and disseminate proposals for spiritual unity, strengthening and preserving the friendship of the people and promoting inter-ethnic relations in Kazakhstan. Speaking at the XIX session of the Assembly, the President stressed that the unity and diversity of the people of Kazakhstan is an important factor in ensuring Kazakhstan's stability and sustainable development.

I wholeheartedly congratulate you on the opening of the XIX Session of the Assembly of the People of Kazakhstan. Every session of the Assembly opens the way for decisions which will play a historic role in the annals of our country. The agenda of the current session includes issues such as stability, unity and modernisation.

Stability is the unshakable foundation of the consensus between us.

Unity is our greatest asset, and no price can be put upon it.

Modernisation is the expressway that will lead us to the future we deserve.

These three concepts are the key to the integrity and inviolability of our country. On them rests the welfare of our glorious homeland.

Let me outline these three concepts and how we plan to use them, in theory and practice, in the future.

Stability, as far as Kazakhstan sees it, means more than 700 new schools and more than 750 new clinics, hospitals and medical centres. It means that 1.5 million Kazakhstanis can celebrate as they move into new apartments and houses.

For the second decade in succession, the country is developing a pattern of stable economic growth. By 2020, we plan to get 1.5 million people in Kazakhstan into work.

The roadmap for industrialisation up to 2014 will lead to the creation of over 100 new production facilities. This year has seen a USD 1.3 billion increase in the resources of the National Fund, allocated for the implementation of the industrial and innovation programme.

The implementation of the Roadmap, "Business 2020", is in full swing. Nowhere else in the world is there such a programme of state support for entrepreneurship. And within this programme, in 2012 alone, we have allocated about KZT 37 billion. In total, the programme is supporting more than 1000 companies, employing almost 130,000 people.

Within the framework of the programme "Employment-2020", nearly 1.5 thousand micro-loans were granted to start-up businesses last year. The micro-loan programme totals more than KZT 1.8 million. This year, the volume of micro-loans will be increased three and a half times, while the number of beneficiaries will increase to more than 8,000 people.

We have started to implement the national IPO project. The national IPO market will include "KazTransOil" JSC "KEGOC", "Air Astana", "Samruk-Energo", "Kazakhstan Temir Zholy", "KazMunaiGas", "Kazatomprom" and others, through a gradual process, by 2015.

The national IPO programme is not just a new mass privatisation. It is the creation of a powerful new class of owners who live a decent life.

In 2012, KZT 16 billion was put into the programme called "Modernisation of housing and communal services". This programme will cover every region, city, town and village.

Every year we are also developing our health care. Health trains, furnished with state-of-the-art equipment, provide medical assistance to more than 100,000 inhabitants in over 200 remote locations. Currently, there are 183 telemedicine centres, where some 20,000 distance consultations are held with patients.

In Kazakhstan our surgeons have been conducting a unique operation at the National Medical Holding Company to transplant an artificial left ventricle. As a result, Kazakhstan is one of twenty-two developed countries where cardio-implantation technology is used. We have completely resolved all our issues in cardiology.

In general, today 87% of the people of Kazakhstan say that they feel there is stability in terms of their social well-being and confidence in the future.

Presently, the whole world anxiously awaits a new global financial crisis. Even in developed countries there are increasing economic difficulties, cuts to social spending and growing public debt. Yet here in Kazakhstan we are creating new factories, issuing micro-loans and increasing pensions, benefits and wages. This is the right way to prepare for any global crisis.

Kazakhstani unity is an invaluable guarantor of Kazakhstan's forward momentum. There are few countries in the world enjoying the same large-scale government support for ethnic and cultural centres, houses of friendship, theatres, schools and the media. Today, 92% of ethnic Kazakhs regard inter-ethnic relations in the country as secure.

All Kazakhstanis share a common future.

This has again been shown by the results of the presidential and parliamentary elections, in which the vast majority of voters backed the "Nur Otan" party.

The basis of Kazakhstan's unity is equality in civil rights and liberties.

For example, freedom of speech is currently ensured in Kazakhstan under our existing legislation. This state of affairs has improved considerably and is more secure than that of any of our partners in the CIS, EurAsEc (Eurasian Economic Community), SCO (Shanghai Cooperation Organisation), etc. In respect of party structures, we lag behind no one.

In fact, we are the closest to European standards for safeguarding the role of the press. In a number of areas, for example controlling the proliferation of ideas related to violence and brutality, terrorism and extremism, our legislation is much less stringent than in many other countries.

Modernisation is an imperative of global development. The world is witnessing a new technological revolution that is providing incredible opportunities for economic development and improvement in people's lives. Kazakhstan has to keep pace with these processes, together with our partners in the Common Economic Space. All Kazakhstanis must realise the historic significance of industrial and innovative development, social modernisation and regional and global integration.

Global peace and globalisation have slowed. Regional integration is playing an increasing role. This means that the Eurasian Economic Union is a necessity and a positive factor, with which we can strengthen our country's economy, independence and future.

I regularly receive warm letters from well-wishers across the country. In the last year and a half alone, through the Assembly I have received about 10,000 letters. Every sentence reveals the noble and sympathetic heart of the entire Kazakhstani people. Kazakhstanis are expressing their wholehearted support for the policy of peace and construction.

From the village of Lyublinka in the Kostanay region, Viktoria Georgievna Kostenko writes: *"We decided to move to Germany, but we left behind our soul. I could not bear to stay there without the Kazakhstani steppe and our native chants.*

I lived off my memories of the motherland, and most importantly of the people – living together, sharing their hopes and fears. Now I am home again – in a prosperous and advancing country. May there always be peace and harmony in our land."

Thank you, Viktoria Georgievna, I hereby pass on your wishes to the whole of Kazakhstan. The whole world seeks a formula for unity and finds it here, among us in Kazakhstan.

During a meeting I had recently with the UN Secretary-General Ban Ki-Moon, he stressed that the principles of the Assembly – respect and tolerance – *"are the principles of the UN"*.

All this indicates that our country is on the right track. Today, Kazakhstanis of all ethnicities and religions are equal citizens of their country. The Kazakhstani people and the state language both act as a unifying core for developing civil society in Kazakhstan. This process is moving ahead purposefully. 70% of state media is published in the Kazakh language. The number of students in schools where lessons are taught in Kazakh is now 63%. We are setting ourselves the goal of achieving 95% mastery of the state language by all Kazakhstanis by 2020. I have repeatedly stated that the language issue is not a matter of politics. The political decision was taken long ago, with the adoption of the Constitution and the relevant laws. The language issue cannot be a subject of political speculation. Now it is a matter of practice.

An important aspect of economic and social modernisation is the development of the trinity of languages. Almost all Kazakhstanis speak Russian. This is our common heritage, which cannot be lost. There is a growing importance and role for English, which for Kazakhstanis, opens a window onto the world of innovation, technology and business.

Today, in any developed country, a clear majority of its population is fluent in two to three languages. Therefore, in the technologically advanced countries, the natural sciences, chemistry, mathematics, physics and biology are taught in schools and universities – mostly in English. However, the humanities – history, literature and the others – are taught in their native language.

A recent example is the experience of Malaysia. The vast majority of the public speaks the country's official language, whilst teaching is in English. Otherwise, they feel, the country will fall behind the global technology community. It is a versatile pedagogical approach. We too must therefore study English. I am instructing the Ministry of Education and Science to consider introducing this international experience.

This year marks two dates that we should not forget.

It is the eightieth anniversary of the mass famine of the early 1930s and also the seventy fifth anniversary of the height of mass political persecution under Stalinism.

The toll taken by these tragedies is irreparable. According to most estimates, starvation and disease in Kazakhstan, Belarus, Russia and Ukraine claimed more than 7 million lives. More than 1.5 million of those who died at that time as a result of starvation lived in Kazakhstan. 600,000 Kazakhstanis were forced to leave their native land to escape from hunger and disease. In 1937-1938 alone, according to official figures, the NKVD in the Soviet Union arrested more than 1.5 million people. We must never forget this.

On 31st May, we will celebrate the annual Day of Remembrance for Victims of Political Persecution and Famine. On this day the monument "Asharshilik Kurbandarina Eskertkish" will be opened in Astana.

In that brutal era, thanks to the hospitality of the Kazakhstani people and the mutual support of all ethnic groups forcibly deported to Kazakhstan, the republic was able to survive those harsh, terrible years. In the modern age we have made the value of unity and concord the foundation of our society, the foundation of our unique Kazakhstani tolerance. We must carefully pass on those values to every future generation of Kazakhstanis.

Strengthening inter-ethnic harmony requires continuous effort. First. Strengthening Kazakhstani tolerance means, first and foremost, strengthening and developing the Assembly.

On my instructions, a draft Development Strategy for the APK up to 2020 has been produced. We need to enhance the quality of the work done by the Assembly in the regions. As you know, in the Majilis Assembly a parliamentary group for inter-party cooperation on peace, social and inter-ethnic harmony has been created. Indeed, this is a new mechanism for interaction between MPs from different parties. This is a great step forward. This practice should also be extended to the level of the regional assemblies. The Akims of the regions should pay attention to the qualities of those selected as Heads of the Secretariats. They must be experienced and authoritative executives.

I would like to draw your attention to the fact that the structure of the APK should not be limited to the official level of the regions and the cities of Almaty and Astana. It is necessary to consider new working arrangements for the Assembly in major collectives from universities, national companies and enterprises. The Assembly is our national treasure. The efficiency of its regional branches must therefore be the personal responsibility of the regional governors.

In this way, it is necessary to finalise and adopt the strategy of the APK up to 2020.

Second. A firm guarantee for the sustainable development of our society lies in strong adherence to the principles of a secular state. Religion is the realm of the human soul and morality. And the high values professed by every religion, whether Islamic, Orthodox, Catholic, Protestant or other creeds, will always be supported by the state.

In a month's time we host the IV Congress for the leaders of global and traditional religions. Hosting this event is the greatest gift that Kazakhstan can make to the establishment of global tolerance – that most vital principle for world order in the 21st century. We have also created the Agency for Religious Affairs in order to strengthen cooperation between all religious communities in Kazakhstan. At the same time we must develop an effective set of measures to shield young people from the influence of pseudo-religious groups.

Third. In accordance with my instructions, the government is developing a concept of local self-government. This concept must take into account all aspects of inter-ethnic and inter-religious cooperation in the regional units. The APK must participate actively in the drafting of this document.

The Assembly of the People discusses the most important issues facing the country. Today, I would like to raise a number of new aspects of social modernisation.

The present priority is the interests of the common man. In society there is a widespread demand for fair and decent work – I have spoken at length about social justice.

Industrialisation is not an end in itself. Our main concern is the whole human being, his interests, fate, education, employment and decent housing. New enterprises and high-performance industrial facilities require highly skilled workers. This means changing society in Kazakhstan and expanding the middle class. In the 21st century, a successful economy is an economy of social responsibility and justice. Our people are actively involved in the modernisation of the economy and expect fair treatment by all employers. It is necessary to ensure fair wages for productive work. We must fully restore the prestige of work and professional life. That is the true aim of our new industrialisation. A total of 1.5 million people will be in employment by 2020 and we are building an innovative economy and creating a fair society, in which everyone can say *"I am a citizen of Kazakhstan, and in my home country all doors are open to me."*

Kazakhstan is a young country, where half the citizens are under thirty years old. In you, my young compatriots, I see great hopes for Kazakhstan breaking through into the future!

For young people in Kazakhstan, all the necessary conditions are being created for good education, decent work, housing and sport.

In terms of the provision of secondary education, we lie in eighteenth place among the 182 countries participating in the Global Competitiveness Index. Technical and professional education has been extended to more than 600,000 people and since independence, our universities have trained more than 2.4 million professionals.

Under the programme "With a diploma to the village", in the national budget KZT 21.6 billion has been allocated for 2012-2014 to attract more than 16,000 young professionals.

In general, the total amount of finance for the national projects "Aul Zhastary" (Rural Youth), "With a diploma to the village", "Youth Practice" and "Zhasyl El" (Green Country) currently stands at KZT 37.7 billion. The activists taking part in the "Zhasyl El" programme alone have planted more than 43 million seedlings across the country. This represents 80,000 hectares of new forest plantations.

By 2020, we are planning to construct 1.2 million square metres of housing for young families. In Kazakhstan, one in four public servants is a young professional.

Young people have plenty of opportunities to engage in sport. Last year alone, we opened more than 1,500 new sports facilities.

An important priority area is employment and youth employment. Within the framework of the programme "Employment-2020", initiatives such as "Youth Practice" are being successfully implemented. This year KZT 2.7 billion has been allocated to this initiative, which will cover 15,000 young graduates.

In the advanced industrial countries – Germany, Britain, the USA and South Korea – there is a tried-and-trusted dual system for training workers. Under this system, students at vocational schools spend part of their time doing apprenticeships in the workplace. This system of training must be rolled out in Kazakhstan too. I will instruct the "Samruk-Kazyna" Fund to come up with a list of basic enterprises and develop a step-by-step plan for the implementation of the dual model.

This will enable us to upgrade the training system for our increasing industrialisation. As our Industrialisation Map records, more than 600 projects are being implemented at a cost of KZT 9.6 trillion. In total nearly 370,000 jobs have been created for young people.

The State is therefore creating all the necessary conditions to support a new generation of Kazakhstanis. We must continue this work.

First, I am instructing the Government, by the first of November of this year, to submit to me the draft Concept for state youth policy up to 2020. Second, by the end of the year it will be necessary to update our legislation on the state's youth policy. Third, I am issuing instructions to create, within the structure of the Ministry of Education and Science, a Youth Committee, and corresponding departments in the regions. The Akims of the Astana and Almaty regions must personally lead the Regional Youth Councils. Fourthly, it is vital to create new opportunities for social mobility for young people. We have already done a great deal to ensure that one of the most effective social sources of mobility is public service. Last year alone, the Agency for Civil Service Affairs employed more than 2,000 people through the personnel reserve, mostly young professionals. However, independent sociological studies show that the top issue for young people is the lack of employment and equal starting conditions. There are frequent cases when, after getting a good education abroad, young professionals cannot find a job and realise their potential. I am instructing the government to prepare a systemic package of legislative and socio-economic measures to create social mobility for young people. Fifth, we need in-depth research into the processes affecting young people. I am instructing the Ministry of Education and Science to look into the establishment of a Research Centre called "Youth" at the Eurasian National University named after LN Gumilyov. Sixth, we must strengthen the work of the youth wing of "Zhas Otan". I am ordering the central apparatus of the "Nur Otan" party to develop and approve the "Zhas Otan" Strategy for Action up to 2020.

I know that on the initiative of the Civil Alliance of Kazakhstan and of youth organisations, support of this message is being underlined through the campaign "The future starts today" which is spreading across the country. Within the framework of this campaign, I will be having meetings with young people.

The APK cannot stand on the side-lines. It needs to pay more attention to the problems of young people and actively support these measures. Together with the "Nur Otan" party, we must establish strict control over this work.

Today, all doors, all possibilities and all roads are open to our people. We are many, but we are one country and one people. All political forces and the entire population of Kazakhstan must focus on achieving these main objectives.

These are: unity and stability; increasing the welfare of citizens; and a healthy and educated nation.

To be useful to their country and responsible for the fate of their homeland is the duty and honour of every responsible politician and citizen of Kazakhstan.

Ahead of us is the Day of Unity of the People of Kazakhstan. I wish to congratulate you all on this, our common holiday!

We are now known around the world as a prosperous secular state of harmony and internal concord. The Assembly has made a special contribution to the creation of this atmosphere of mutual understanding and stability. I believe that this institution, which has quickly become the cradle of constructive consensus in our society, can look forward to still more striking achievements.

Our country is thriving. People of different nationalities live in peace and harmony. Long live united and indivisible Kazakhstan, protecting the fate of so many people! May the foundation of our common home be tranquillity, may its support be stability and may its aspiration be peace! I wish you every success!

Speech at the XIX session of the Assembly of the People of Kazakhstan
"Kazakhstan's way: stability, unity and modernisation"
Astana, 27th April 2012

FOUR

FOREIGN INVESTMENT

The Foreign Investors Council was created in 1998 to establish direct dialogue between the Government and foreign investors to promote foreign economic relations and further improve Kazakhstan's investment climate.
At the XXV plenary session, the President of Kazakhstan presented an ambitious "New Silk Road" programme aimed at increasing the transit/transport potential of Kazakhstan. He called on foreign investors to participate actively in the implementation of the state programme focussing on Kazakhstan's industrial/innovations development.

Once again I would like to congratulate all those attending the XXV anniversary meeting of the Council and thank you for your active involvement in our collaborative work. In the fourteen years since the establishment of the Council, Kazakhstan has come a long way. During this period, the economy has grown in real terms more than two and a half times – to USD 186 billion. In 2011, GDP growth was seven and a half per cent. Labour productivity in the manufacturing sector as a whole has increased by 20%. Kazakhstan's foreign trade turnover in 2011 increased by 40% on the previous year and amounted to USD 126 billion.

We marked the 20th anniversary of independence last year by recording significant progress in diversification and the transition to an innovation economy. Over the years, 70% of total foreign direct investment in Central Asia has been attracted to Kazakhstan. That is almost USD 150 billion. Last year alone, investment totalled USD 18 billion.

The programme of economic industrialisation has been successfully implemented. In two years we have built about 400 new production facilities, which have already turned out products worth more than USD 3 billion. The implementation of another 220 projects is ongoing. Of these, more than thirty are large industrial facilities with investment of between USD

300 million and more than 1 billion. Total investment in the manufacturing industry over the past three years has amounted to 8.5 billion dollars.

I freely admit that these advances rely heavily on the active role played by our foreign partners. For this reason, I would like to thank all members for their invaluable contribution to improving the investment climate and economic development of Kazakhstan. To consolidate these gains, we have adopted a new development strategy up to 2020 and a number of important state programmes. However, our achievements and external estimates indicate that Kazakhstan is able to formulate and solve much more ambitious goals than that.

Today I would like to invite you to join us in launching the large-scale project "New Silk Road". Kazakhstan must revive its historic role and become the largest business and transit hub in the Central Asian region, a bridge between Europe and Asia. As a result of this mega-project, by 2020 the volume of transit cargo travelling through Kazakhstan should increase almost twofold, with additional revenues of at least 50 million tonnes.

Why Kazakhstan? Primarily due to our favourable geographical position which in a globalising world is a hugely significant factor.

With Kazakhstan being located in the heart of the Eurasian continent, linking the major markets of China, Europe, Russia and the CIS countries and providing transport routes to Central Asia and the Persian Gulf is greatly beneficial to investors, guaranteeing them a link between producers and consumers. Kazakhstan is traversed by the major transcontinental routes "North-South", "East-West" and "South-East Asia – the Central Asian region".

The second factor is the constant growth of cargo flows. These flows now connect China, the world's second-biggest economy, the EU countries and the CIS. It is expected that by 2020 the volume of trade between Kazakhstan's neighbouring countries will grow by 1.5 times and reach USD 1 trillion. The annual volume of trade between China and Europe now exceeds USD 500 billion, with average annual growth of eight per cent. By 2020, it will amount to USD 800 billion. The land transit route from China to Europe through Kazakhstan has a distinct advantage: it is significantly shorter than the route by sea, through the Suez Canal.

The third element is direct access to the markets of the Customs Union. The single economic space will become fully functional in July this year thus ensuring free movement of capital, goods and labour.

The fourth reason is the favourable investment climate. In the "Doing Business" rating, Kazakhstan ranks forty-seventh globally, and for the indicator "protection of investors" we were in thirty-fourth position. Additionally the Government has been set the task of achieving the most advanced standards among the OECD countries in this field.

The fifth factor is political and economic stability. Over a period of twenty years of independence, we have been able to significantly strengthen peace and harmony in multi-ethnic Kazakhstan. This is an important factor for attracting global capital.

How can we realise such an ambitious project?

My vision is the creation, in the key transport corridors of Kazakhstan, of a unified set of international hubs for trade and logistics, finance and business, innovation and technology and tourism.

The competitive advantage of the "New Silk Road" will be based on the implementation of the "5S principle", standing for speed, service, cost, safety and stability. As a result of territorial and functional linkages it should be possible to achieve a true synergy, the main source of competitive advantage for the "New Silk Road", following the example of Dubai or Singapore.

The main element of the "New Silk Road" as a transport and logistics hub will be developed around the following projects. Firstly, in "Kazakhstan Temir Zholy" we have created a world-class multi-modal transportation and logistics company.

Secondly, we are actively developing the "Khorgos" international centre for cross-border cooperation on the border with China. This is the "Eastern Gate" of Kazakhstan. To the west of Kazakhstan, projects will be implemented to expand the seaport of Aktau and construct a logistics centre in the city of Aktobe. These will form the republic's "Western Gate", with access to the Caspian region, Russia and beyond that to Europe.

Third, we will rapidly build a "transcontinental corridor" between "Western Europe and Western China". This project will be completed by

2015 and will reduce the delivery time for goods sent from China to Europe by road by almost three and a half times compared to sending them by sea.

Fourth, work will continue on expanding the capacity of the country's railway network through the construction of the railways "Zhezkazgan-Beineu" and "Arkalyk-Shubarkol", with a length of 1,200 kilometres. This is in addition to the railways that have already been built, namely "Uzen – Turkmenistan – Iran – Persian Gulf" and "Khorgos – Zhetygen" – the second railway crossing to the Caspian Sea.

Fifthly, on the entire route from China to Russia, i.e. in the FEZ "Khorgos – Eastern Gate" and in the cities of Almaty, Aktau and Aktobe, class "A" multifunctional logistics centres will be built. The development of business activity and services for foreign nationals in Almaty will create additional conditions for a tourist hub around the city.

The bulk of investment will then be directed towards development in the field of ski resorts for winter holidays and the Kapshagai resort area for the summer season. In addition, relatively nearby there is the great potential of the Lake Balkhash and Alakol region.

Infrastructure development in the port of Aktau and the services cluster adjacent to the oilfield will boost the construction of the seaside resort recreation area "Kendirli".

To support the integrated development of tourism the issue of visa facilitation is being resolved. The Ministry of Foreign Affairs is considering the abolition of visa requirements for thirty-four countries. Innovative enterprises focused on providing services to large companies will also be established.

Together, these conditions will make it possible to create, by 2020, on the basis of the existing free economic zone "Park of innovative technologies", a fully-fledged hub for international innovation and technology. Even today, 121 companies are registered at the Park, with plans to locate the research departments of national companies there. We will continue to invest in the development of world-class infrastructure and grant additional benefits and guarantees, in particular by the placing of state orders for R&D.

Work will continue on the establishment in Almaty of a modern transport infrastructure and service cluster, meeting world standards. Almaty is to become a leader in the country for the implementation of the "technology city of the future", with a suitable level of safety, environmental friendliness and convenience for foreign nationals. Almaty will witness the "single window" for foreign businessmen and investors being implemented. We will offer a complete package of services under a simplified scheme, from obtaining visas and various permits, to contacts with government agencies and registration of companies. The Almaty model will be used in every city where a similar large-scale transformation is to be carried out.

In partnership with exchanges in Asia and Europe, it will be necessary to create an international commodity exchange in Almaty, to serve freight flows through Kazakhstan. The increasing volume of commercial operations and turnover should give impetus to the development of the "Regional financial centre of Almaty". I am ordering the Government, together with members of the Foreign Investors Council, to discuss the above-mentioned objectives and by the end of the year to develop a comprehensive plan for implementation of the project "Kazakhstan – the New Silk Road".

Let me start a new practice for holding meetings of the Foreign Investors Council. At each meeting I propose that it should be mandatory to consider two issues.

The first of these is the implementation of an investment policy in Kazakhstan for the protection of investors' interests. This will provide assessments for the relevant state bodies.

The second issue is the development of Kazakhstani content. We have already dedicated the twentieth plenary meeting of the Council to this issue. However, given its importance, I propose to hold discussions on it at every meeting. The emphasis will be on the development of technology. We have devoted a great deal of attention to the development of Kazakhstani innovation and policy content, and would like to see a greater element of high-tech and technology-intensive goods and services. In this regard, I propose that the next meeting of the FIC be dedicated to innovative development.

The Government is currently developing a concept for the innovative development of Kazakhstan up to 2020, on my instructions. I invite investors, given your extensive experience in implementing large-scale projects in various sectors, to help us build the policy for Kazakhstan's technological development.

It is necessary to intensify the activities of the working groups during the year. Accordingly, I propose to instruct the Ministry of Industry and Trade, together with the Association "Kazakhstan Foreign Investors Council" to make proposals for a qualitative review of the composition of the working groups, and of the Council itself, in order to achieve maximum focus.

Speech at the XXV plenary session of the Foreign Investors Council
Astana, 22nd May 2012

FIVE

GLOBAL ECONOMIC GROWTH

The Astana Economic Forum, created in 2008, is now one of the major international platforms to address the global economic outlook and devise mutually acceptable solutions and recommendations for economic growth, employment and the development of an effective global financial system.

The world economy is going through a critical period, full of fast-moving and unpredictable structural changes. This is further exacerbated by a rampant global crisis which is threatening sustainable development. In this difficult situation, the importance of our collective discussion of the problems facing the world economy cannot be over-emphasised.

The Astana Economic Forum has become a significant part of the global dialogue between politicians, scientists and experts. This is demonstrated by the quality of those taking part. Applications to participate in the various sections were received from over 8,000 people in more than ninety countries. The participants include twelve Nobel Prize winners and four members of the global "100 thinkers" list. I particularly welcome the many current and former heads of state and government who have come to Astana and world-famous politicians, heads of international organisations and regional associations.

Over four years of work, the range of issues discussed at the forum has expanded. The Astana Forum in real terms has, in essence, become an amplifier for the broad "Eurasian perspective" on the problems of global development.

This is especially important in the context of the successful work of that new geo-economic reality of the 21st century – the Common Economic Space of Kazakhstan, Russia and Belarus.

The agenda for the Forum includes the key issue of global economic transformation. This issue has been discussed for many years. However, the large number of ideas and proposals cannot make up for the shortage of practical solutions at the global level. The global monetary and economic crisis has turned into a global social crisis affecting many developed countries.

The International Labour Organisation highlights the threat of global unemployment which in the leading countries of Europe has greatly exceeded the figures for the last century. In Italy and the United Kingdom the level is eight point three per cent, in Germany six per cent and in France nine point seven per cent. In these four "locomotives" of the European Union, there are a total of almost 11 million unemployed, and about half of them are young people. In the other EU countries there are still more. In total, every third employee of working age throughout the world, or 1.1 billion people, does not have a job or is living with his family on two dollars a day.

Substantial funds have been set aside to save individual national economies and maintain the balance of the World Bank and the International Monetary Fund. Unfortunately, this is limited exclusively to the positive measures taken in the G8 and G20 formats. However, each new billion dollars has the potential to generate a billion new social problems. As they say, it is like trying to put out a fire with gasoline.

The half-hearted nature of the global anti-crisis measures is clear evidence of a different kind of systemic crisis – in the form of a corrosion of international relations. The creation of the G20 has significantly expanded the breadth of dialogue on the reform of the world economy. However, today, four years after the first summit of the anti-recessionary G20, this format seems inadequate. At the last World Economic Forum in Davos, many world leaders finally agreed that capitalism, or more precisely, the neo-liberal modified version, needs to be fixed. At the end of last year, I proposed the approval, within the Astana Forum, of a new format for dialogue, which we have called G-Global.

This idea has received broad support in political, expert and business circles throughout the international community. In just a few months, daily visits to the official page of the Astana Forum on the internet site G-Global have increased forty-fold. More than 30,000 users from 140 countries have become permanent visitors. In fact, the network has launched an intensive search for ways of forming a new world economic order.

It is symbolic that the theme of interactive debate on the G-Global platform is rapidly addressing the issues of reforming the world economy and the financial system. We are discussing a wide range of issues related to innovative development, nuclear and environmental safety, ethnic and religious tolerance, geopolitics and other matters. In other words, G-Global is acting as a potential unifying idea for a multipolar world.

Almost every online message underlines the hope for a stable and just world order in the 21st century. What conclusions can we draw from all the suggestions?

Firstly, the international community is going through one of the most controversial and difficult stages in global history. Never before has mankind had such great potential for both successful development and self-destruction. Awareness of this makes it imperative to address global issues in a comprehensive manner.

Today it is just not enough to solve the problems of the economy and "global warming". It is not possible to ignore the nuclear threat, smouldering conflicts, lack of tolerance or distortions in social policy which are leading to significant dependency, at the level of both social groups and individual states.

Secondly, never before has there been such a level of development in global communications. Today, and even more so in the future, the capacity exists to reduce the distance and "compress" the time needed to overcome historic, political and many other barriers. This potential cannot just remain an instrument for provocative communications and the deliberate reduction of moral principles and public order in "dysfunctional" societies. It must be used for constructive purposes, including fostering a global dialogue in the interests of the stable development of the world.

Third, the world is now learning to live in new circumstances. And this is not an easy lesson to learn; some people have great difficulty with it. First of all, I am referring to society's ability to follow the path of progress, through evolution to new technological structures and levels of social relations. Today it is important to know and actively learn from the successful experience of many countries. In this regard, Kazakhstan is ready for such cooperation.

We are willing to learn and share our own experience with all our friends.

Fourth, the structure of the global world in the 21st century will depend on many factors. Among them it is now important to recognise the desire for justice of billions of people around the world. Justice in the 21st century is not just a moral category. It is one of the key conditions for successful national and global development.

In the 21st century, those socio-economic models that are based on the extraction of natural resources from the "third world" are no longer acceptable. At the same time there is no future in endless external borrowing for non-productive purposes and the abandonment of industrial development and of investment in the development of the human potential of a country.

This is also the lesson of the "Arab Spring" and to some extent of "the Eurozone crisis".

Fifthly, it is important to bring the whole system of international relations out of stagnation. An important task here is the formation of transparent world politics. A foundation of mutual trust and responsibility between states is essential to secure the present and the future of each region and the world. The idea of G-Global has aroused extraordinary interest in just six months. It represents an opportunity to find a solution to the systemic crisis affecting the global economy, peace and international relations.

G-Global takes into account the increased level of influence in geopolitics and geo-economics of non-state players such as NGOs, private entities, multinational companies, politicians and citizens. As a civilised concept for the information age, G-Global is aimed at all countries, all areas of the Internet and the millions of users of the World Wide Web who are interested in global reform and the establishment of a just and secure world order. I am convinced that together we can achieve the main goal of G-Global, which is to offer the international community an attractive and effective model for international relations in the 21st century.

Two decades ago, Kazakhstan was a fragment of a collapsed superpower. We had to create a new state and a new economy from scratch. Our starting point was a completely ruined economy, with hyperinflation at 2,100%.

Thanks to the reforms and the efforts of the whole society, Kazakhstan has achieved impressive success.

In a short, historic period, per capita GDP has grown from USD 700 to USD 12,000. This represents sixteen-fold growth. None of the countries of the "South-Eastern Tigers" have achieved such results in twenty years. They have only grown by a factor of three or four. The country has attracted about USD 150 billion of foreign investment.

Thanks to the skilful anti-crisis measures in the teeth of the global crisis, we have maintained the positive development dynamic of our country. In the past year, our economy grew by seven point five per cent, and we expect the same growth this year. Last year alone, the country attracted USD 20 billion.

Now Kazakhstan is implementing an ambitious programme of accelerated industrial and innovative development. The goal is the creation of a non-oil economy, which will allow an increase of at least 50% in the economy by 2020.

Virtually every six months, scores of new businesses are opened around the country. As far as the map of industrialisation is concerned, we plan to introduce more than 350 innovative entities in manufacturing, agricultural production and infrastructure. In two years we have created about 100,000 new jobs. Kazakhstan has, for the first time in its history, started to manufacture cars, trains and aircraft. We are implementing large-scale infrastructure projects. For example, in the next few years we plan to build more than 1,500 kilometres of new railways and thousands of kilometres of motorways.

At present, we are forcing through social modernisation in Kazakhstan. Within the framework of the "Employment-2020" programme, we are addressing the ambitious task of providing gainful employment to 1.5 million Kazakhstanis.

In the next five years, we are planning annual construction of 6 million square metres of housing, including affordable accommodation for young people. We are actively engaged in modernising our education and health systems.

It is in Kazakhstan's interests to ensure growth in foreign investment, so we will continue to improve the conditions for productive activity for foreign business. I have offered major investors the joint opportunity to implement the mega-project "Kazakhstan – the New Silk Road" and I invite all interested business people to participate actively in the implementation of our strategic plans.

Independent Kazakhstan made a contribution to peace more than two decades ago by closing the Semipalatinsk nuclear test site and renouncing all nuclear weapons. Today Kazakhstan is one of the leaders of the movement for a nuclear-free world. This is indicated by the new Kazakhstani anti-nuclear initiatives put forward at the Global Nuclear Security Summit in Seoul. We have a suitable share of responsibility for the fate of the region of Central Asia, Eurasia and the world. And we accept it with dignity, by offering and seeking a number of regional and global initiatives.

Kazakhstan, as a country which has proved in practice the success of its approach, recognises that our prosperity and the prosperity of other countries would be inconceivable without a stable and secure world. And for the world continuously to progress, it is essential to develop, on a binding basis for all states, the fundamental principles of world order in the 21st century. A constructive approach to the development of human civilisation, in my opinion, can be achieved on the basis of the following five principles, which I propose to call the principles of G-Global.

The first principle is evolution, not revolution. I believe that mankind reached the limit of revolutions and world wars in the last century. Today, therefore, the entire wisdom of humanity should be directed to sustaining peace. The alternative is self-destruction. In the 21st century, the successful modernisation of the global world order can only be evolutionary.

As demonstrated by the "Arab Spring", revolution only hinders the development of societies, throws them backwards, complicates interstate relationships and generates still more problems. Revolution in the 21st century will be possible and permissible only in the field of science and technology. In political practice and social life, it is destructive. Especially if it takes root in soil that is not economically prepared for it. The path of reform is the only way to progress in the 21st century.

The second principle is justice, equality and consensus. In the 21st century, the division of countries into major and minor, master and slave, civilised and uncivilised, is out-dated. The inertia created by the domination of some by others, does not lead to progress. It carries the risk of leaving individual countries and regions on the side-lines of global development. This is a dead end for us all.

The alternative to this practice is to simply place the geopolitical foundations of the global economy, monetary system and policies on an equal basis among all states.

Another important aspect is the transition to a new paradigm for global social development based on social partnership and responsibility. This is the path to empowering ordinary people so that they can actively enjoy the benefits of economic growth and profitability. It is vital that in the long term, global solutions at all levels – the United Nations, international organisations, regional associations, forums and summits – are accepted only by consensus. It is important to note that fundamental changes to the world economic system will be impossible without a transition from the "Washington" consensus to a global consensus. To achieve this we must take account of the new system of global governance in the interests of both the developed and developing countries.

The third principle is global tolerance and trust. I am impressed by the conclusion drawn by the authors of the modern concept of the "creative class", namely that in the 21st century, tolerance is an important factor of economic growth.

Here in Kazakhstan we have known this for a long time and have initiated a dialogue between religions. In developing a scientific approach to this, I would say that one of the levers for lifting the world economy out of recession is global tolerance. And not only in terms of mutual inter-ethnic, inter-religious and inter-cultural respect. Tolerance must form the basis for the relationship between states, regardless of their geopolitical weight and influence, historic experience or level of economic and social development.

In the 21st century, the world's diversity provides great opportunities for cooperation on economic and cultural matters and information. Without tolerance there can be no global confidence. Twenty years ago, addressing an assembly of the United Nations, I initiated the process of the CICA (Conference on Interaction and Confidence Building Measures in Asia), which is now a respected international organisation. The experience of CICA demonstrates that confidence-building measures could be extended to the entire UN system, because without global confidence, real, concerted anti-crisis measures will be impossible to achieve.

The fourth principle is global transparency. Peace in the G-Global format means a transparent community of nations. There must be no "double standards", or dividing nations into large, medium-sized and small. We need maximum openness and transparency in international affairs. Kazakhstan will urge this on all its partners during its presidency of the OSCE (Organisation for Security and Co-operation in Europe) and in the context of the only Astana summit of the OSCE in the 21st century. Only in this way will it be possible to develop the global economy successfully and raise the prosperity of every nation. And the world will also be able to get rid of many problems related to poverty, hunger and disease.

The fifth principle is constructive multi-polarity. The creation of a multi-polar world is a trend of global development in the 21st century. However, what will be the relationship between the different poles? Will it be honest and fair competition and peaceful competitiveness? Or will the world become a field for fierce ideological and political confrontation, the scene of a new "arms race"? This would once again ignite pockets of smouldering regional conflict. If mankind does not control the spread of nuclear weapons, this will increase the risk of international terrorism and extremism. The only alternative to these threats and challenges is to build constructive multi-polarity.

It must be a balanced system of geopolitical checks and balances, with no bloc thinking, which is a negative legacy of the bipolar world. There must be no geopolitical snobbery. It should enable powerful integration associations to coexist peacefully and cooperate closely. One such grouping will be formed in the near future, in the shape of the Eurasian Economic Union.

I am convinced that only in a constructive, multi-polar world will it be possible to solve the pressing problems of the global economy and achieve sustainable development.

I am sure that the potential of the G-Global idea will grow through the broad support of the world community. So I consider it important to create a particularly impressive Internet portal. It should be broken down by the main ideas of G-Global.

This is the reform of the world economy and monetary system which I described in my articles *Keys to the Crisis* and *The Fifth Way*. It means the creation of a nuclear-free world and the strengthening of global security, first and foremost, in the Euro-Atlantic space and Eurasia, as well as enhancing dialogue between cultures and civilisations, the implementation of the concept of global energy and environmental development, including Kazakhstan's "Green Bridge" initiative.

These areas could be part of a global strategy for the future both into the 21st century and for subsequent centuries. For the large-scale scientific and expert study of this project, I propose that an International Institute for Forecasting be created, based at the Eurasian Economic Club of Scientists.

I believe that the 21st century will be the era of great human wisdom. We have proposed the G-Global project with the sole purpose of taking a step towards that era. A step towards a world without economic crises and with a valid new global currency.

Speech at the V Astana Economic Forum
Astana, 23rd May 2012

SIX

INTER-FAITH PERSPECTIVES

The idea of hosting the Congress of World Religious Leaders was initiated by Nursultan Nazarbayev, President of Kazakhstan. The Congress, which was created in 2003, is a unique platform for establishing dialogue between the leaders of world and traditional religions. It seeks to develop a culture of tolerance and mutual respect in contrast to ideological hatred, extremism and terrorism.
The main theme of the IV Congress was "Peace and harmony as the choice of mankind". The forum was attended by 85 delegations from 40 countries.

Today, the light of the highest spirituality and blessing is shining brightly here in Kazakhstan.

Nine years ago, the first congress took place, attended by seventeen delegations from seventeen different countries. Today it is clear for all to see that there has been both a qualitative and quantitative increase in the global significance of our forum. The congress for leaders of global and traditional religions has become a unique component of the international dialogue. We are grateful for the interest shown in the congress on the part of the UN, UNESCO (United Nations Educational, Scientific and Cultural Organisation) and ISESCO (Islamic Educational, Scientific and Cultural Organisation), and by the leaders of a host of other international associations, prominent politicians and experts.

Beneath the peace and harmony of the Astana Palace's pyramid, the topical issue of how to strengthen mutual understanding between religions and cultures has long been a subject of discussion. In the difficult period at the start of the third millennium, the noble initiatives adopted by previous congresses received the backing of the global community. They played a considerable part in helping to ensure that the world did not slide into the abyss of a "clash of civilisations".

In spite of all the complexities of global development, the powerful, instinctive desire for dialogue remains a trend that is much in demand amid the universal processes taking place throughout the world.

The Council of religious leaders includes representatives of the world's leading faiths: Islam, Christianity, Judaism, Buddhism, Hinduism, Shintoism and Zoroastrianism. In essence, it is the first functional mechanism for interaction between religions, in a multi-layered format. The creation of the Council is something that is capable of bringing all inter-faith dialogue to a whole new level.

Firstly, it will be within the Council that cooperation will be established with the other structures involved in the international dialogue. Secondly, a new, permanent body is being created with, in time, the potential to become an invaluable tool for global peace-making. Its authority and potential enable it to accept pleas and appeals, particularly at times when there may be conflicts in progress. Thirdly, it is important that the Council should oversee the establishment of a global system of monitoring to ensure that the rights and freedoms of believers are maintained. Fourthly, the spiritual power of religions, united within this new Council, is capable, I am sure, of playing an important balancing role in the processes of global development. Fifthly, work related to the planning and staging of all subsequent congresses will be stepped up a level.

I am grateful to all the leaders of global and traditional religions, who welcomed our initiative so positively and agreed to be the first members of the Council.

Over the nine years in which they have been taking place, the congresses for the leaders of global and traditional religions have always been held at times when complex global processes seem to have reached their most serious levels. The first congresses were convened as a response to the threat of the "clash" of religions and the use of religion to serve the evil objectives of international terrorism and extremism. The third and most recent congresses were held at a time when the most powerful financial and economic crisis the world has known was at its zenith. The current forum is likewise being held at a decisive moment for the whole world.

A global transformation of the world order has begun. In essence, mankind is going through a phase of systemic crisis. The global recession, on the brink of which the world found itself, brings the threat of major social upheaval to many societies. Among the more than 1 billion unemployed in today's world, half are young people, and these include many who are well-educated. As they lose the ability to enjoy gainful employment and see cuts in social guarantees, growing numbers of young people are turning to radicalism and crime.

At the same time, there is a growing crisis of morality. We cannot help but see that in many societies, "false freedom" is being promoted and is taking root. Perverted views of the nature of relations between people are portrayed as the norm in modern society.

The desire to engage in honest labour is being displaced by the urge to make a quick buck in any way possible. This 'anti-morality' is sometimes taken to extremes. A typical sign of the growing crisis of morality in the world are the incidents of aggressive denigration of those who are members of religious faiths, and attempts to force religion onto the side-lines of society. Cases of sacrilegious contempt being shown for holy sites are taking place in many countries, throughout virtually all religions. These include public burnings of holy books; desecration and destruction of mosques, temples, synagogues and other religious edifices; the discrediting of religious ministers, and the beating or killing of members of their congregations.

Why is this happening? Religion is one of the strongest protective barriers against lack of spirituality and greed, known to man. Many times throughout history, religion has been the only thing safeguarding the wisdom of our people, their culture and traditions.

Kazakhstani society is aware of this given its own experiences under the Godless Soviet regime, particularly during the period of persecution brought about by Stalin. For example, we have the historical and architectural memorial which honours the victims of political persecution, and which was erected at the site of one of the "islands" in what was once the notorious "Gulag archipelago". This island was known as the ALZHIR – the Akmolinsk camp for the wives of those accused of betraying the motherland.

In those years of the former USSR, millions of innocent people lost their lives. Among them were tens of thousands of people who administered the faiths of Islam, Christianity and other religions. This was the terrible price the religions paid for the unwavering stance taken by those who believed in, and preached faith in, God the Creator.

The immoral acts that we see being committed against religions today are a similar phenomenon to what occurred in the 1920s and '30s, when attempts were made to "overthrow" churches. We condemn such attacks unreservedly and wish to express our support for all religious leaders, for all religions and for their resistance to the outbreak of militaristic Godlessness.

The modern world is at a crossroads. It is for this reason that this central issue cannot be overstated. Throughout mankind's history, no values have ever been more cherished than peace and harmony. One cannot fail to notice that there is a dearth of positive ideas about peace-making in today's world.

Humanity, as evidenced on more than a few occasions in the past, is making use of new breakthroughs, given to it by a higher intelligence, but not always in the interests of peace. Extremely advanced information technologies and cutting-edge communications, designed to bring peoples together, are often applied in such a way as to divide people and erect fresh barriers within societies and between nations. Rather than being used as a tool for the dissemination of knowledge, the knowledge networks at our disposal are often used to promote sin, propagate falsehoods and promote base human instincts, persuading brother to kill brother and to incite hatred.

The things that morally bind any society together – family, bringing up children, continuity from one generation to the next and much else – are being undermined. All this is part of the bitter reality of modernity.

I, in turn, wish to express my own point of view, which stems from my experiences as a politician. It is abundantly clear that in a globalised world, it will only be possible to bring the world's economy out of the stupor of recession through the combined efforts of the entire community of nations. This is something that is acknowledged by everyone. It is for this reason that I have proposed an effective model for global interaction to be drawn up and implemented in the 21st century. I call it "G-Global – the Great world".

It involves a flourishing global economy, with firm safeguards in place against crises, an efficient global currency, and a just system for trade and cooperation. It is a world in which advanced technologies are put to use in the name of the happiness and wellbeing of all people. It is a world of justice and faith between peoples and states, with firm foundations for religious and global security. It is a tolerant community of nations, in which all problems are solved on the basis of harmony and respect. It is our planet, rescued forever from the threat of nuclear destruction, free from weapons of mass destruction.

It is my belief that mankind has the knowledge and experience necessary to create such a model, based on five fundamental principles. Number one: the evolutionary nature of development in our socio-political systems and a rejection of revolution as a form of political progress. In the 21st century, it is revolutions, rather than religions, that have become the opium of the masses. Number two: justice, equality and consensus in interaction between all states. Number three: global transparency, the rejection of all forms of "double standards" and "behind-the-scenes deals" in international relations. Number four: a constructive, multilateral approach as a system of geopolitical balances, free of the mass psychology of the last century. And finally, number five: global tolerance and trust as the primary ingredient for interaction between cultures, religions and states in the 21st century.

I believe that multiculturalism and ethnic and religious diversity are not a challenge to society, but rather a great strength. In the 21st century, tolerance is becoming the key factor in the development and growth of the innovative economy. It's noticeable that over the last thirty years, the countries that have enjoyed the greatest success have been those renowned for their ethnic and cultural diversity.

In today's world there is a need to build on this experience and broaden it even further. Leaders of global and traditional religions could play the leading role in this dialogue with an objective focus on building, ideologically and spiritually, the foundations for a just world order in the 21st century.

Global dialogue is about more than just international forums and meetings. Through interactive communication, a growing number of people are taking part in this dialogue across the world. Similarly the

G-Global idea and format is opening up new opportunities for mutual global understanding and tolerance. I therefore propose to create an online resource dedicated to strengthening global tolerance and trust. This could become part of a general electronic portal for G-Global.

An effective model for peace and harmony is key to the successful development of our country. Independent Kazakhstan is a nation in which 140 ethnicities live together in peace and harmony. We were among the top-three most dynamic economies in the first decade of the 21st century. We have created our own model for harmony between different ethnicities.

Kazakhstani citizens enjoy equal rights whatever their ethnic or religious affiliation, and each of them is an integral part of a single civil community. We are creating the conditions necessary for every person to be able to preach their religion freely, and study their native language, culture and traditions.

The lofty values that are preached by each religion – whether Islam, Orthodox Christianity, the Catholic Church, Protestant teachings, Judaism, Buddhism and others – have always been supported by the Kazakhstani state. This explains the spiritual renaissance that has been taking place in our society for more than twenty years now. New mosques and churches are being built. We are working on the draft version of a programme for the strengthening of inter-faith harmony up to 2016.

At Kazakhstan's initiative, the international year of bringing cultures closer together took place in 2010, whilst UNESCO has declared the period 2013-2022 as an international decade for bringing cultures closer to one another. During Kazakhstan's chairmanship of the OSCE (Organisation for Security and Co-operation in Europe) in 2010, we proposed that our partners expand security measures in the Euro-Atlantic and Euro-Asian regions as well as strengthening tolerance.

The Declaration by the Astana Summit of the OSCE reflected a number of our ideas on developing inter-faith dialogue and strengthening trust between states. During the course of the year, Kazakhstan took charge of the Organisation of Islamic Cooperation, which occurred at a difficult time for the umma.

We put forward a range of initiatives aimed at developing collaboration with Muslim states to solve some of the most pressing socio-economic problems in the humanitarian field. Uncertain processes are currently taking place in the Muslim world. There are some dynamic economies and there are also countries with serious socio-economic problems. Islam represents a formidable layer of humanity's cultural and material legacy, and it is one that is growing. It is impossible for the global community to imagine a world without Islam, either in the present-day or in the future. All forms of impediment to it are short-sighted and, indeed, dangerous. We must approach what is happening in this part of our huge and diverse world with understanding.

Kazakhstan is a country in which Muslims represent a majority among the population. The religion of Islam is one of the spiritual foundations of our society. We have devised a unique formula for nationwide unity and harmony among all Kazakhstanis, regardless of their religious beliefs or ethnicity. Congresses for the leaders of global and traditional religions are a noble gift bestowed by Kazakhstan on the whole world.

Next year will mark the 10th anniversary of the first congress. In order to mark this occasion, I would like to propose that a special appeal be drafted and adopted by the Council of religious leaders, emphasising the importance of dialogue and the relevance of it, and calling for an increase in the peace-making role played by religious and spiritual leaders.

The congresses for leaders of global and traditional religions held in Astana go to show that the theory that irreconcilable differences exist between our religions is nothing more than a fantasy. It is not religions that do battle with one another, but rather people and nation-states. The world's great thinkers describe religion as a formula for morality.

The great Abay once spoke these wise words: *"It is the duty of the believer to do good. But what value is there in good deeds that are done without faith?"*

The higher meaning of any religious credo consists in turning man, and mankind, onto the path towards this lost ideal.

Speech at the 4ᵗʰ Congress for Leaders Of Global and Traditional Religions
Astana, 30ᵗʰ May 2012

SEVEN

IN REMEMBRANCE

The famine of 1932-1933 is one of the most tragic events in Kazakhstan's
history resulting in the death of more than 1.5 million people.
The monument to the memory of victims of the 1932-1933 famine was
inaugurated in 2012 – the 80th anniversary of the start of this terrible disaster
and the 75th anniversary of the beginning of political repression in Kazakhstan.

Astana has been at the centre of the world's attention. At this time, Kazakhstan
is once again carrying out its historical role. Over the last two days, the
leaders of global and traditional religions have been gathered together on
Kazakhstani soil to discuss the pressing problems facing humanity. Astana
is championing the strengthening of global peace, stability and cooperation.

Nine years ago, when the first congress was held, Kazakhstan was described
as a land of peace and harmony. One of the foundations for this harmony
is our unanimous recognition of the eternal values of kindness, peace and
justice. We are equally unanimous in our rejection of the evil, violence and
brutality that took place in our past. On the Memorial day for the victims of
political persecution and famine, we remember two tragic dates in particular,
the eightieth anniversary of the outbreak of a mass famine in our land, and
the seventy fifth anniversary of the start of political persecution.

There was a famine not only in Kazakhstan, but also in Russia, Ukraine
and Belarus. A total of seven million people lost their lives. 1.5 million
of these came from Kazakhstan. We have gathered together today to
immortalise the nation's memory of these people and officially open the
monument 'Asharshylyk kurbandaryna eskertkish'.

The Bolsheviks' policy of collectivisation proved to be a brutal
experiment. It laid waste to a rural way of life that had existed for a hundred
years. The foundations of a one thousand-year-old nomadic civilisation that
had existed on our land were undermined. All this led to great suffering

on the part of millions of people. The famine and its terrible consequences were the greatest humanitarian catastrophe of the Soviet period. Our nation suffered enormous losses. More than 1.5 million people lost their lives as a result of the famine and over 600,000 Kazakhstanis were forced to flee their historic homeland, to escape famine and persecution.

This is a source of pain to our nation that will never go away and never be forgotten. It will remain forever in the hearts of the Kazakhstani people and in the nation's collective memory.

As we attempt to make sense of history, we must show wisdom and not allow this subject to become politicised. The reason for the famine, deportations and mass deaths lay in the brutal policies of the Soviet regime. The chief perpetrator of the persecution was the inhumane, totalitarian system.

At the same time, we must also remember the flip-side of our shared history. In spite of all the hardships they faced, thanks to the hospitality of the Kazakhstani people all those who were deported acquired a new life in Kazakhstan. Their descendants live among us today as our fellow citizens. Together we are building a strong, independent Kazakhstan, which is on the road to peace and creativity! Our record of twenty years of successful, independent growth speaks for itself.

Yet today, we see the economic crisis continuing throughout the world. It is turning into a crisis of social values. In many countries, mass lay-offs of workers are taking place. Salaries and pensions are being cut and companies closing down. The deficit in foodstuffs is growing and prices are increasing for other goods.

In spite of all of this, Kazakhstan is enjoying sustainable, continuous growth. We have overcome these crises. We are putting our programme of industrial development into effect. Every six months or so, dozens of new companies are opening their doors throughout the land. In just two years, around 100,000 new jobs have been created. According to our map showing industrialisation in Kazakhstan, by 2015 more than 350 sites of innovation will have been erected in the recycling industry, agricultural production and infrastructure.

Over the next few years, we are to build thousands of kilometres of new railways and modern highways. As part of the 'Employment-2020' Programme, we will provide gainful employment to 1.5 million Kazakhstanis. We are implementing a campaign to modernise society and increasing the nation's wealth.

Our main goal is to ensure the welfare of all Kazakhstanis. The foundation for all our achievements is peace and stability. This is the key condition for our successes in the future! Stability, peace, unity – these are the firm guarantees that will ensure our country flourishes and becomes prosperous, with every Kazakhstani family provided for. And we must take good care of these guarantees. This must be remembered and passed on to future generations.

We are a young nation with our eyes set firmly on the future. We celebrated the twentieth anniversary of our country's independence just last year. During the first few years of Soviet rule, huge numbers of people were forced to leave Kazakhstan. At that time, our nation's population fell to just four million. Since independence, we have managed to welcome back to the Motherland around a million of our compatriots who left the country. Kazakhstan is now seeing steady growth. The people are becoming more prosperous, the birth rate is rising and the population is increasing with each passing year.

Thanks to the continuity with which the state has provided support in health insurance, the pre-natal mortality rate and the mortality rate in child-birth have fallen significantly. In the last four years alone, average life expectancy has risen from sixty five to seventy. That is a notable achievement. The country's population has been growing steadily at a rate of 1.5-2% a year. There are already some seventeen million people living in Kazakhstan. My aim is to see the country's population rise to twenty million, and this is certainly a realistic target.

There are a great many things we need to do over the coming years. Yet even as we embark on this journey, we must remember our past and pay our respects to the memory of our ancestors. It is essential that we preserve the unity of our nation, peace in our country and harmony in our multi-ethnic society. The large-scale events that have been organised here in Kazakhstan have caught the whole world's attention. As you know, our country hosted the biggest ever meeting for the leaders of the Organisation for Security and Cooperation in Europe. And we are currently hosting the fourth congress for leaders of global and traditional religions.

We are doing all of this so that our country can make a name for itself across the world. This same task is also being performed by other initiatives taking place in Kazakhstan: the battle for a non-nuclear world, regional and global security, benevolent and neighbourly partnerships between nations.

I therefore wish to call on you, once again, to remember the lessons of the past, hold your ancestors in high esteem, roll up your sleeves for the work ahead of us, move forward, and bring up our young people to be hard-working, passionate in their love for their country and native land, and true patriots. May you stay healthy, and may our nation enjoy good health and peace!

Speech at the triumphal opening ceremony in Astana for the
Monument commemorating the victims of the famine of 1932-1933
Astana, 31ˢᵗ May 2012

EIGHT

OLYMPIC SUCCESS

At the ceremony for Olympic competitors, Nursultan Nazarbayev congratulated the Kazakhstani Olympic team which won seven gold, one silver and five bronze medals at the Summer Olympics in London and took twelfth place among the 205 national teams which competed.

I wish to congratulate you, wholeheartedly, on Kazakhstan's superb victory in the Thirtieth Summer Olympic Games! For two weeks, all of the Kazakhstani people were watching and supporting their athletes, as one, after seeing them off to these top-level championships with high hopes. And those of our young men and women who set off to this prestigious competition, with the cheers of the nation ringing in their ears, lived up to these hopes honourably!

Kazakhstan's sportsmen and women achieved successes that are unprecedented in our country's history. At the medallists' podiums in London, the sky-blue flag of Kazakhstan was hoisted above the flags of all the world's other states no fewer than seven times. On seven occasions, the national anthem of Kazakhstan was played beneath London's skies. Our team won medals for the national team's collection on the very first day of competition, and didn't stop until the final moments of the Games.

Whilst the Olympics were taking place, the heartfelt empathy of millions of Kazakhstani sports fans, as they watched the fierce competition for medals unfold, unable to take their eyes off their TV screens, inspired each and every one of the sports stars that Kazakhstan sent to the Games. Inspired by our nation's success at the Olympics, the sense of delight felt by all Kazakhstanis could not be any greater. And this makes us feel confident that in the future we will reach even greater heights.

The essence of our Olympic athletes' triumph in London is wrapped up in three figures: seven, thirteen and twelve! Competitors from Kazakhstan won seven Olympic gold medals. That represents an increase by a factor of three and a half on our haul of gold medals from the previous Games, in Beijing. Like all the other people of Kazakhstan, I am proud of the fact that in honour of our Olympic athletes' victories in London, on seven occasions our country's national anthem was played and the flag of Kazakhstan was raised.

Thirteen is the total number of Olympic medals awarded to our competitors! In addition to the golds, we also won one silver and five bronze medals. And twelve stands for Kazakhstan's current Olympic ranking – twelfth.

Our national team has made extraordinary progress. After finishing in twenty ninth place at the Olympic Games in Beijing, it has jumped right up to twelfth place in the medals table for the London Olympics. Kazakhstan has become one of the leading sporting states among all 205 national teams. This represents a massive victory for our whole nation!

All of us were impatient to see our Olympians achieving magnificent victories! For sixteen days, the whole country followed your progress avidly and supported you. I'm sure that the energy that came from this nationwide support was something you could feel as you competed on the London stage. You lived up to the hopes of a nation, and my own personal hopes! On behalf of all the people of Kazakhstan I wish to thank you and your coaching staff, and everyone who helped to shape your great Olympic victories!

I invited the parents of our champions to attend this ceremony. I wish to thank them for bringing up these heroes, who have brought back sporting glory to our multi-ethnic nation!

There were three sources that helped to create Kazakhstan's Olympic triumph. The first was the support given by the state to physical exercise and sport. Sport and a healthy lifestyle are one of the key priorities in the 'Kazakhstan-2030' Strategy. We are doing a great deal to complete the tasks required to encourage mass participation in physical exercise and sport.

Kazakhstan's twenty most successful Olympians come from no fewer than fourteen of the country's sixteen regions. This speaks volumes about the serious amount of work that has been achieved by local sports authorities throughout the country. I saw to it that funding for elite sports development programmes has more than tripled since 2006. Almost KZT 10 billion were set aside for these goals in the budget for 2012. More than 33,000 sports facilities have been built and are in operation throughout the country. There are more than 70,000 sports associations in our country. A total of three million Kazakhstani citizens regularly practise sport. We will continue this policy of supporting sport in the future.

The second source of the success is the talent, determination and will to win shown by each and every Kazakhstani Olympian, as well as the peerless mastery of their coaching staff. We all witnessed the intense drama of the sporting contests in which our competitors took part. We saw just how difficult and, therefore, how hard-earned each Kazakhstani victory was! The winning performance in the road race by Alexander Vinokourov, who brought us our first gold medal on the first day of the Games, formed the prologue to Kazakhstan's Olympic success.

The weightlifting golds won by Zulfiya Chinshanlo, Maiya Maneza and Svetlana Podobedova continued our Olympic team's winning streak. Ilya Ilyin set a world record in winning his weightlifting event, becoming the first double Olympic champion in Kazakhstan's history as an independent nation. Ilya and Zulfiya both set new world records, whilst Svetlana set an Olympic record in the Clean and Jerk. And we mustn't forget Olga Rypakova and the leap that took her to Olympic gold in the triple jump.

The 'golden' success of our acclaimed boxer, and the captain of the Olympic national team, Serik Sapiev, represented a winning finale for Kazakhstan at the London Olympics. Serik achieved victory in the welterweight category and won the Val Barker Trophy for best boxer. Following his disappointing results at the Beijing Games, I decided to give him my personal backing.

Other contributions to Kazakhstan's overall list of Olympic achievements were made by the boxer Adilbek Niyazmbetov, who won silver, and the following competitors who all won bronze medals: the boxers Marina Volnova and Ivan Dychko and the wrestlers Guzel Manyurova, Daniyal Gadzhiyev and Akzhurek Tanatarov.

Seven of our athletes achieved honourable fifth-place positions in Olympic competition, in boxing, weightlifting, Greco-Roman wrestling and freestyle wrestling. This means that we have much potential for the future. Kazakhstani athletes were also successful in a host of other Olympic disciplines. This is testament to the great potential our sport has.

The third source of Kazakhstan's Olympic success is the friendship that exists between all the different ethnicities in our country, and the unity of our nation! Kazakhstan's Olympic team was, in a very real way, a "sporting Assembly of the nation". Our Olympic champions and medallists included representatives of no fewer than six different ethnicities which are present in Kazakhstan. They come from nine different regions, and also from the cities of Almaty and Astana, and thus the majority of our homeland's regions have a representative on the team. The coaching team for the country's Olympic squad also contains a wide range of nationalities.

Our team performed in London as one big family, and that is exactly what our nation is too. The victories achieved by Kazakhstani Olympians served to make our people even more close-knit, showcasing the great power of patriotism, unity, equality and brotherhood among all those who live in our shared home – the Republic of Kazakhstan.

The feats achieved by our Olympic athletes are a fine example of hard work, patriotism and belief in your ability, both for our young people and for all the citizens of our country! I have no doubt that the Olympic triumphs we have witnessed will inspire thousands of young hearts. Since Kazakhstan became independent, it has had sixty three medallists in the summer and winter Olympics, including eighteen Olympic champions. One hundred and sixteen Kazakhstanis have won medals at various world championships in the same period. In Kazakhstan, more than 250,000 children and teenagers are currently enrolled at 418 sports academies for children and young people.

I am firmly of the belief that the example set by our athletes will bring hundreds of future champions to our stadiums. Sporting achievements in global events are the best way to showcase a state's abilities. In the 21st century, only nations that are strong and fit will be able to compete with the rest of the world. I have therefore set the Government the task of getting 30% of the population involved in physical exercise and sport by 2020. What better way could be there be to promote a healthy way of life than to point to our athletes' achievements. And if every Kazakhstani strives to reach their goal as passionately as our Olympians did, Kazakhstan is destined to become a country that is ahead of the game.

The victories you won are direct evidence that there is a good reason why Kazakhstan has been granted the right to host global championships and sporting events. Having hosting a successful Asian Games, we already have rich experience in this field. The entire country will be busy preparing for the Universiade-2017, which will be held here in Kazakhstan. Next up for our athletes are the Winter Olympics in Sochi in 2014. And, of course, we must start getting ready for more triumphs at the Thirty First Olympic Games in Rio de Janeiro.

We have set the bar high, and we must keep it there. I am confident that sport in Kazakhstan can look forward to plenty more great victories and achievements in the years to come.

Success at the Olympics is a wonderful thing to achieve for your native land. For this reason, I have signed a Directive on the presentation of state awards to our outstanding athletes and coaching staff. On my orders, every Olympic champion will receive USD 250,000 from the state, every silver-medallist will receive USD 150,000 and each bronze-medallist will receive USD 75,000. I have ordered the mayors of all the regions to mark the Olympic successes of all our outstanding countrymen in a fitting way.

The country will show the esteem in which it holds our Olympians and take care of them at all times. One example of which I am aware is that a new athletics facility in Ust-Kamenogorsk will be named after Olga Rypakova. This decision has my full backing. It is quite right that our sports academies and stadiums should bear the names of our Olympians.

The results achieved at the London Olympics will be written into the history books of Kazakhstani sport in gilt-edged lettering. At the Thirty First Summer Olympic Games of 2016 in Rio de Janeiro, Kazakhstan will be one of the strongest nations taking part. Our task, therefore, is not to allow the high standards we have set to slip. We can't wait to see you setting new records and earning sensational victories in the future! Move forward boldly from one victory to the next! May our country's sporting glory grow and expand! Long live Kazakhstan!

Speech at the ceremony to honour the Kazakhstani athletes who
won medals at the 30th Summer Olympic Games held in London
Astana, 17th August 2012

NINE

A NUCLEAR FREE WORLD

A special conference was held to mark the International Day against nuclear tests initiated by the UN at the suggestion of Kazakhstan. At the conference President Nursultan Nazarbayev underlined Kazakhstan's important contribution to nuclear disarmament and its work in strengthening the non-proliferation regime, suggesting five principles comprising the G-Global initiative aimed at improving global nuclear safety.

The present forum is being attended by the heads and members of parliament, members of governments, representatives of international organisations and associations, famous politicians and scientists from over seventy countries. The fact that so many famous people have gathered together in Astana once again confirms how relevant the agenda of our forum is. In March of this year the II Global Summit on Nuclear Security was held in Seoul. The International Conference opening today is a new step towards the implementation by Kazakhstan of the tasks discussed at the spring summit. It is our duty to create an anti-nuclear movement at a global level, which would make an important contribution to ridding humanity of the nuclear threat.

Today, the world marks the International Day Against Nuclear Tests for the third time. It was established by the United Nations at the initiative of Kazakhstan, the first state in history to close down its nuclear test sites. This historic act, accomplished twenty one years ago at the will of the people of our country, is of tremendous significance to civilisation.

I would like to highlight three main points.

First. For Kazakhstan this was a decisive step towards true sovereignty and independence. For the people of Kazakhstan nuclear weapons and radiation were not a distant theory. They were a cruel, implacable evil, to which our land had fallen prey for more than four decades. In total, almost

500 atmospheric, surface and underground tests were carried out in our country for military and so-called "peaceful purposes". That's half of all tests carried out in the world for as long as nuclear weapons have existed. On a daily basis, radiation has poisoned the steppes, rivers and lakes, slowly destroying all life around. The nuclear demon has ruined the fates and undermined the health of over 1.5 million Kazakhstanis living around the sites. The consequences of nuclear testing are felt to this day.

The widespread popular movement to support my initiatives against nuclear testing has given me confidence and strength in defending the interests of the people. Despite tough opposition from the Soviet leadership and the military and industrial complex, I signed the Decree on the Closure of Test Sites.

Second. The twenty ninth of August has become a point of reference in the process of acquiring the status of a nuclear-weapons-free region for the whole of Central Asia. Kazakhstan voluntarily rejected the world's fourth largest nuclear arsenal, inherited from the Soviet military machine. This consisted of more than 110 ballistic missiles with 1,200 nuclear warheads, capable of reaching any point on earth.

At the time, and often today, you can hear opinions belittling the importance of this courageous step by Kazakhstan. For example, there are those who claim that the failure was due to Kazakhstan's lack of ability to maintain a nuclear arsenal. I would point out that Kazakhstan has the world's second largest reserves and is the world's largest producer of uranium. The economic potential of our nation is equal to or greater than the GDP of some "threshold" countries.

After the collapse of the Soviet Union, we had the experts and the necessary infrastructure to implement military nuclear programmes. Therefore, two decades ago the emergence of Kazakhstan as a new nuclear power was only a matter of political will and time. But we have shown political will in another area: we have fundamentally and irrevocably renounced our membership of the "nuclear club". In cooperation with the USA and Russia, warheads and bombs have been disposed of. In September 2006, together with other countries in the region, we signed the Semipalatinsk Agreement, which declared Central Asia a nuclear-free zone.

Third. With the closure of the Semipalatinsk test site, a new phase of the global process of nuclear non-proliferation and disarmament was launched. Prior to twenty ninth of August 1991 mainly restrictive measures were taken in the area of nuclear safety. Kazakhstan was the first to impose a complete and unconditional ban on the testing and, hence, perfecting of "doomsday" weapons. Sixteen years ago, by a decision of the UN, the Comprehensive Nuclear Test Ban Treaty was opened for signature. And Kazakhstan was amongst the first to sign it. 183 states have already joined the treaty and 157 have ratified it.

All powers belonging to the "nuclear club" observe the moratorium on testing. After the closure of the Semipalatinsk test site, the planet's other major test sites – in Nevada, Novaya Zemlya, Lop Nor and Mururoa – have remained silent. Hence, the twenty ninth of August is a watershed moment for the whole world; the date on which the danger of a nuclear apocalypse was averted. I am convinced that the awareness of how critically important this date is to the world community will continue to grow in the years to come.

For sixty five years the British magazine "The Bulletin of Atomic Scientists" has been measuring the level of the global nuclear danger on a symbolic "doomsday" clock. Earlier this year, the clock's hand moved a minute closer to a potential nuclear disaster.

Why has this assessment been made? Without any doubt, the specialists wanted to draw the attention of the participants of the summit in Seoul to an array of problems in this area. We can certainly observe today a reduction in the strengthening of global nuclear safety. And this is in spite of regular summits held on this topic.

First, a regime of non-proliferation of nuclear weapons has not yet been universally achieved. "New" nuclear and some "threshold" countries are excluded from the agreement in question. Second, the Prague Treaty between the USA and Russia was signed two years ago, which revived the process of reducing strategic offensive weapons. However, this did not set an example for other countries in the official "nuclear club". Third, the Comprehensive Nuclear Test Ban Treaty cannot become effective. This still requires a number of signatures of countries in the "threshold" group. Fourth, the issue of the global monitoring of the development of national nuclear power programmes has not been regulated. The lack of clear unambiguous norms casts a shadow of suspicion of "nuclear ambitions" or even "support for nuclear terrorism" on almost any state that strives to use nuclear energy for peaceful purposes. This manifest injustice is not conducive to strengthening the regime of non-proliferation, and perpetuates distrust in nuclear safety.

There are fears that the amendments to the Convention on the Physical Protection of Nuclear Material will not come into force, as planned, by 2014. The reason for this is the deadlock in the process of ratification by a number of countries. Fifth, the accident at the nuclear power plant in Fukushima last year has clearly highlighted to the world the issue of maintaining modern security technology at peaceful nuclear facilities.

This is not by any means an exhaustive list of the issues that have hampered the process of forming a global system of nuclear safety. But all of these are the effects rather than the causes. The underlying source of this problem goes far deeper.

The current state of global nuclear safety is strongly influenced by flaws in modern world politics, largely inherited from previous eras. These include inertia in thinking as a bloc, the lack of trust and transparency in relations between countries and the lack of responsibility of individual states.

The situation is exacerbated by the chaotic nature of the objective process of piecing together a multipolar world. The opium of military nuclear energy still intoxicates the minds of some political and military figures. There are forces in the world which narrowly view the global multipolar world primarily as the totality of the centres of nuclear power.

I am convinced that there should be no place for the exotica of "nuclear umbrellas" in the world of the future. It is immoral to make nuclear safety a bargaining chip in dealing with other issues of interstate relations. At the same time, the twenty-first century is inconceivable without nuclear power. According to experts, by 2035 the world economy's demand for energy will double. There are currently around two billion people in the world who have no access to electricity. For many countries the problems of poverty, unemployment and food shortages can be solved by the implementation of peaceful nuclear energy projects, certainly, under the strict supervision of the UN and the IAEA (International Atomic Energy Agency). Therefore, our raising the issue of a nuclear-free world has nothing to do with radiophobia or a utopian desire to assign the secret of energy from nuclear fission to "oblivion". A nuclear-free world is a complete ban on the military use of nuclear energy. This is the essence of my proposal for the development and adoption of the Universal Declaration of a Nuclear-free World. I was and remain a consistent supporter of this idea.

From the standpoint of political realism, I have to admit that the solution to the key problems of global nuclear security is inseparable from the overall process of transforming the modern world order. Recently, I made an appeal to form a new world order in the format and on the principles of G-Global. Its major feature should be humanity's attainment of freedom from the fear of nuclear self-destruction. I am convinced that on the basis of the proposed five principles of G-Global a breakthrough in global nuclear safety is possible.

First, we need a step by step plan for a comprehensive reduction of strategic offensive weapons with the participation of all nuclear-armed states, developed and adopted under the auspices of the United Nations. Above all, it is important to ensure that the Comprehensive Nuclear Test Ban Treaty comes into force.

I believe that the world community has the right to push for all member states of the "nuclear club" to assume obligations to reduce their nuclear military arsenals. Not all at once, but gradually. For example, these states can adopt the practice of refusing to modernise and decommissioning obsolete nuclear weapons as well as the means of supply.

Naturally, this should be implemented in parallel to the process of disarmament by the two leading nuclear powers; the USA and Russia. Over the longer term, measures to wind down the "nuclear umbrellas" are viewed as realistic. This only concerns limiting the distribution and storage of nuclear weapons within the boundaries of the national territory of the state that possesses them.

Second, it is important to have robust international guarantees of safety for all the participants in the regional nuclear-free zones. It is necessary to develop mechanisms to encourage states to fundamentally reject military nuclear programmes. Only on this basis is it possible to provide a just solution to the problems associated with the prospects of nuclear power in individual countries. To date, thirty states have adopted national obligations in the field of nuclear safety. In international anti-nuclear law and practical politics there should be no "double standards" and exceptions.

Third, nuclear disarmament and a nuclear-free world are inconceivable without clear mechanisms to underscore the confidence of all participants in this process. The principle of confidence is a sensible alternative to the military concept of deterrence, including nuclear.

In a month's time we shall be marking the twentieth anniversary of Kazakhstan's initiative of the CICA (Conference on Interaction and Confidence Building Measures in Asia). CICA is a developing and promising structure of regional and global security. It involves twenty seven states, which are home to half the world's population, and accounts for over a third of the total world product.

The successful development of the CICA shows that in the twenty-first century any issues arising in relations between states, can only be resolved constructively on the basis of trust. The global system of nuclear safety must fully exploit the potential of regional groupings – CICA, OSCE (Organisation for Security and Co-operation in Europe), the Organisation of Islamic Cooperation, etc. Accordingly, it is important to broaden their "basket" to include the issue of creating a nuclear-free world.

In proposing the idea of G-Global, I stated that global tolerance was one of the fundamental principles of the new world order. Unfortunately, false promises are still being made in global practice to "reinforce" the strength of one religion or another through the power of nuclear weapons. Let me remind you that twenty years ago Kazakhstan resolutely rejected the advice of certain "well-wishers" and the dubious honour of being the first Muslim nuclear power. Nuclear weapons spell suicide for humanity. And suicide as a direct challenge to the Creator is condemned by all religions of the world.

And from this point of view, the desire to develop a military nuclear power is absolute blasphemy.

A nuclear-free world is our common goal, a goal for which humanity should strive. Only by acting together can we make our world a safer and better place. We have the opportunity to remind the world once again of the tragic consequences of nuclear testing, to urge the global community to take more decisive action to bring about their final and irrevocable prohibition. It is for this purpose that Kazakhstan is launching the international "ATOM" Project.

The name of the project is composed of the first letters of the four words in English "Abolish Testing. Our Mission". As part of the project, anyone anywhere on earth who is opposed to nuclear weapons may subscribe to the online petition directed to the world's governments, to renounce permanently nuclear testing and to push for the Comprehensive Nuclear Test Ban Treaty to become effective as soon as possible. I call upon all people of good will in the world to support the "ATOM" Project and to make the construction of a world without nuclear weapons our most important goal.

Fourth. I regard global transparency as one of the foundations for a future nuclear-free community of nations. Through its own anti-nuclear experience, Kazakhstan has demonstrated to the world its openness in matters of nuclear disarmament and non-proliferation. We recently carried out, in a transparent manner, a project for the transportation of 210 tonnes of spent nuclear fuel to safe storage.

Transparent work is on-going to convert Kazakhstan's reactors to reduced-enrichment fuel. In cooperation with the IAEA, a unique automated system of accounting, monitoring and physical protection of natural uranium is being created. Work is underway to implement Kazakhstan's bid to the IAEA to place the International Nuclear Fuel Bank in our country. These are all examples of the indisputable benefits for our country, which has renounced nuclear weapons for good. At the same time it sets an example for other states.

Fifth, the movement towards a nuclear-free world is the path to constructive multipolarity. Positive cooperation, for the sake of the security of mankind, is demonstrated by the participation of many countries in the work to transform the former Semipalatinsk test site into "a territory of the world". The high level of cooperation on this matter between Kazakhstan, the USA and Russia was noted in the joint statement of the Presidents of the three countries, adopted during the Seoul summit. A significant contribution to the various rehabilitation projects was made by Japan, Canada, the Netherlands, Switzerland and a number of international organisations. We are deeply grateful to everyone for this help. A variety of UN programmes also play an important role in overcoming the consequences of nuclear testing.

Two years ago Secretary General Ban Ki-moon personally visited the territory of the former test site. I am grateful to him for his support for, and appreciation of, Kazakhstan's anti-nuclear policies and initiatives.

Today, humanity has a unique chance to put an end to the endless balancing on the brink of nuclear collapse. For this, it is important now more than ever to unite the efforts of all nations, of all people of good will!

At the same time I would like to draw the participants' attention to the on-line communication medium G-Global. It has already enabled millions of users to engage in dialogue on a wide range of issues relating to the formation of a new fair world order in the twenty-first century. I have no doubt that the most important component of this world order will be a nuclear-free world. I urge you to participate actively in an interactive discussion in the format of G-Global and to work for a nuclear-free world, for our future and the future of our grandchildren.

Introduction to the International Conference
"From nuclear test ban to a world free of nuclear weapons"
Astana, 29th August 2012

TEN

RELATIONS BETWEEN SOCIETY & STATE

*The Constitution of Kazakhstan was adopted by a referendum in 1995
and became a fundamental document, which defines the social and state
structure, the relationship between society and the state, as well as that
between citizen and state. The Constitution is one of the vital
instruments in the democratic development of Kazakhstan.*

As you are aware, our Fundamental Law starts with the words *"We, the
people of Kazakhstan, are united by a common historical destiny."*

From the moment it was adopted, our Constitution has served as a
platform for the harmony and stability of our multi-national people. Using
our Fundamental Law as a basis, we laid the foundations for a re-born
Kazakhstani national identity and set out on the path to robust development.
Our Fundamental Law, having become a unique code of honour of a free
nation, encompassed the breadth of the boundless Kazakhstani steppes
as well as the heroism of its people and its propensity to higher ideals.
The Fundamental Law, having laid the cornerstone for the indestructible
foundation of our independence, is now the sacred book of our nationhood.
Reflecting the interests and aspirations of the people and summoned into
existence by their own heart, our Constitution is a guiding star, keeping
us on the right track in these testing times, full of unknown ordeals. The
Constitution is a life-giving source, the origin of all our laws, guaranteeing
the steady development of our country.

The Kazakhstani people have a wise saying: *"Progress only comes to the
country that respects its laws and knows how to obey them."* We are striving
towards a state in which the Fundamental Law is followed unfailingly, and
its letter is turned into the inviolate law governing our lives. It is thanks
to this that our achievements have become possible, and our country has
attained international authority. And we are now celebrating the supremacy

of our Fundamental Law, harmonising the noble past of our people with their bright future; our state can only look forward to success.

We in Kazakhstan very much appreciate the attention given by legal science throughout the world to our experience of constitutional development. A constitution is the foundation of the entire pyramid of a state's structure. Peace and harmony are those values that this political and judicial innovation sought to corroborate when it was first introduced in the 18th century.

In a few days' time – on the 17th September – the 225th anniversary of the adoption of the first constitution in the world, the Constitution of the United States of America by the Convent in Philadelphia will be celebrated. The Constitution of the Republic of Kazakhstan is thirteen times younger than that of the USA. But it is based upon the same great principles of freedom, a striving towards equality of rights and the prosperity of its people. And seventeen years ago Kazakhstanis showed wisdom, cohesion and unity by voting in a referendum to adopt the Fundamental Law.

We studied over twenty of the world's constitutions before settling on our own. It was necessary to consider the tendencies of worldwide development, the best articles of the constitutions from around the world and to take into account our own traditions and history. And this synthesis was accomplished by our own specialists and those from abroad.

Discussions with the experts gave rise to the idea and initiative for the Constitution of Kazakhstan, which had the backing of the whole nation. Today we can proudly announce that the Constitution of 1995 was the most important factor for Kazakhstan's success. Firstly, it laid the foundation for building a new modern state and we creatively applied the multi-faceted experience of the world's developed democracies.

Ensuring all institutions of power are elected and accountable to the people and safeguarding human rights and freedoms – these are the basic foundations of our state structure. Kazakhstan's independent judicial system is being improved and national institutes for the protection of rights are being developed. At the same time the Constitution takes full account of the mentality and legal traditions of our nation. The pivot of the constitutional order is the provision on equality for all citizens living in Kazakhstan, irrespective of their ethnic, religious, social or other affiliation, What is unique is the constitutional status of the Assembly of the Nation of Kazakhstan – the principal mechanism for securing inter-ethnic harmony. The Assembly selects its representatives from the Majilis (lower house of Parliament), ensuring the interests of all 140 ethnicities in our country. This is not found in any other country in the world.

Secondly, our Constitution resolves the issues of the basic principles of economic development. A central provision is the stipulation that economic growth should be directed towards the benefit of the people and society as a whole. For the past one and a half decades our economy has been growing at an average of seven per cent every year. In comparison with the initial period of independence, the country's GDP has increased more than sixteen times. The GDP per capita is currently around USD 12,000. Let us not forget that in 1993 it was a mere USD 700. Throughout the years of independence USD 150 billion of foreign investment has been injected into our economy.

Thanks to state support, the number of small and medium-sized businesses has increased in Kazakhstan thirty five times. By 2020 the proportion of products of this sector of the economy will constitute 40% of the country's GDP. This is a graphic illustration of how social modernisation is materialising on the basis of the Constitution – a mass middle class is growing.

Thirdly, the constitutional provision regarding the social character of our state has proven to be the basis that is successfully helping the economy survive the effects of the most hard-hitting global crisis. Since 2010 the country has built around 440 new industrial facilities, with almost 50,000 highly qualified staff. Over 250 further enterprises will be set up in the next five years, creating around 150,000 jobs for Kazakhstanis.

Over the last decades the financing of education and science, the health service, and the social security sphere has increased several times over. 370 new schools have been built, and the number of children's pre-school centres has grown seven and a half times. Dozens of major medical centres have been built with the most advanced equipment. Quite recently

Kazakhstan became one of twenty two countries in which heart transplant operations were carried out successfully. We are planning to build around 400 new health care centres by 2016. The level of pension provision is one of the highest and most reliable in the CIS.

Fourthly, Kazakhstan's predisposition to an open foreign policy is clearly defined in our Constitution. We are developing economic integration with Russia and Belarus – our partners in the Currency Union and the Common Free Market Zone. Given Kazakhstan's contribution to the global anti-nuclear movement, we believe we have the moral right to preside over this movement to ensure that the world becomes nuclear-free, and that mankind is not wiped off the face of the earth in a nuclear war. We were the first to close down the largest test site in the world. We voluntarily renounced our nuclear arsenal, and showed the world that nuclear bombs are no guarantee of security.

The CICA (Conference on Interaction and Confidence Building Measures in Asia), convened at my own initiative, promotes the strengthening of security. This year will mark the twentieth anniversary of this process. Thanks to its position of authority, Kazakhstan has successfully presided over the largest regional organisations – OSCE (Organisation for Security and Co-operation in Europe) and the Organisation for Islamic Cooperation. As a responsible member of the international community, Kazakhstan proposes that the whole world works together to form a new world structure in the format, and on the basis, of the five principles of G-Global.

The main aim of social modernisation is the formation in Kazakhstan of an Association of Universal Labour. The "concept of the consumer society" that has been drummed into the world over the last half a century, has turned out to be an illusion. In this environment the value of labour has been negated, and the right to freedom of labour has been narrowly and selfishly perceived by some as the "opportunity" to live at the expense of support from the state. Therefore in the idea of an Association of Universal Labour I see an alternative to the growth of social parasitism and to the illusion of "making a quick buck" without the support of social security contributions.

Our state is meeting the needs of its citizens in practically every respect.

We are implementing the "Employment 2020" Programme whereby the state provides people wanting to work in rural locations with micro-loans, and those moving to the cities with qualifications and places of work.

Over four million people currently receive welfare payments, benefits and pensions in Kazakhstan, which adds to the burden of every working person in the country. What are welfare payments and benefits? These represent money earned by some people which the state then gives to others. Therefore, to secure true social equality for everyone a "golden medium" is needed, so that there is no adverse effect on the rights of those who work conscientiously and contribute towards the state's support of vulnerable citizens.

The social policies of a modern state should provide not only for the protection of the vulnerable amongst its citizens, but also the support of the working population. Social welfare is often only understood in the sense of welfare benefits. But social welfare not only refers to wages, pensions and other payments. It is a package of fundamental conditions the state has created for the health and prosperity of Kazakhstanis. These include the health service, education, sport, housing construction, and so on.

I am certain that with an Association of Universal Labour, hard-working people will see themselves as the masters of their own destinies and lives. This is the very basis of social modernisation.

The main idea behind modernisation is the planned implementation of the social potential of our Constitution. And in this plan we are faced with a list of tasks. Firstly, a new reading of our Constitution is needed for the XXI century. The Fundamental Law is not a dried-up legal relic. It is a living mechanism that should provide the framework to enable people to access legal and social innovations that satisfy the new conditions and quality of Kazakhstani society. This is the path all developed countries have taken. It is also our path towards successful development. Therefore, the task of the legal experts, and in particular specialists in the field of constitutional law, is to open up the pioneering spirit of the Constitution. It is important to turn the energy of the Fundamental Law into the strength to make practical decisions – of the new laws and legal norms, to secure the progress of our country.

Secondly, I have set the task of carrying out a complex inventory of the social legislation of Kazakhstan, and also of drawing up new laws. These are draft bills to secure work places in the social sector, a system of professional qualifications, etc.

Thirdly, we are currently paying particular attention to the development of the mechanisms for "feedback" from government bodies to citizens by using the facilities of the information society. There are currently around eight million users of the World Wide Web in Kazakhstan, which is practically half of all Kazakhstanis. An important task, therefore, is to develop an "electronic government", a three-level system of "electronic local administration". The "Information Kazakhstan" programme is currently being developed. The transfer of all authorisation procedures to an electronic format has been planned for as early as 2013.

Fourthly, a successful society in the 21st century is a society of people well versed in the law. The basis for this legal literacy is first and foremost a knowledge of the Constitution. Therefore, educating the population in the legal culture is an important issue for social modernisation. We need to start in kindergartens and schools. And continue in colleges and universities, in the work place. This is a task for all government bodies, national companies and employers of all forms of ownership.

Our great predecessor Töle Biy once said: *"A country that respects its laws is that much more content than all the others."*

We are the successors of ancient civilisations, whose representatives had to be respected and obeyed. The Fundamental Law was a deed of honour. Our closest ancestors also implicitly complied with the decisions of the Biys – experts and architects of the law of the steppes. Our contemporaries, learning from past history, are steadfastly carrying on the wise traditions of unity and continuity of the generations. May our Fundamental Law – the heart of our nation state and bastion of our independence – be celebrated in centuries to come! In our conquest of new heights let us breathe easily and deeply!

Introduction to the International Scientific-Practical Conference,
dedicated to Constitution Day of the Republic of Kazakhstan
Astana, 30ᵗʰ August 2012

ELEVEN

EDUCATION AND DEVELOPMENT

*Nazarbayev University was opened at the initiative of the President of
Kazakhstan, Nursultan Nazarbayev, in 2010 with the aim of modernising the
education system in Kazakhstan and attracting international experience
and high-level teaching staff in a range of scientific fields. The Head of State
shared his views on the further development of education as an integral part
of the political and economic development of Kazakhstan.*

There is an old saying that still holds true today: *"He who is strong will defeat
one man, but he who has knowledge will overcome a thousand."*

The wisdom of this Kazakhstani proverb is more relevant today than ever. We
are living in an age in which our job is to rely not on force, but on knowledge.
The modern world has reached a level where each state's potential is measured
first and foremost by the state of science and education within the country. And
it is assessed by means of how, within that particular country, people are able to
apply the knowledge they have gained for the benefit of society.

There would be little colour to life without the knowledge that has
been acquired through focused and determined effort, which at times
can seem like digging a well with a needle. That's why, as I see it, our
knowledge is the foundation for our independence, and our ideas are the
security for our freedom.

Nazarbayev University is already setting its own standard – one that is very
high by all international measures – of teaching and academic research. The
Kazakhstani higher education community, and also our education system
as a whole, is currently oriented toward our own system of educational and
investigative values and traditions.

Some years ago, when we were beginning to plan and construct this
university, our aim was for it to be the best higher education institute in
Kazakhstan. We needed a new university. A university that would be a leader,

with a new mentality that would become a model for higher education institutes in Kazakhstan in the 21st century. Thus this unique university, to which I agreed to lend my name, came into being.

The university's potential is growing stronger with great dynamism with over 1500 students currently enrolled. There were ten people competing for every place this year and professors from the world's leading universities give lectures here.

The Life Sciences Centre, Centre for Energy Research and Inter-disciplinary Instrumental Centre are all making great progress. Around seventy scientific and technical projects are being implemented here, and this figure will have risen to a hundred by the end of the year. Scientific studies have been published in some of the world's most prestigious scientific publications. Four patents for inventions have already been obtained.

We will continue developing the university as we move forward. Today we are opening the School of education. By the end of the year we plan to open the Business School and the School of state policy. We are not all that far from the day when we will be able to open the Medical and Mining Schools.

It is on the campus of a leader in university education that a new future for our country is being born, along with a new elite for our state. Those whose role will be to shape Kazakhstan in the 21st century, ensuring that the Kazakhstani people enjoy peace and a flourishing future.

Over the course of twenty years of stable and successful growth, Kazakhstan has achieved its most important historical objective. For the first time in centuries of our nation's history, a state was formed on land that has been Kazakhstani since time immemorial, enjoying full international legitimacy. I have to say that the recognition of its state sovereignty represents a massive and highly-prized resource for any nation. Throughout those years, the country worked towards gaining sovereignty and political clout in the world as well as recognition of this sovereignty. Twenty years later, the goal has been achieved.

Throughout the years of independence, within just one generation, Kazakhstan has been transformed from a developing country into a country with a medium level of income and a growing economy. Quality of life has improved dramatically, because right from the start we set high standards for Kazakhstani people's lives. By way of example, the poverty level has fallen four-fold over the last ten years, whilst the economy is sixteen times larger than it was a decade ago.

Our balanced, measured foreign policy has enabled Kazakhstan to achieve great success in the global arena. Long-term, carefully planned investment in human resources has endowed us with a talented and – I have no doubt of it – successful younger generation. We have created the most favourable conditions possible for your education and self-improvement, so that, we produce professionals, in demand across the globe, bringing success, prosperity and acclaim to Kazakhstan in the 21st century. This is, if you like, the mission for the future and responsibility before previous generations.

The first decade of this century began with an outbreak of international terrorism, after which the world was hit by a global financial and economic crisis of unprecedented proportions, in which the global economic order that had existed for decades was held hostage. The crisis that began in 2007 in the USA spread to Europe in 2008, and ever since then Europe has been in its clutches. Today, every country is forced time and time again for a new place in its global surroundings and change itself, in order to remain competitive.

The model for the global economic system is currently being reassessed, and the foundations of a consumer economy and global finances are undergoing transformation. The biggest global financial and economic crisis in the planet's history has not yet been overcome. It is continuing to exert a powerful influence on every country, including Kazakhstan.

Also on the agenda are a range of external risks such as global political shifts, volatility in energy prices and conflicts over resources. The new order also brings challenges for each country's internal security. In many countries, this could lead to social tension, incitement to civil disorder, conflict between different races and religions, and to threats from terrorist organisations. Our task is to reduce these risks as much as possible, and for that reason we are currently working systematically on these crucial issues.

Firstly, in our pragmatic foreign policy, the main emphasis will be on:

- developing new relationships and partnerships;
- economic diplomacy;
- further strengthening of Kazakhstan's role in providing regional and global security.

The international community, which has been through such a deep crisis, must be in no doubt that Kazakhstan knows what it wants; knows what it has to offer, is well aware of the cost of this issue and will always fulfil its obligations.

Secondly, the economic policy of this new phase in our development demands significant adjustment to our investment policy. Investment will go wherever it will lead to the greatest profit. In Kazakhstan's modern economic model, the motivation to secure profits and make a return on investment will be no different from how it is at the world's leading corporations. We are currently establishing a new approach to international economic collaboration. The new areas for growth will be small and medium-sized businesses. All of this is extremely important for new Kazakhstani industry and Kazakhstan's key strategic strengths are its raw materials.

At present, we are working on issues related to making efficient use of our energy and mining industry, in order to create new economic growth in the country and productivity in these sectors, and ensure the greatest possible increase in the levels of manufacturing and profit. In order to ensure stability, we are optimising our policies in respect of social welfare, labour and employment. In healthcare, we will continue the reforms that have been commenced. We are re-focusing our plans with regard to residential housing and providing the country with water security.

A very important factor during this new stage is administrative reform. In this field we are working on issues related to de-centralisation, protecting private property, strengthening the institutes which govern contractual relations and ensuring equality before the law.

These key areas will determine the new direction that Kazakhstan takes in the new world order. This direction is currently being developed by the Government and by our experts.

Today, Kazakhstan is a young and dynamic nation. The average age of the population is below thirty five. The 'baby boom' which began in 2005 is forecast to continue until 2016. There will be 1.2 million more children than in former years. This younger generation will one day take up the baton passed on by those who are shaping Kazakhstan's new future. It is not too early to start putting in place all the conditions required in order for them to get the very best out of life.

I have issued a raft of orders on the strengthening of the state's policy in relation to young people. A Committee on youth issues has now been created. Departments on matters related to young people are being formed in every region. A new Concept for youth policy, lasting until 2020, is currently being drawn up. Young Kazakhstanis must remember that citizenship of a country not only confers rights, but also, and more importantly, brings with it a great responsibility in respect of yourself, your family and your Motherland. In the 21st century, the people of Kazakhstan must become a nation that enjoys longevity. Good health is sometimes thought to be connected only to medicine. Good health is something that individuals themselves must strive to attain. I call on all of you, and on all students, to quit bad habits that can damage your health, take up sport and lead an active lifestyle.

We are moving towards a post-industrial world, in which the triad of 'health, science and innovation' will hold sway. International organisations attached to the UN, European leaders, a large number of famous economists and politicians have already officially recognised the concept of the Third industrial revolution.

A very clear description of this concept has been given by the well-known American academic Jeremy Rifkin. The first revolution was related to the invention of the steam engine, the second – with the invention of electricity and the first communications devices, and the third began at the same time as digital communications.

Over the coming years, internet technologies and renewable sources of energy will come together to create new infrastructure for the third industrial revolution. The "Energy Internet" will enable millions of people to produce clean energy in their homes and offices and at energy plants, and to exchange it freely with one another.

A fascinating project is currently in the pipeline in Africa, involving the construction of solar and wind power stations in the Sahara. The energy will be supplied by means of an underwater cable beneath the Mediterranean to Europe. Renewable energy enables us to bring back to life certain types of industry which became traditional for our people, and also distant-pasture cattle-rearing. Any rural shepherd who had at his disposal a small wind and solar power station could build himself a complex with a mobile home, communications and a water supply. 90% of the land in our country is not polluted by chemicals. It is therefore possible to grow clean natural crops which are in demand throughout the world. The world's demand for foodstuffs is set to grow by 40% by 2050. All this represents the advantages that the 'green economy' gives us, which will form the basis of the industrial revolution.

It is very important to develop institutes which ensure stability and harmony in relationships between different ethnicities and religions. We must strengthen the legal sanctions and bring in measures outlawing discrimination on religious or ethnic grounds, as well as crimes in this field. We must further enhance the role played by the Assembly of the People of Kazakhstan. The Kazakhstani people will have no truck with extremism and radicalism. Our citizens have always spoken out against empty rhetoric and social discord.

We are all aware of the political, inter-ethnic and religious conflicts taking place all over the world. Nobody has any safeguards against these things in the 21st century. And there can be no winners when they are taking place. The only thing that wins in such conflicts is evil, which leads to poverty, destruction, famine, a protracted civil war and a backward step towards the Dark Ages. Today, in the 21st century, we are living in a 'glass world'. It is a world that is both transparent and fragile. It is not the kind of place in which anyone should be throwing stones. It needs to be looked after.

I would like to underline three key Kazakhstani successes in which our nation can take pride.

Number one. The unity we have among all Kazakhstanis – representing 140 ethnicities – is a value unlike any other. Our mission is to take care of it, protect it and encourage its proliferation. We must not allow anyone to rock the boat, as we set a successful course through the world's oceans.

Number two. Tolerance, a trait that is typical of our nation as a whole and each of us in particular. Peaceful understanding and respect for ethical and religious differences. Thanks to this, our diversity, rather than dividing us, unites us. If it were not for our tolerance, we could be blown off course, and would no longer be safeguarded against disaster. We would be transformed into seafarers who have suffered disasters and are issuing a distress call.

Number three. The shared nature of our historical fate. Our aim is not only to survive in the new conditions of the changed world in which we live, but also to continue our development, building on our past achievements and expanding our ability to influence this new world.

Industrialisation based on innovation has become the new guiding value for our society. The second attribute that we can hold up as a value is our hard-working nature. I have been receiving a great deal of positive feedback in response to the article in which I outlined the programme 'Twenty steps to a society of universal labour'. This is not surprising, because hard work always has been, and always will be, a distinguishing feature of the people of Kazakhstan.

Kazakhstanis are one big, indivisible family, in which the country's flourishing depends on the labour, knowledge and experience of every single citizen. Today, there are just as many openings in the labour market as there are unemployed people. There is a shortage of skilled workers at the moment. All those who are willing to work can quite easily earn money doing not one, but two jobs.

This is a situation that requires careful handling. The solution is a redistribution of manpower: skilled hands and smart minds are in demand everywhere. By dint of having grown so quickly, we have become accustomed to the good life. Our people often forget what is going on in other countries. There, ordinary people have little to say about the level of their salary, pensions, benefits or whatever else it might be. They have only one dream: to secure gainful employment of some shape or form.

Here in Kazakhstan, the time has already come when everyone is able to enjoy stability in their lives and not only put food on the table for their family, but also give their children a good education and plan for the future. The main principle throughout the world is not that the work goes where the people are, but that the people go where the work is.

Each and every individual strives to go to wherever they will have the opportunity to earn money and make a living. This axiom holds true for all of the world's developed countries. If we want to achieve a world-class standard of living, the work we do must be at the same level. Therefore discipline and the quality of our work take on a special importance. Without these simple rules, we can't even begin to talk about a successful modernisation of society.

However much effort the state might put into raising the population's prosperity, it will only grow if each and every Kazakhstani citizen becomes a hard-working master of their fate, and seeks to cherish and promote all that is good about this country. No longer can we simply sit back and do nothing. Today, every person in Kazakhstan must ask him or herself the question: what have I done to make things good in my country, and to make our Motherland richer? If every citizen thinks along these lines, I am positive that the whole country will get a massive boost to its development. The main thing is to remember the following: discipline and order before all else.

I started out in life as an ordinary worker, and it is my belief that in any production process and in any workforce, you need discipline among the staff. It is therefore important to bring in a new format, in which the state, rather than being forever a donor, is a partner, creating the requisite conditions for increasing the prosperity of society as a whole and each of its members.

There's another abiding value, too: the desire to further our knowledge. World experts are predicting there will be a drastic shortage in skilled labour. According to their forecasts, by 2020 the global market is going to need an additional 40 million employees with a degree-level qualification and 45 million specialists with professional technical qualifications. Even now there is a particularly acute shortage of engineers, doctors, chemists, biologists and other professionals from the 'exact' and 'natural' professions.

Consider this: countries such as Japan, China, South Korea, Singapore and Malaysia are getting ahead thanks to the mastery with which they implement their ideas and technologies, and to their determination and hard work.

According to one of the most famous theoretical physicists of our times, Stephen Hawking, mankind is entering an era in which it will determine its own evolution, an era in which constant modernisation is required.

The knowledge you have is the result of the work you do. The more you work and strive to educate yourself, the more you will know. We look on knowledge as an economic resource for the state, a factor in our manufacturing. We are slowly but surely modernising our national education system, bringing it ever closer to international standards.

Over the last three years, Kazakhstan has been in the top four countries in UNESCO's Development Index, out of some 129 countries from around the world.

By tapping into the potential of young talent, we have seen a dramatic increase in the number of awards won by our schoolchildren in international intellectual competitions. Whereas in 1998 our schoolchildren won only eight medals, the tally this year already stands at 957. This represents growth by a factor of almost 120.

In 1993 we took a decision that was firmly oriented towards the future. The 'Bolashak' programme was the first cornerstone in the implementation of the Kazakhstani model for innovative education.

The 'Balapan' programme is now being implemented in dynamic fashion in the field of nursery education. We have brought in funding on a per capita basis and are developing private-public partnerships. The number of pre-school organisations has risen by more than 3,500. In just two years, the percentage of children attending nursery school has risen from 36% to 65%. We will ensure that by 2020, all children in Kazakhstan will be able to go to nursery school.

We must continue to modernise pre-school education: by doing so, we will lay the foundations for building a well-rounded character in our children in later life. I am therefore tasking the Government with the following:

Firstly: on the model of advanced international experience, introduce modern teaching methods in nursery education. These must be innovative, whilst the education technologies used must be creative.

Secondly: devise detailed systemic proposals on how to increase the number of children with access to pre-school education.

Thirdly: ensure that trilingual teaching is introduced throughout the country at the level of pre-school education.

In so doing, we will be able to construct a logical system for language learning: the alphabet in kindergarten, a basic level at school, and a professional level in the language studied at university or college. In the secondary education system we are continuing our preparations for the introduction of twelve-year teaching. New standards in education are being developed. The infrastructure of secondary education is being improved, and the three-tier system is being done away with. By the end of 2014, 522 new schools will have been built.

Active steps are currently being taken to expand the network of Intellectual Schools. Their practices will gradually be expanded to the whole of the secondary education system. This year, thirty five academic institutions will start work following the same standards as the Intellectual Schools. In order to promote advanced technologies, digital teaching is being introduced in secondary education. In 2012 it will be introduced in 581 schools. Now, children from rural schools and children with disabilities will be able to enjoy access to teaching materials.

We must continue to modernise our secondary education system. It is essential that we provide a phased transition of secondary education towards per capita funding. If a child moves to a different school, the money given to his former school will go with him. We will thereby increase competition between schools.

I am ordering the Government to get to work on implementing per capita funding in a number of pilot schools.

Special attention must be paid to increasing the level of qualifications among teachers and the incentives on offer for them. We have brought in a new three-level programme for re-training teachers, devised on the basis of the best pedagogical practices. I am ordering the Government to ensure that 120,000 teachers receive training over the next five years under a new programme of further training.

We must increase schools' autonomy and create supervisory boards within them. In essence, at school level we will begin to devise new mechanisms for primary local self-governance. A network of world-class colleges is being created in Kazakhstan, which will be the flagships in our drive to enhance professional technical education. At these colleges, we will test a corporate format for managing academic institutions with the involvement of business, new educational standards and international accreditation in teaching programmes.

I am ordering the Government to open an Inter-regional centre for professional and technical education in the city of Atyrau by the end of the year. In 2014, the new colleges in Astana and Almaty will open their doors. We must also improve the quality of higher education. Successful universities are, first and foremost, those institutions that have an autonomous status, academic freedom and are oriented towards research and development. These are the principles that govern how Nazarbayev University operates. It is essential that we translate this experience to the country's other educational institutions as well.

Nazarbayev University must become a hub for intellectual activity and innovation. What must be done in order to achieve this? Firstly: taking the best practices from around the world, work on a solution to the issue of creating a special economic zone attached to the university. Secondly: work must be initiated to create an industrial, high-tech forum. The national companies Kazatomprom and Kazkosmos are already establishing scientific and manufacturing centres for solar power and aerospace technologies next to the university. I am ordering the Government and the Samruk-Kazyna Foundation to devise specific plans on how to continue locating high-tech manufacturing centres and sector-specific R&D institutes for national companies around the university. Foreign companies operating in Kazakhstan must not be left on the sidelines of this project either.

Thirdly: in the long-term, for the sustainable development of a technology cluster, additional space will need to be allocated for the University.

Fourthly: it is essential that we activate a collaboration between science and business, as I have been saying for some years now. There are some pretty good examples of this sort of collaboration around the world. For example, in the early 1980s in the United States, a programme was launched by the National Science Foundation to create joint centres between industry and universities. There are currently around 50 such centres in operation, with more than 700 professors and somewhere in the region of 800 post-graduate students and 200 students. Since the centres were set up, the centres have invented approximately one thousand breakthrough technologies. I am ordering the Samruk-Kazyna Foundation, in conjunction with the university, to work on the issue of creating an engineering centre which operates on the basis of orders from industrial concerns.

Fifthly: we should set about creating elements of the innovation infrastructure such as a technopark, a business incubator, a centre for the commercialisation and transfer of technologies and venture funds. It is essential that we continue developing higher education institutes focusing on research in Kazakhstan. Most of the innovation taking place in the developed world is happening in university science and in the results produced by universities' commercialisation offices. Furthermore, it is at universities young people are being taught courses in entrepreneurship and innovation management, which are essential to any academic who wishes to make financial profit from the results of his research. For example, Cambridge University has some world-renowned, efficient institutes for an innovative ecosystem, such as a science office, Cambridge School of Business, an innovation centre, a science technopark, an ideas incubator and an office for the commercialisation and transfer of technologies.

Thus potential scientists have a wide range of institutions and tools from which to choose. It has a choice that the scientists themselves are able to make. There are no prescribed formulae for the steps they need to take to commercialise their research. The university's job is to create all the effective infrastructure required in order to commercialise the results of their scientific work. It should be noted that Cambridge reached this point by way of an evolutionary process, over many years.

In the Kazakhstani context, it may be that to begin with we need to set up a similar system of institutes: an innovation cluster, oriented towards our current needs and potential key projects. This approach will be a source of high-quality human capital and lay the foundations for building a knowledge-based economy and society.

One of Harvard University's mottoes is: *"learning throughout one's entire life is no longer an alternative but an essential need"*. In connection with this, the high-quality education that Nazarbayev University students are receiving is merely the initial intellectual capital. There must be constant work to improve education and professional competencies.

As the German philosopher G. Zimmel once said, *"an educated man is one who knows where to find what he doesn't know."* I call on you to grow as individuals in every way, get involved in sport and the arts, learn foreign languages, and enjoy the profound legacy of Kazakhstani and world literature, which is something the Internet can never replace. It is only through hard work that dignity, prosperity and attaining a new quality of life can be achieved.

A great writer from our times, Mukhtar Auezov, once said: *"Knowledge is a tool for achieving equality between nations and people."* We are a people who have made progress our *raison d'etre*. And we firmly believe that in our era "only he who has obtained the key to mastery shall flourish."

The state's supreme ideal is to create the requisite conditions in order for every citizen to enjoy a dignified life, free from adversity and hardships. These things are also the focus of my article *'The modernisation of society in Kazakhstan: Twenty steps towards a society of universal labour'*. The Kazakhstanis say: *"honest toil leads to the reward it deserves"*. The tendency to look for easy ways to make a quick buck must therefore be made unacceptable in our society. We must make it the norm for people to feel that the route to success lies solely in honest, determined toil combined with profound knowledge. This is a requirement of our times.

In every profession, people become successful trailblazers only when they adopt innovative approaches and new ways of solving complex problems. Following in others' footsteps down much-trammelled paths and choking on the dust left in their wake is not for us, and it is not the choice made by the young people of Kazakhstan. It is for the youth of our independent Motherland, to blaze a trail of your own, one that will later turn into a highway leading to the further development of our nation! A rich and vibrant future for our Homeland is directly dependent on the knowledge and professional mastery of our students.

Lecture at Nazarbayev University
'Kazakhstan on the road to a knowledge-based society'
Astana, 5th September 2012

TWELVE

REGIONAL SECURITY AND STABILITY

*The Conference on Interaction and Confidence Building Measures
in Asia (CICA) is an international forum which aims to promote
peace, security and stability in Asia. The idea of establishing the
CICA was first announced by President Nursultan Nazarbayev at
the 47th UN General Assembly session, October 5th 1992.
At the CICA jubilee session Nursultan Nazarbayev emphasised the
importance of further strengthening the role of Asian countries in ensuring
global safety and building on the strong foundation of CICA as a fully-
fledged initiative to support peace and stability in the Asian region.*

On 5th October 1992, from the floor of the 47th meeting of the UN's
General Assembly, I put forward a proposal to the effect that an inter-state
forum for dialogue should be established on the continent of Asia, in order
to draw up confidence building measures in various areas of cooperation.
Today, some two decades letter, CICA (Conference on Interaction and
Confidence Building Measures in Asia), now transformed into an effective
forum for multilateral diplomacy, incorporates twenty four states covering
more than 90% of the territory of the Asian continent, where half of our
planet's population resides. I would like to express my extreme gratitude
to all these countries for the support they have shown for the initiative,
and for the support throughout the last twenty years that has enabled the
organisation to grow.

Over the years, we have completed a colossal amount of work and
achieved some very significant results. Firstly, CICA has united the
majority of the states in Asia, which represent various cultures, civilisations
and models for development. Three summits have been held and three
ministerial meetings have taken place. Secondly, we have drawn up and
adopted articles of association which laid the political and legal foundations

for our cooperation within the framework of CICA. Thirdly, the forum has successfully been institutionalised. The Secretariat and its working bodies are now operating successfully. Fourthly, we have adopted concepts and action plans for practically all areas of CICA's activity. The fifth point to make is that the process of forming the basis for expansion of cooperation between our countries is taking place. We have been given the 'green light' for the creation of a Business Council, whilst CICA business forums are being held regularly. The sixth point is that we have established ties with international and regional organisations and forums.

In 2010, Kazakhstan handed over the mandate for the chairmanship of CICA to the Republic of Turkey, which will shoulder the responsibility this role entails until 2014. Over the last two years, CICA has substantially expanded its geographical coverage. Vietnam, Iraq, Bahrain and Cambodia have all signed up to become members of the forum. Bangladesh and the Philippines have joined us as observers. We are grateful to our Turkish partners for the sizeable contribution they have made to the development and strengthening of CICA, and also to enhancing its authority in the international arena.

Kazakhstan welcomes the intention shown by the People's Republic of China to accept the chairmanship of CICA for the period 2014-2016. I would like to emphasise the fact that China has the unique historical, political and cultural experience required to promote the complex process of building confidence and developing cooperation in Asia. I have every faith that China's chairmanship will give a huge boost to the strengthening and further development of CICA, and enable us to promote the concept of indivisible cooperative security in Asia through multilateral dialogue, taking mutual interests into account and striving to achieve consensus.

The Asian continent is being transformed into the main forum for global international relations in the 21st century, both in terms of its economic potential and in terms of its degree of influence on global politics. The countries in this region already produce over 57% of the world's total GDP. At the same time, regrettably, unresolved problems between states in Asia, related to territorial disputes and disagreements, are becoming more acute.

At the same time, the Asian region is the zone that contains the greatest concentration of states with nuclear weapons and which are actively expanding their military potential.

The frenzied development of the countries in Asia is being accompanied by an intensification of existing conflicts, leading to a rise in the level of distrust and geopolitical rivalry. We are still facing the ongoing problems of illegal immigration, the illegal profits made by drug-dealers, territorial claims and separatism, religious extremism and terrorism. It is abundantly clear that unless we strengthen trust between the Asian countries, it will be hard to achieve any significant breakthroughs in solving global security issues. In connection, it is essential that we make the greatest possible use of CICA's potential for joint decision-making on issues of security and cooperation in Asia.

Kazakhstan is one of the leaders in the movement for global nuclear disarmament. We made a historic contribution to this process, by closing the Semipalatinsk Test Site and forever rejecting the nuclear weapon which Kazakhstan used to possess. We call on all nations to ratify the Universal Declaration on a Nuclear-Weapon-Free World.

A new Kazakhstani initiative put forward at global summits on nuclear security in Washington and Seoul, concerning the creation of an International nuclear fuel bank in Kazakhstan under the auspices of the IAEA (International Atomic Energy Agency), has been fully reviewed and developed. In addition to this, as part of the international ATOM (Abolish Testing. Our Mission) project initiated by our Republic, anyone on Earth can speak out against nuclear weapons by signing up to an online petition which will be sent to the world's governments. Creating a world without nuclear weapons is our most important goal for the future.

We also believe that the issue of the complete destruction of North Korea's nuclear programme should be resolved by means of six-way negotiations. As for Iran's nuclear programme, I would like to stress once again that the only way we will be able to find a solution for this problem will be by using diplomatic methods.

A global transformation of the world order has begun. The turmoil we have seen in the Middle East and North Africa provides a clear example of this. Kazakhstan has declared on numerous occasions that it backs efforts to find a peaceful resolution to the crisis in Syria. We are firmly of the belief that the country's future lies solely in the hands of the Syrian people, and that therefore the parties must come together around the negotiating table.

One of the most topical tasks that we face is the implementation of a whole range of measures aimed at resolving the problems faced by Afghanistan.

During its chairmanship of the OSCE, Kazakhstan made a serious effort to re-establish normality in Afghanistan. We are continuing to provide full assistance to Afghanistan today, in all kinds of ways. We are teaching young Afghan students in our institutes of higher education, supplying humanitarian aid and helping to fund the construction of social facilities. We are working on the expansion of the transport infrastructure, so that Afghanistan can play a full part in the regional transportation system. Within the framework of international organisations, we are also fine-tuning the work we have been doing with our partners in order to step up the battle against drug manufacturing and drug trafficking.

As expert communities have been pointing out with increasing frequency, the time has come for large-scale reforms to the global economy, in which there is still a considerable risk that we will see another wave of crisis events.

Kazakhstan is calling for a radical expansion in the number of parties involved in the search for global anti-crisis solutions. In order to achieve this goal, we put forward an initiative on the creation of the G-Global communications platform, which will be based at the Astana Economic Forum.

The deepening of our partnership in the field of transport looks likely to have strong prospects. Kazakhstan, as a firm believer in central Asian integration, intends to become the region's biggest hub for transit and logistics, a 'bridge' between Europe and Asia. There are various multilateral associations, both regional and trans-regional, operating in the Asia-Pacific region. At the same time, by contrast with Europe and its developed institutions in the field of security, Asia does not have a system that covers the entire continent, as the OSCE does. In light of this, CICA takes on a special significance and meets a particular need in its capacity as an institutional tool for maintaining security and cooperation in the region.

In the Declaration of principles, the Almaty Act and the CICA Catalogue of confidence building measures, the political and legal foundations for a security system in Asia have been set down in writing. They provide a consolidated vision for CICA's member states on the key issues of security in the world and the region. All of this suggests that the Council has the potential required in order for it to be transformed into an organisation.

This is precisely the reason why it is essential that all members of CICA work together over the next few years. It is my hope that by the time of the fourth CICA summit, we will have some definitive results on the founding of the organisation. By this time we must also raise the status of the head of the CICA Secretariat from Executive Director to the level of Secretary General. I propose that we re-examine the issue of creating a Permanent Committee for CICA and make the relevant changes to the current Procedural Rules. It is also essential that we continue to enhance cooperation between CICA and OSCE, which could be transformed into a joint platform for Euro-Atlantic and Eurasian security.

Today, as Asia experiences a period of stormy development, it is more essential than ever that we have an all-encompassing and effective institute for security and cooperation. In this context, CICA must take up its rightful place in the new global architecture of security. I am firmly of the belief that there will be no problem that cannot be solved in Asia, as long as we bring to bear effective cooperation and constructive trust between our nations. Once we grasp this, it will sow hope and strengthen faith in a bright future for our sub-continent and for the entire planet.

Speech at a the meeting of the Council of Foreign Ministers of
the member states of CICA, held to mark the 20th anniversary of CICA
Astana, 12ᵗʰ September 2012

THIRTEEN

EXPO 2017: NEW & GREEN TECHNOLOGIES

*On 22nd November 2012 at the 152nd session of the General
Assembly of the International Exhibitions Bureau, Astana, the
capital of Kazakhstan, won the right to host the International
exhibition EXPO-2017 on the theme of "Future Energy".
In his address to the people of Kazakhstan, President Nursultan Nazarbayev
hailed the EXPO as a great opportunity for Kazakhstan to promote
new energy and "green" technologies, as well as to make a significant
contribution to global innovations and technological development.*

Kazakhstan has deservedly won the right to host the International special exhibition 'EXPO-2017' in Astana.

We beat off competition from a serious challenger in the shape of the Belgian city of Liege, which has already hosted an international forum in the past. This is a tremendous success for Kazakhstan.

The 'EXPO' exhibitions are global in scope, comparable in terms of their significance to world economic forums, and are as popular with tourists as the world's most famous sporting events.

Over more than 160 years since these international exhibitions were first established, they have taken place predominantly in countries which are considered to be economic powerhouses: the USA, France, Germany, Japan, Brazil, Canada, Great Britain, Spain, China and others. Kazakhstan has now joined this illustrious group of countries. This achievement serves to underline once again that we have become a country that is respected throughout the world. A clear majority of the member states of the International Bureau of Exhibitions voted for us as the hosts of 'EXPO-2017'. In effect, the world opted for Astana! The staging of 'EXPO-2017' is therefore a huge responsibility for Kazakhstan.

We must now undertake a huge amount of preparatory work: we need to build an exhibition centre, erect new hotels, build roads and improve the transport infrastructure, and ensure we are ready to welcome our guests in style. It is a task of epic dimensions. Over the course of three months, the exhibition will attract somewhere in the region of five million foreign visitors. All those countries involved are preparing their pavilions in line with the exhibition's theme, 'Energy of the future'.

Experience has proven that hosting an exhibition on this scale has a huge impact on the development of the cities and countries in which they take place. This is a magnificent opportunity for our country to acquire new technologies in the field of energy and new 'green' technologies. There will be billions of dollars of investment pouring into Kazakhstan during the planning and hosting of 'EXPO-2017', and indeed when these facilities are used for other purposes after the exhibition.

I have created a State Commission to deal with all matters related to the planning and staging of the exhibition. A site has been chosen in Astana for the construction of the new Exhibition Complex and this will represent a further focus for the people in Kazakhstan.

Astana's success in securing the right to host 'EXPO-17' is a victory for all the people of Kazakhstan. I have no doubt that all Kazakhstanis will become actively involved in the preparations for the International exhibition. I firmly believe that 'EXPO-2017' will be yet another golden chapter in our history. I call on all my compatriots to join forces and play an active part in preparing our country for this prestigious international event.

Speech to the people of Kazakhstan about the
International exhibition 'EXPO-2017' in Astana
Astana, 6ᵗʰ December 2012

FOURTEEN

ECONOMIC REFORM

In this speech, President Nursultan Nazarbayev presents a new Strategy for the development of Kazakhstan up to 2050, with the key aim of implementing further economic reforms and becoming a member of the world's thirty most developed countries.

On 16 December 1991, we, the people of Kazakhstan, made our choice in favour of sovereignty, freedom and openness to the world. Today, these values form an integral part of our daily lives. Back then, as we started out on this journey, the global and domestic situation was completely different. Yet now, thanks to our joint efforts, the country has undergone a transformation and progressed beyond all recognition. Today, we are a successful state – one that has its own identity, its own distinguishing traits and its own stance on events. Crossing that first threshold has come at a high price. The country has worked on strengthening its sovereignty and political weight for more than twenty years. Twenty years on, this goal has been achieved. We have successfully completed the important phase of establishing our credentials. Kazakhstan, at the start of the 21st century, is a nation that is independent and sure of itself.

The changes that are taking place in the world due to the impact of the prolonged global crisis do not scare us. We are prepared for them. Our main task now, whilst we hold on to all that we have achieved since securing our sovereignty, is to continue developing sustainably in the 21st century. Our key objective is to create, by 2050, a welfare-based society founded on a strong state, a well-developed economy and the opportunities afforded by universal labour.

A strong state is particularly important in terms of securing the conditions we need for rapid economic growth. A strong state is one with a policy based not on survival, but on planning, long-term development and economic growth.

I would like to outline my vision of our country's prospects for growth. It is the new political course that we are going to steer.

I. Kazakhstan finds it feet – how the crisis tested our statehood, the national economy, civil society, public harmony, regional leadership and international authority.

In 1997, we adopted a Strategy for the development of Kazakhstan up to 2030. We had not yet fully overcome the post-Soviet chaos, South-East Asia was embroiled in crisis as were a number of other markets. We were also having a tough time of it.

Throughout the years since then, our strategy has lit the way, like a beacon, allowing our forward progress, never losing sight of our most important goal.

After the speech I gave in Parliament, there was confusion and disarray. Many people were asking themselves: "What is this – propaganda? A promise of manna from heaven?" This tells you just how ambitious the tasks were that we originally set ourselves. But, as they say, what the eyes may fear, the hands will achieve. We faced a monumental objective: the task of changing the course of events. The task of building a new country. In order to complete it, we had to undertake a three-fold process of modernisation: build the state and effect the breakthrough towards a market economy; lay the foundations for a social state and reawaken the public's consciousness. We had to determine our own path. This path was set out in detail in the 'Kazakhstan-2030' Strategy. This document provided a vision of our strategic aims and objectives and represented a breakthrough, in terms of our world-view, of monumental importance.

There is a folk saying in Kazakhstan: «*Maksat – zhetistiktin zhelkeni*». Only those objectives that have been correctly set will lead to success.

I believe that we made the right decision. The global crisis of 2008-2009 confirms this. Kazakhstan withstood this challenge. The crisis did not destroy our achievements and only made us stronger. The political, socio-economic and foreign policy development model that we chose for the country has demonstrated its effectiveness.

1. A strong and successful state.

Our most important achievement has been the creation of an independent Kazakhstan.

We enshrined our state borders in law. We established an integrated economic zone for our country. We restored and strengthened the country's manufacturing network. At present, all our regions are operating in close communication with one another, tied together by unbreakable bonds. We brought in some historically important constitutional and political reforms, which created a modern system for state governance, founded on the separation of powers. We built a new capital city for the country – Astana. It is a modern city which has become the pride of the nation. We have used the potential of our capital to show the world our capabilities. For this very reason, the international community chose Kazakhstan as the host country for the Universal exhibition 'EXPO-2017'.

This would not have happened if it were not for Astana. This is an honour that has only been bestowed on a privileged few. Our country has become the first in the entire post-Soviet region to be awarded the chairmanship of OSCE (Organisation for Security and Co-operation in Europe), to hold a summit for this organisation and to host 'EXPO-2017' – an event of global significance.

2. A sustainable process of democratisation and liberalisation.

We are progressing in line with a clear formula: "The economy first, politics thereafter". Every stage of the political reform process has been linked to the level of economic development. We are therefore moving along a path of political liberalisation. Only by doing so will we succeed in modernising the country and ensuring its competitiveness.

Our society is moving closer, step by step, to the highest standards of democratisation and human rights. We have enshrined fundamental rights and freedoms in the country's Constitution. Today, all citizens of Kazakhstan have equal rights and opportunities.

3. Peace and harmony between diverse social, ethnic and religious groups.
We have restored the justice and fairness which historically existed in our country with respect to the people of Kazakhstan, our culture and language. Despite our ethnic, cultural and religious diversity, we have also managed to preserve peace and political stability throughout our country. Kazakhstan is now home to people from more than 140 different ethnicities and seventeen different faiths. Civil peace and harmony between ethnic groups – this is our most important tradition. The model of peace and harmony, and the dialogue between cultures and religions in our multicultural country are rightly recognised as a global template. The Assembly of the People of Kazakhstan has become a unique Eurasian model for dialogue between cultures.

Kazakhstan has therefore been transformed into a centre for global interfaith dialogue.

4. The national economy. Our role in the international distribution of labour.
We were the first country in the Commonwealth of Independent States to create a modern model for a market economy, founded on private ownership, free competition and principles of openness. Our model is based on the active role of the state in attracting foreign investment. We have managed to attract more than USD 160 billion of foreign investment into the country. We have created the basic conditions required for entrepreneurial activity and a modern system of taxation. We are slowly but surely diversifying the national economy. Through the programme of industrialisation, I set the task of transforming our economy within two, five-year periods and ensuring its independence from fluctuations in global prices for raw materials.

In the fifteen years that have elapsed since the 'Kazakhstan-2030' Strategy was adopted, our state has risen to become one of the five most rapidly-growing economies in the world. As a result, we will be one of the fifty largest economies in the world in terms of GDP by the end of 2012. This is based on a reputable ranking used by all countries to measure development.

Six years ago, I set an objective of nationwide scope: we were to become one of the top fifty most competitive countries in the world. Kazakhstan already occupies fifty first place in the rankings compiled by the World

Economic Forum. Today, we are just one small step away from our goal.

5. A strong social policy, which gives our society stability and harmony.
The main criterion, as far as I am concerned, has always been and will always be the quality of the life of the people. Over the last fifteen years, the Kazakhstani people's incomes have grown sixteen fold. The number of citizens whose income is below the poverty line has fallen seven fold, whilst the number of people out of work has been halved. We have laid the foundations for a socially-oriented society.

We have succeeded in making significant progress towards improving the nation's health. In order to improve efficiency in healthcare, the system by which it is organised, managed and financed has been reformed. Over the last five years, the mortality rate among women giving birth has fallen three times, whilst the birth rate has risen one and a half times.

We are creating a situation where everyone has an equal opportunity to receive a good education. Over the last fifteen years, the investment in education has risen by a factor of 9.5. A state programme for the development of education is being implemented, focusing on radical modernisation of all levels of education – from nursery school to higher education. Thanks to our policy of long-term investment in the development of our human potential, we have produced the current generation of talented young people.

6. A country with a strong reputation in the global community.
In global politics, our country is a responsible and reliable partner, which enjoys undisputed international authority. We are playing an important role in enhancing global security and supporting the global community in the battle against international terrorism, extremism and the illegal drugs trade. We initiated the CICA (Conference on Interaction and Confidence Building Measures in Asia) – an international platform for dialogue that is important to our security. Today, CICA has twenty four member states, with an aggregate population of more than three billion people.

Over the last two to three years, the Republic of Kazakhstan has held the chairmanship of the Organisation for Security and Cooperation in Europe, the Shanghai Organisation for Cooperation, the Organisation for Islamic Cooperation and the CSTO (Collective Security Treaty Organisation). At the Astana Economic Forum, we proposed a new format for dialogue: G-Global. The essence of this initiative is to combine the efforts of all parties in order to create a just and secure world order.

We are making a valuable contribution in ensuring global security in both energy and food supply.

7. Our active role in promoting the non-proliferation of nuclear weapons. Our initiatives aimed at strengthening the non-proliferation of nuclear weapons have made an invaluable contribution to global stability, good order and security. Having achieved a world first by shutting down the Semipalatinsk Test Site and rejecting nuclear weapons, we received firm international guarantees of our security from the leading nuclear states – the USA, Russia, United Kingdom, France and China. We played a key role in creating a zone that is free from nuclear weapons in Central Asia and are actively supporting the establishment of equivalent zones in other parts of the world, first and foremost in the Middle East.

We are backing the efforts by the international community to counteract the threat of nuclear terrorism. We are now discussing the need to take more decisive measures to dispel the nuclear threat in the future. We believe that the Agreement on the non-proliferation of nuclear weapons was, and remains, the cornerstone of the non-proliferation regime. As an important catalyst in strengthening the non-proliferation regime we need the immediate ratification of the Agreement on the universal banning of nuclear testing. Three years ago, the General Assembly of the UN backed my proposal that the twenty-ninth of August should be declared the International Day of action against nuclear testing.

All of these initiatives amount to an acknowledgement of our important role in global politics. Thanks to this responsible policy, Kazakhstan is rightly regarded as a leader of the non-proliferation regime and as a role-model for other states.

8. The 'Kazakhstan-2030' Strategy: key outcomes.

In the 'Kazakhstan-2030' Strategy, we set out plans for the country's success. We have since moved steadily and determinedly towards fulfilment of the goals we set. Even when the global crisis of 2008-2009 was at its worst, the national economy continued to grow. It is a great honour to outline the results of our implementation of the 'Kazakhstan-2030' Strategy, which has seen the completion of a whole host of its parameters ahead of time.

(1) National security.

We faced the task of developing Kazakhstan whilst keeping our territorial integrity intact. We managed to achieve even more than we set out to do. For the first time in history, our state now has clearly-defined borders which are recognised by the international community. We have delineated the state border – all 14,000 km. Kazakhstan is firmly in control of the situation regarding its part of the Caspian Sea. The threat of any territorial disputes arising in the future has now been dispelled. We will not be leaving any territorial disputes with our neighbours for future generations to deal with.

We have created a strong, modern army, capable of defending the country, and an effective system of law enforcement; these provide safeguards which protect the security of the individual, society and the state.

(2) We have preserved and strengthened the internal political stability and national unity in our country, which is home to 140 ethnicities and seventeen different faiths.

Our policy has been a great success. We are steadily creating the institutions of a civil society, on the basis of a democratic growth model. The institution of the human rights ombudsman has been established. Whereas in the past we did not have a multi-party system, the country now has a wide range of political parties drawn from across the political spectrum. There are numerous parties represented in Parliament and our Government has a parliamentary majority.

Civil society is developing and we have independent media outlets. There are more than 18,000 NGOs in operation, in all manner of fields. Approximately 2500 media publications are being printed, with 90% of them privately owned.

Kazakhstan is currently an important international centre for cross-cultural and inter-faith dialogue. It was in our country that the first four congresses for the leaders of global and traditional religions took place. In the 21st century, Kazakhstan must become a bridge for dialogue and cooperation between East and West.

(3) Economic growth, founded on an open market economy with a high level of foreign investment and domestic savings.

We set ourselves the task of achieving real, sustainable, accelerating rates of growth. We managed to achieve this task within a very short time-frame by historical standards. In the 'Kazakhstan-2030' Strategy, the emphasis was placed on economic growth. As a result, within fifteen years we have seen the national economy grow from KZT 1.7 trillion in 1997 to KZT 28 trillion in 2011. The country's GDP has increased more than sixteen-fold. Annual growth in Kazakhstan's GDP since 1999 has been 7.6%, a figure that enabled us to catch up with the most advanced developing countries. GDP per head of the population has increased by a factor of more than seven – from USD 1,500 in 1998 to USD 12,000 in 2012.

From the outset, Kazakhstan has led the CIS countries in terms of the amount of direct investment which we have attracted per head of the population. Today, this figure stands at USD 9200. We have seen a twelve-fold increase in domestic trade, whilst the volume of industrial output is twenty times higher than it was at the outset. In the same period, oil extraction has risen three-fold and we are now extracting five times as much natural gas as when we introduced the Strategy. We have put the profits made from our raw materials resources into the National Fund. This will provide a reliable shield against future economic or financial turbulence. It is a guarantee of our security for current and future generations.

Within the context of our programme of industrialisation, since 2010 we have implemented 397 investment projects at a total cost of KZT 1797 billion, and created more than 44,000 jobs. Over the two years since we introduced the programme 'Road-map for business – 2020', 225 projects have been approved, with a total of KZT 101.2 billion worth of loans granted. We are now a dynamic country with an average level of per-capita income, relative to the rest of the world, and a rapidly growing economy.

(4) Health, education and the well-being of the citizens of Kazakhstan.

It was vitally important that we radically altered the livelihoods of our people and improved their quality of life. The results of that work are clear for all to see. Average monthly wages are 9.3 times higher now than they used to be and the average pension payment has increased ten-fold. The nominal monetary value of the population's income has risen sixteen-fold. Every year, investment in healthcare increases – from KZT 46 billion in 1999 to KZT 631 billion in 2011. We have created a medical cluster which incorporates five innovative healthcare institutions: a children's rehabilitation centre, centres for maternity and childhood, neurosurgery and emergency care, and a cardio-surgery centre. In every region of the country, we are creating the right conditions to provide high-quality medical services. On-call medical services are growing at a rapid pace, providing medical services to the most far-flung corners of our country. Our national screening system is making it possible to identify and prevent disease at an early stage. We have introduced free or discounted medicines for certain illnesses. Over the last fifteen years, the population has increased from fourteen million to almost seventeen million people. Life expectancy has risen to seventy.

We are steering firmly down a path of introducing accessible, high-quality education. Our implementation of the 'Balapan' programme has enabled us to increase the scope of nursery education so that it is now available to 65.4% of children. We have brought in mandatory pre-school training: today it is provided to 94.7% of all children attending nursery school. Since 1997, 942 schools have been built throughout the Republic, along with 758 hospitals and other healthcare institutions.

We are developing a network of specialist 'intellectual' schools and world-class professional and technical colleges. Over the last twelve years there has been a 182% increase in the number of grants awarded to those wishing to go into higher education. In 1993, we adopted the unique 'Bolashak' programme, enabling 8,000 talented young people to enjoy a first-rate education at some of the world's best universities. In Astana, we have created a modern science and research university, operating in line with international standards.

(5) Energy resources.

Kazakhstan's oil and gas complex is the engine for our entire economy and allows us to achieve growth in other industries. We needed to create a modern, effective oil and gas and mining sector for our economy and we have achieved this task. We are now using the profits from our raw materials sector to construct a new economy for the future. There has been steady growth in the share of GDP represented by the oil and gas sector, from 3.7% in 1997 to 14.7% in 2006 and 25.8% in 2011. We have diversified export markets and consolidated our position, thereby reducing dependency on any one area for the sale of our products.

(6) Infrastructure, particularly in the fields of transport and communications.

We set ourselves the task of developing the country's infrastructure and we proved to be up to the challenge. In the years that have elapsed, a plethora of major strategic facilities in industry, transport infrastructure and infrastructure for everyday needs has been implemented. These include major arterial roads and railways, pipelines, logistics centres, transport terminals, airports, stations, ports and so on.

These initiatives have given employment to many Kazakhstanis, and led to the county's integration into regional and global communication networks.

With every passing year, the number of consumers in the telecommunications sector is growing. This holds true for landlines, mobile networks and the internet. The 'digital government' has made interaction between citizens and the state much easier. Over the last eleven years, KZT 1263.1 billion has been invested into the development of the roads. In this period, we have built, or renovated, more than 48,000 km of roads and 1,100 km of railways. We are currently working on restoring the New Silk road, creating an arterial transport corridor – 'Western Europe to Western China'. We have opened up access to the Persian Gulf states and the Far East, by building a railway line from Uzen to the border with Turkmenistan. By constructing a road between Korgas and Zhetyen, we have thrown open the gates to the East, creating a pathway to the markets of China and the entire

Asian sub-continent. We have commenced construction of the Zhezkazgan to Beineu railway line.

(7) A professional state.

We needed to rid ourselves, once and for all, of the managerial traditions of the administrative and command system and create a contemporary, effective body of managers. The system for recruiting and promoting staff, whereby all citizens have equal rights and opportunities, has resulted in high levels of professionalism and transparency within the state apparatus. We managed to effect a revolution of sorts, in the way the state is governed, shifting its focus towards increasing the quality of the services that the state provides to the people. Thus, the key tasks that were set in the 'Kazakhstan-2030' Strategy have been completed, whilst further tasks are in the process of being fulfilled.

We can now confidently say: "The 'Kazakhstan-2030' Strategy worked, and our plans for a modern Kazakhstan have come to fruition. This is the result of unity, determination and painstaking work; it is the living embodiment of all our efforts and hopes." Great pride can be taken in these achievements.

The global crisis confirmed that we have found our feet as a state and as a society. Our borders, our political system and our economic model are no longer cause for debate either within the country or beyond its borders. There is now a new task ahead of us. We must strengthen the country's onward trajectory for further growth in the long term.

II. 10 global challenges in the 21st century.

Mankind is currently facing some new global challenges and I will outline the ten key challenges facing our country and our region. We must consider each item if we are to achieve new successes in the future.

The first challenge: the acceleration of the pace of change.

The speed of change, in the context of world history, is growing ever faster. The world is undergoing a period of intensive transformation and the speed of these changes is striking. Over the last sixty years, the planet's population has tripled, and by 2050 there will be nine billion people on the planet. In the same period, global GDP has risen eleven-fold.

Whenever an acceleration occurs in the course of history, new and unlimited opportunities open up for states, and I am proud of the fact that we have taken full advantage of these opportunities. In just over twenty years, we have modernised every aspect of society, at an extremely fast tempo. We have also managed to achieve things which would take many countries centuries to achieve. Yet we still have certain social groups which have not been properly integrated into the general process of modernisation. There are some objective reasons for this. There exists a certain lack of balance in society, which impacts our people's morale and their expectations of society. We must remove this lack of balance and provide every layer of society with the opportunity to become integrated into the modernisation process, to find their true place in society and make full use of the opportunities provided by the new political path we have taken.

The second challenge: the imbalance in global demographics.

With each day that passes, the imbalance in global demographics grows more acute. Global trends demonstrate that the world's population is ageing. In forty years' time, the number of people aged over sixty will be greater than the number of people under fifteen. Low birth-rates and an ageing population is inevitably leading to problems in many countries regarding the labour market, particularly in terms of the shortage of labour resources. The growing demographic imbalance is creating new waves of immigration and ramping up social tension all over the world. In Kazakhstan, we have had to confront the pressure caused by immigration in certain parts of the country, where illegal immigrants have been destabilising the local labour markets.

We must also understand that it is highly likely that in the foreseeable future we might face the reverse process: a wave of people leaving our country to work elsewhere. We are a young nation. The average age of our population is thirty five. This means that we have a massive opportunity to safeguard our human potential and position ourselves correctly in the world. And today we have a sound basis from which to move forward. There is much work available in our country – enough for all those who are seeking it. Moreover, in our country everyone has the opportunity to create work for themselves and be able to make a living. This is one of our great achievements.

I am leading Kazakhstan towards a society of universal labour, whereby those who are out of work won't just sit back and receive benefits, but will master new crafts; whereby people with disabilities will be able to become actively involved in creative activity, with corporations and companies providing dignified working conditions.

Young people must study hard, absorb new knowledge, master new skills, and make proficient and effective use of their knowledge and of technology in their everyday lives. We must create all the opportunities required for this purpose and ensure the best possible conditions.

The third challenge: the threat to global food security.

High rates of growth in the world's population are placing intense pressure on food supplies. Tens of millions of people around the world are going hungry even today, and around one billion people suffer chronic food shortage. Unless we make radical changes to the way we manufacture foodstuffs, these frightening numbers will only grow worse. As we see it, there are some massive opportunities hidden away in this challenge. We are already among the world's biggest exporters of grain. We are blessed with vast swathes of ecologically clean land and are able to produce foodstuffs that do not have a negative impact on the environment. It is entirely within our power to make a huge advance in agricultural production. To do so, we need a new kind of thinking at state level.

The fourth challenge: the acute shortage of water.

The world's water resources are also under a huge amount of stress. Over the last sixty years, consumption of drinking water has risen eight-fold. By the middle of this century, many countries will be forced to import water. Water is a resource that is severely restricted, and the battle to control water sources is already becoming an extremely important geopolitical factor, and one of the causes of tension and conflict on the planet. The problem of water supply is one that is also acutely felt in our country as well. We simply do not have enough high-quality drinking water. A whole host of regions have an acute shortages. There is a geopolitical aspect to this problem, too.

We are already facing a serious issue in terms of our use of water resources from rivers that flow across our borders. However complex this issue may be, we must not allow it to become politicised.

The fifth challenge: global energy security.

All developed countries are increasing their investment in alternative and 'green' energy technologies. By 2050, the application of these technologies will enable us to generate up to 50% of all the energy we consume. It is abundantly clear that the age of the hydrocarbon-based economy is gradually coming to an end. We are moving into a new era, in which mankind's activities will be founded less on oil and gas than on renewable sources of energy.

Kazakhstan is one of the key elements in ensuring global energy security. Our country, which has significant reserves of world-class oil and gas, will not retreat from the policy of being a reliable strategic partner and providing mutually beneficial international cooperation in the energy sector.

The sixth challenge: natural resource exhaustion.

Given the limits of Earth's natural resources and the process of resource depletion, the unprecedented growth in humanity's consumption is intensifying both negative and positive processes in a wide range of fields. Kazakhstan has a host of strengths on this front. The Almighty has blessed us with an abundance of natural riches and our resources will be in great demand among other countries and peoples. It is of fundamental importance that we revise our approach to these natural resources. We must learn to manage them in the correct way, saving the profits we make from their sale and, above all, efficiently transforming the natural wealth of our country into sustainable economic growth.

The seventh challenge: the third industrial revolution.

Mankind is on the threshold of a third industrial revolution, which is changing the concept of manufacturing. Technological breakthroughs are radically changing the structure and demand of global markets. We are living in a totally different technological reality from the one of old. Digital and nanotechnologies, robotic technologies, regenerative medicine and many other scientific advances are becoming an everyday reality, transforming not only the world around us but also man himself. We must be active participants in these processes.

The eighth challenge: growing social instability.

At present, one of the biggest global problems is the ever-increasing level of social instability – the main cause being social inequality. In the world today there are some 200 million people who are unable to find work. Even in the European Union, unemployment is at its highest level in recent decades, prompting numerous incidents of mass civil unrest. Against this backdrop, it must be said that the situation in Kazakhstan is looking fairly promising. We have the lowest level of employment ever seen in our recent history. It goes without saying that this is a significant achievement. Nonetheless, we can't afford to rest on our laurels. The global economic crisis, which is turning into a socio-political crisis, will inevitably put great pressure on Kazakhstan and test the durability of our society. The issue of social security and social stability is therefore at the top of the agenda. An important task is to strengthen social stability.

The ninth challenge: the crisis of values in our civilisation.

The world is suffering an acute crisis in values and perspectives. With increasing frequency, the cry goes out that we face an impending clash of civilisations, the end of history, the collapse of multiculturalism. It is of fundamental importance that we do not get drawn into this discourse on world-view, and that we preserve the values we have, which have withstood the test of time. On the basis of our own experiences, we can safely say that we have transformed what they used to call our Achilles' heel – the diversity of ethnicities and faiths in our society – into a great strength. We must learn to live in such a way that different cultures and religions can co-exist. We must be committed to dialogue between cultures and between civilisations. It is only by engaging in dialogue with other nations that our country will be able to achieve success and be influential in the future. In the 21st century, Kazakhstan must consolidate its position as a regional leader and become a bridge for dialogue and cooperation between East and West.

The tenth challenge: the threat of new global destabilisation.

We can all see what is currently taking place in the world. It is not a new wave of the crisis, but a continuation of the crisis of 2007-2009, from which the world's economy has not yet emerged. The global economic system may suffer serious problems as soon as 2013-2014, prompting, in particular, the collapse of global prices for raw materials. From our perspective, such a scenario would be highly undesirable. A potential recession in the EU and/ or the United States could lead to a reduction in the developed countries' demands for raw material resources. A potential default on the part of even one of the Eurozone member states could trigger a 'domino effect' and put our international reserves and the stability of our export supplies in jeopardy. The reduction in the currency reserves is ramping up the pressure on the currency markets and on inflation, which could, once again, have a negative impact on the socio-economic situation. We must devise a carefully thought-through, approved and coordinated plan for all the branches of the executive, the state and society, so that we are able to guard against any scenario as international events unfold.

III. The 'Kazakhstan-2050' Strategy: a new political path for the new Kazakhstan, against the backdrop of rapidly changing historical circumstances.

The paradigm of tasks that we are required to solve has changed markedly. If we are to cope with the new challenges that we face, we need to go beyond the confines of the 'Kazakhstan-2030' Strategy. It is important to expand the horizon of our plans for the future, and that, just as we did fifteen years ago, make another leap forward in terms of our world-view. First of all, Kazakhstan is a modern state. Our society has reached maturity. The agenda today, therefore, looks rather different from the one we had when our state was still finding its feet.

The nature and depth of the transformation taking place in the world, and the level of global interdependency, mean that sustainable, long-term development is crucial. Many countries are already attempting to look beyond the period 2030-2050. 'Controllable forecasting' is being turned into an important tool for states' development in these current unstable times.

Secondly, the 'Kazakhstan-2030' Strategy was created for the period when our state was still emerging. All of the basic parameters, have now been implemented. Thirdly, we are now encountering the challenges and threats born of this new reality. These are of an all-encompassing nature, in which countries and regions are becoming embroiled.

When we devised the 'Kazakhstan-2030' Strategy, nobody imagined that a global financial and economic crisis of such unprecedented scale was looming – one that would create utterly unforeseeable economic and geopolitical circumstances. The 'Kazakhstan-2030' Strategy was produced in 1997 as an open document. Right from the outset, we incorporated the ability to make adjustments. Aware that the global situation is constantly in flux, and that life can sometimes make adjustments of its own, a working group was established to make sense of the situation in which we found ourselves and our potential strategy in new circumstances.

Taking these adjustments into account, I am now proposing that we devise a new political course for our nation up to year 2050, within which we will continue to implement the tasks we set in the 'Kazakhstan-2030' Strategy. We must remain fully conscious of the fact that both time and changing circumstances will make their own adjustments to our plans, as occurred with the 'Kazakhstan-2030' programme. The year 2050 is more than just a symbolic date. It is a genuine deadline on which the global community is currently firmly focused. The UN has devised a global forecast for the development of civilisation up until 2050. A report forecasting likely scenarios to 2050 has been published by the World Food Programme.

Currently, many countries are drawing up and implementing long-term strategies such as these. China is looking ahead to exactly the same threshold in its strategic planning and even major trans-national corporations are devising strategies for development for the next half-century.

One and a half decades ago, when the 'Kazakhstan-2030' Strategy was adopted, the first generation of Kazakhstanis to be born were just about to start school. Today, they are either busy earning or completing their studies. And in two or three years' time, the second generation of Kazakhstanis born into an independent Kazakhstan will appear. It is therefore important that we start thinking, even at this early stage, about giving this generation some accurate coordinates by which they can be guided.

Our main objective is to be among the thirty most developed countries in the world by 2050. Our tradition of achievement combined with the Kazakhstani model for development must form the basis of our new political direction. The 'Kazakhstan-2050' Strategy represents the harmonious transition of the 'Kazakhstan-2030' Strategy into a new phase and provides an answer to the question of who we are, where we are going and where we want to be by 2050. I firmly believe that this is precisely what the younger generation are interested in knowing.

By 2050, Kazakhstan must be among the top thirty most developed countries in the world. Competition for membership of this elite club among developing countries is going to be fierce. Kazakhstan must be prepared for global economic confrontation, and clearly appreciate that only the strongest are guaranteed a place in the sun. We must work tirelessly and in an inspired manner, never losing sight of our primary objectives:

• The continuing development and strengthening of our statehood.
• The transition to new principles in our economic policy.
• Universal support for entrepreneurship – the greatest force in the national economy.
• The formation of a new social model.
• The creation of modern, efficient systems of education and healthcare.
• An increase in the responsibility, effectiveness and functionality of the state apparatus.
• The production of an international and defence policy that is able to cope with new challenges.

The following is my vision for the key areas of the 'Kazakhstan-2050' Strategy.

1. The economic policy of our new course: universal economic pragmatism based on the principles of profitability, return on investment and competitiveness.

President Nursultan Nazarbayev addressing the Diplomatic Corps, 2nd March 201

2

Left: President Nursultan Nazarbayev delivering a lecture at Nazarbayev University, 5th September 2012

Below: President Nursultan Nazarbayev delivers a speech at the G20 Summit in St. Petersburg, Russian Federation, 5th September 2013

Right: President Nursultan Nazarbayev speaks at the solemn meeting, devoted to the Day of Independence of Kazakhstan, at Astana Opera House, 14th December 2014

3

5

The Samruk-Kazyna Transformation Forum, Astana, 6th October 2014

6

VI Con   nber 2013

Above: Conference of the Istanbul Process, 26th April 2013

Below: President Nursultan Nazarbayev speaks at the Eurasian Forum of developing markets, The Palace of Independence, Astana, 10th September 2013

Above: President Nursultan Nazarbayev speaks at the Ceremony of the national contest 'Mereili otbasi', 19th September 2014

Opposite: Annual meeting with the Diplomatic Corps, Astana, 5th February 2014

Below: XV Session of the Council of Foreign Investors, 22nd May 2012

Above: President Nursultan Nazarbayev speaks at the at the XV Session of the Council of Foreign Investors, 2nd June 2014

Below: President Nursultan Nazarbayev attends the Forum of Bolashak Students to mark the 20th Anniversary of the Presidential Scholarship programme, 29th November 2013

The essence of the economic policy in our new plan is universal economic pragmatism. In effect, this is a radical break with our current views and approaches. What does it signify? Number one. All economic and governmental decisions, without exception, shall be taken from the standpoint of their economic viability and long-term interests. Number two. New niches in the market will be identified, in which Kazakhstan can participate as an equal business partner. New outlets for economic growth will be created. Number three. We will create a favourable investment climate, with the aim of increasing our economic potential, profitability and return on investment. Number four. We will create an effective private sector and grow public-private partnerships as well as providing state incentives for exports.

The key condition for the success of this new economic policy will depend on our management ability. To this end we must:

• Perfect management resources – and we have the reserves needed for this. It is essential that we introduce modern management tools and the principles of corporate management to the state sector.

• At the same time, we must also benefit from the internationalisation of labour, and attract external staff resources to implement some of the tasks involved in our new plan, in a programme of outsourcing. We must also hire the best foreign specialists on the open market and invite them to work here in Kazakhstan.

The use of management cadres with extensive international experience and knowledge will provide a dual effect: we will not only modernise the way our production systems are managed, but we will also train our own domestic workforce. This is a new practice for us.

It is of fundamental importance that by 2050 we ensure that the following tasks are solved:

Firstly, the state's macro-economic policy must be modernised. For example, in the field of budget policy:

• We must arm ourselves with a new principle of budget policy: spending only within the limits of our capabilities and cutting the deficit to the lowest possible level. It is essential that we increase our reserves in case troubled times lie ahead, thereby ensuring we will be safeguarded in the long-term.

• Our attitude towards the process of budgeting and financing must be just as carefully thought through and responsible as our attitude towards private investment. In other words, not a single tenge from the budget must be spent in vain.

• The state's budget must be focused on projects of nationwide scope that will be fruitful in the long-term, such as the diversification of the economy and the development of infrastructure. It is essential that we adopt stringent criteria when choosing which facilities to invest in, ensuring that they are viable and will provide strong returns. It is important to remember that even the most cutting-edge facilities become a burden on the budget, if they require ongoing maintenance costs but do not bring in profits and do not solve the problems faced by our country's citizens.

In the field of tax policy:

• It is essential that we introduce a favourable taxation regime for those operating in manufacturing and new technologies. This work has now been started and I am setting us the task of fine-tuning it: conducting a review of all the existing tax exemptions and making them as efficient as possible.

• We must continue our policy of liberalising the tax system and introducing a systematic customs administration. We must simplify and minimise the paperwork involved in tax returns. We must give the market players incentives to be competitive, rather than encouraging them to look for ways of avoiding paying tax.

• A pragmatic reduction in the amount of tax oversight ought to minimise the dialogue between economic entities and the tax service. Over the next five years, it is essential that we make the transition towards digital, online tax returns.

• From 2020 onwards, we must introduce the practice of providing tax credits. The main task here is to encourage investment activity by entrepreneurs.

• The new tax policy must be one that is socially-oriented. To this end it is essential, starting from 2015, that we devise a set of incentives, including measures stipulating a practice of reducing taxation on companies and citizens who invest in education and medical insurance for themselves, their families and their colleagues. Thus, our future tax policy at the level of business must stimulate domestic growth and promote Kazakhstani exports, while, at the level of citizens, persuading them to save and invest.

In the field of monetary policy and lending:

• Given the unfavourable situation in the global economy, we must protect the incomes of all Kazakhstanis and maintain a level of inflation that is acceptable for economic growth. This is not only a micro-economic issue but also an issue related to the country's social security. And it is the most important issue facing the National Bank and the Government.

• Kazakhstan's banks, for their part, must do what they exist to do – ensure that the credited loan requirements of the economy are provided. At the same time, we must not loosen control over the financial system: we must purge the problem-loans from the banks and tackle issues related to state funding head on. To this end, the National Bank and the Government, coordinated by the President's Administration, will draw up a conceptually innovative system for monetary policy and lending, to provide the economy with sufficient monetary resources.

In the field of national debt and foreign debt policy:

• We must maintain constant control over national debt levels. We must cut the budget deficit in relation to GDP from 2.1% in 2013 to 1.5% in 2015. National debt must remain at a moderate level. This is a task of fundamental importance, because it is only in this way that we will ensure budget stability and national security against the backdrop of global instability.

• It is essential that we provide strict monitoring of the level of debt in the quasi-state sector of the economy.

Secondly, we need a radically new approach to infrastructure development. Our infrastructure should enhance and expand our capacity for economic growth. It must be developed in two areas: we must integrate the national economy into the global environment, and also move into the regions within our country. It is important that we focus attention on creating manufacturing, transport and logistics facilities beyond Kazakhstan's borders, taking careful heed of our own interests. We must venture beyond the bounds of existing ideas and create joint enterprises in the region and throughout the world – in Europe, Asia and the US, such as ports in coastal countries, and transport and logistics hubs in key transit points around the world. With this goal in mind, we must devise a special programme entitled 'Global infrastructure integration'.

We must enhance our transit potential. Today, a host of major infrastructural projects of nationwide importance are being implemented, which should result in a two-fold increase in the amount of transit passing through Kazakhstan by 2020. By 2050, this figure is set to rise ten-fold. Everything must be made subordinate to our key task – that of promoting exports in those global markets in which there will be long-term demand for our goods and services.

The creation of infrastructure must also be subject to the laws of profitability. It is crucial that we only build in locations where construction will lead to the development of new businesses and the creation of jobs. Within the country, we must create 'infrastructure centres' so that we can supply remote regions, or regions with a low population densities, with vital infrastructure. It is crucial that we create cutting-edge infrastructure for our transport system.

Thirdly, the modernisation of the system by which we manage state assets. Kazakhstan has a relatively small economy, in global terms. And it must be managed extremely efficiently. The country should operate like a single corporation, and the state must be its kernel. The strength of corporate mentality lies in the concept that all processes are viewed as a single whole. Civil servants, at all levels, must learn to adopt this business mentality. I repeat: we must both allocate the country's budget and also invest in a carefully thought-through and well-adjusted way.

The chief criterion for efficiency is the level of return obtained from our investments. The faster we grow the country's manufacturing potential, the faster Kazakhstan will become a fully-fledged player in the international market, as opposed to an appendage to it. The driving force behind our transition to a new economic policy must be the National Fund. The resources contained in the National Fund shall be used first and foremost for the benefit of our long-term strategic projects. The saving and collection of resources in the National Fund must be continued, but these resources must be used in an extremely rational and carefully planned way. The state, as embodied by national companies, should stimulate the development of the economy in the future, taking into account the sectors which will emerge as a result of the third industrial revolution. Kazakhstani industry must consume the cutting-edge composite materials that we need to produce right here in Kazakhstan.

The state must stimulate the growth of our transit potential in information technologies. By 2030, we must be a transit hub for 2-3% of the world's information flows. By 2050, this figure must be at least doubled. We must also give private companies incentives to invest in research and innovation. I would particularly like to emphasise the following: the implementation of innovations is very important, but it is not an end in itself. The country will only receive the real benefit when our new technologies find real markets. We must bring an end to the practice of selective backing for particular companies or industries. We must back those industries which are carrying out socially important, strategic functions, but also demonstrate their effectiveness.

Fourthly, we must bring in a radically new system for the management of natural resources. We must use these resources as an important strategic tool for providing economic growth, and large-scale foreign policy and external economic agreements. It is essential, starting right away, that we accelerate the volume of raw materials released onto international markets. Our key importers might drastically reduce their expenditure on raw materials, thereby reducing prices. Our strategy of getting ahead of the game will enable us, before the markets start to become destabilised, to save sufficient funds very quickly, which will then help the country to survive a period of potential global crisis.

The technological revolution is changing the shape of the way raw materials are consumed. By way of example, the introduction of innovative technology in composites and new types of concrete is rendering reserves of iron ore and coal far less valuable. This is yet another factor which should encourage us to pick up the pace with which we extract natural resources and supply them to world markets, so that we can exploit the current high global demand for the good of the country.

Whilst remaining a major player in hydrocarbons we must develop the production of alternative types of energy, and actively introduce technologies which use solar and wind power. By 2050, no less than half the country's entire energy consumption must stem from alternative and renewable energy.

If the nation wishes to make use of the profits from resources in thirty five years' time, we must start preparing for this today. We need to devise a special strategy to determine our priorities and identify our partners, so that we can plan over the coming years, following the example of corporations. This is the key lesson we can learn from our own history: we began the preparations and negotiations regarding Kashagan almost twenty years ago, and it is only now that we are beginning to see the results.

In order for the regions to have a vested interest in attracting investment, it is essential that we cancel the moratoriums on the use of subsoil. We must effect a transition from simple supply of raw materials towards cooperation in renewable energy resources and exchanging the latest technologies. By 2025, we must ensure that our domestic market is fully supplied with fuel and combustion materials, in line with the latest ecological standards. We must attract investors not only in the most advanced extraction and recycling technologies but also in exchange for the creation of state-of-the-art manufacturing facilities in Kazakhstan. Kazakhstan must become a regional magnet for investment, becoming the most attractive site in Eurasia for investment and technology transfer. We must show investors the strengths that we can offer. In addition, all extraction companies should only introduce manufacturing technologies that are environmentally friendly.

In the interests of our nation's future and the security of our state, we must create a strategic 'reserve' of hydrocarbon raw materials. This strategic reserve will form the foundation for the country's energy security. We will thereby create yet another defence mechanism against the possibility of further economic turbulence.

Fifth, we need a plan for the next phase of industrialisation. In two years' time, the first five-year-plan for the implementation of the programme of innovative industrialisation will conclude. The Government must draw up a detailed plan for the next phase of industrialisation. It is essential that we are ready for the various scenarios emerging from future technological developments.

As a result, the share of non-primary exports in overall export levels must double 2025, and triple by 2040.

What do we need to do to achieve this?

• By 2050, Kazakhstan must renew its production assets in accordance with the very latest technological standards.

In the most competitive sectors, we must develop strategies for exploiting new markets for Kazakhstani manufacturers. This will allow us to avoid the potentially destructive effects of de-industrialisation, particularly in light of our potential accession to the WTO (World Trade Organisation). Goods manufactured in Kazakhstan must become globally competitive. On 1st January 2012, the practical phase of the creation of a Single Economic Zone involving Kazakhstan, Russia and Belarus began. This vast market with an aggregate GDP of USD 2 trillion, incorporating 170 million consumers, should encourage Kazakhstani business to be competitive. However, during this economic integration process, Kazakhstan must not lose a single part of its political sovereignty.

• We must develop new manufacturing sites, focused on the non-primary sector and oriented towards exports.

• We must focus the state programme for industrial and innovative development on importing industrial capabilities and technology exchange. To this end, we need a sub-programme for the creation and development of joint international companies and partnerships which will be profitable for the country.

• By 2030, Kazakhstan must expand its niche in the global market for aerospace services and complete a number of existing projects. In particular, the assembly and testing complex for space-craft in Astana, the aerospace system for distance reconnaissance, the national system of space monitoring and land-based infrastructure, and the system of high-tech satellite navigation.

• We must continue to develop the two leading innovative clusters – Nazarbayev University and the Innovative Technologies Park.

• We must accelerate the pace of our transition to a low-hydrocarbon economy. I propose that in 2013 we create an international organisation called 'Green bridge', and that we also begin implementing the 'Green-4' project at the four satellite towns around Almaty.

The forthcoming 'EXPO-17' exhibition in Astana should give a powerful impetus to the country's transition to a 'green' path for development. The world's greatest achievements in terms of science and technology will be on show in the capital. Many Kazakhstanis will be able to see the 'energy of the future', which we are striving to achieve, with their own eyes. I have raised some of the fundamental issues on which our country's preparations for the third industrial revolution will depend.

Sixth: it is essential that we implement large-scale modernisation of agriculture, particularly given the growing global demand for agricultural products. In order to become a leader in the global food market and increase agricultural production, we must:

• Increase the area on which crops are grown. There are not many countries that have the ability to do this.

• We must ensure there is a significant upturn in harvest volumes, primarily by introducing new technologies.

• We have a great deal of potential for creating the food supply necessary for world-class animal rearing.

• We must create competitive national brands, with the emphasis placed on environmentally friendly approaches. As a result, I am setting our agricultural-industrial complex the goal of becoming a global player in the field of ecologically clean production.

The key task is to develop farming and small and medium-sized business in renewable agriculture and trade. In this regard we must:

• Change the culture of farming to promote new scientific, technological and managerial achievements which arise from our animal rearing tradition.

• Determine which products to back in terms of mass production, so that we can move into major export markets.

The measures we take should result in a five-fold increase in the share of the country's GDP represented by agriculture by 2050. I have tasked the Government:

• To adopt a new development programme for the country's agricultural-industrial complex up until 2020.

• Increase the volume of state support for agriculture by 4.5 times by 2020.

• Devise a system of legislative and economic incentives for the creation of medium-sized and large agricultural production facilities, oriented towards the application of cutting-edge agricultural technologies.

• Bring in higher tax rates for land which remains uncultivated for a specified period.

Seventh: we must devise a new policy in respect of our country's water resources. For our future agricultural needs, we will require colossal volumes of water. In connection with this, we must:

• Conduct a painstaking study of cutting-edge practices which are solving water supply problems in other countries, such as in Australia, and make use of them in our country.

• Implement the most advanced technologies for the extraction and use of underground water, of which we have sizeable reserves.

• In the agricultural sector, we must effect a full-scale transition to energy-saving technologies.

We must alter our society's mentality. We must stop squandering water – one of our most precious natural resources.

By 2050, Kazakhstan must resolve the problem of water supply once and for all. I have asked the Government to devise a long-term state programme for water, with the first phase setting out how to solve the problem of potable water supply until 2020, and the second phase dealing with irrigation and lasting until 2040.

2. Universal support for entrepreneurship – the greatest force in the national economy.

Entrepreneurship in Kazakhstan is the driving force of our new economic course. The share of our economy taken up by small and medium-sized businesses must at least double by 2030.

Firstly, we must create the right conditions so that people can test their skills in business, playing a full role in the economic transformation taking place in the country, rather than sitting back and waiting for the state to solve their problems. It is important to raise the overall level of business culture and encourage initiative on the part of entrepreneurs.

To this end, we must:

• Encourage the efforts of small and medium-sized businesses to join associations and cooperate, and create a system to support and encourage their endeavour.

• Grow the domestic market by encouraging local business initiatives and through minimal, though firm, regulation.

• Make provision for the introduction of a new, more stringent, system of responsibility for civil servants who sometimes create artificial obstacles to business.

• Taking into account the new reality, including involvement in the Eurasian Economic Union and our forthcoming accession to the WTO, we must perfect mechanisms for supporting home-grown manufacturers and take the necessary steps to protect and promote their interests.

The task we face today is to create the right conditions for the transition of small businesses and individual entrepreneurs to the ranks of medium-sized enterprises. Regrettably, the skewed nature of the taxation system for small and medium-sized businesses is hindering their development and growth. The Government must, therefore, bring in legislative changes, to provide a precise definition of the concepts of micro, small, medium-sized and large businesses.

I am hereby ordering the Government to cancel all the permits and licences which do not directly affect the security of the citizens of Kazakhstan and replace them with notifications. Through legislation we must create the conditions whereby business will be able to regulate the quality of the goods, work and services provided. We must also devise a new system for protecting the rights of consumers.

Secondly, in order to build a dialogue based on public-private partnership, we need to secure the involvement of all entrepreneurs in the implementation of this new strategy. An analysis of international practices shows that bringing entrepreneurs into government can contribute to the efficiency of the economy: wherever this has been done, the principle of 'strong business – strong state' has been put into practice. In conjunction with the 'Atameken' Union, the Government has drawn up a conceptual model for the compulsory membership of entrepreneurs in the National Chamber. This model will ensure that the National Chamber will be able to delegate to entrepreneurs a wide range of powers and functions held by state bodies in the fields of professional and technical education, complex service support for small businesses, particularly in rural areas and industrial towns, and foreign investment. The National Chamber will be a reliable and competent partner for the Government.

Thirdly, the state must change its role. We require a second wave of wide-ranging privatisation. This is no easy step, since it will involve the redistribution of responsibilities between the state and the market. Yet it is a step we must take in order to preserve the high rate of economic growth we have been enjoying. Private business always operates more effectively than the state, and this holds true everywhere. We should therefore hand over enterprises and services of a non-strategic nature into private hands. This is a step of utmost importance toward strengthening entrepreneurship in Kazakhstan.

The first step on this path was the successful start of the 'National IPO' programme. It involves, first and foremost, the distribution of our national wealth into the hands of the people. JSC 'KazTransOil' announced a share issue to the value of KZT 28 billion, and bids are already outstripping demand by almost double.

3. New principles in social policy: social guarantees and personal responsibility.

Our main objective is to provide social security and welfare for our citizens. This is the best possible guarantee of stability in our society. There is growing demand in Kazakhstani society for an updated and more efficient social policy, capable of coping with the challenges of our times.

As practices all over the world have shown, there is no ideal, universal model for social policy. Just as there is not a single society in which all the citizens are satisfied with the existing social system. Finding solutions to the issues of social security and the welfare of citizens is a difficult and serious task, which concerns each and every Kazakhstani citizen. We therefore need a comprehensive, carefully thought-through approach. I wish to set out my vision of the principles to which we must hold fast; if we take these principles into account, we will be able to amend our approach to the issues of social justice and social welfare.

Firstly, the state, particularly given the global crisis, must guarantee its citizens a minimum social standard. The most important task is not to allow poverty to rise. Poverty must not be a prospect for a single Kazakhstani citizen. We must establish minimum social standards and guarantees for our citizens, which must be directly dependent on growth in the economy and the budget. This must involve:

• First and foremost, an expansion of the list of the individual's needs and the inclusion of education and healthcare (this goes for the unemployed and those not fit to work too, with a view to integrating them into society), a healthy diet and a healthy lifestyle, satisfying intellectual and information requirements and so on.

• The value of the individual's needs must be calculated based on real prices (consequently we must perfect our statistical methodology).

• A gradual qualitative increase in the standards of living, tied to economic growth.

Adherence to these standards must determine the budget financing for social welfare. This will increase the transparency of budget processes and provide more precise targeting in the way we allocate resources

Secondly, the State must provide social support only to those groups who need it.

What do we need to do to achieve this? The state will bear full responsibility for targeted support for socially vulnerable sections of society: pensioners, those with disabilities, those who are not fit to work, children with diseases and so on. It is essential that we seek to perfect our system of social support and pensions, and take all possible steps to protect mothers and their children's upbringing. We must have clearly defined teaching and training programmes for the employed, tied to the needs of the labour market. The state must provide social support to the jobless, on condition that those who fall into this category seek to master a new trade or undergo re-training. It is important to create the conditions in which employers actively seek to hire socially vulnerable sections of the population, ensuring that they are paid a living wage.

First and foremost this concerns people with disabilities – this is how things are done in the world's developed countries. We must create the necessary conditions for them to enjoy gainful employment to the full. State benefits must only be paid to those who are genuinely unable to work. The companies and corporations which hire people with disabilities and create the conditions necessary for them must be encouraged to continue doing so.

Thirdly, we must concentrate on tackling the problem of social imbalances in the development of our regions. The poor economic growth in a number of regions is currently leading to a situation in which not all are guaranteed work. A polarisation in income levels is taking place among the population. First and foremost we must strengthen the coordination of state bodies in regional development. Our mission is to synchronise all state and industry programmes with our attempts to solve key priorities in regional development.

Over the last year, we have started to implement a development programme for our industrial centres. Considerable resources have been allocated to creating new jobs, resolving social issues among the population, and fine-tuning the way companies and firms work. We will increase the quality of management in the regions. At the same time, we need new, effective mechanisms for levelling out the socio-economic conditions in the regions. I am ordering the Government, in conjunction with the regional Akims, to adopt a programme to develop our small cities. This must be a long-term programme to create a whole range of industry in these cities. Their task is to build a system of regional specialisation of industrial and manufacturing satellite cities for major conglomerations and ultimately increase the quality of life for local people and create work for young people in rural areas.

We also need to take measures to provide full-scale solutions to the problem of migration, which has an impact on regional labour markets. It is crucial that we tighten control over the flows of immigrants from our neighbouring states.

As one of the tasks for the future, we must create favourable conditions for a highly qualified home-grown workforce, to reduce numbers leaving to work in foreign labour markets.

Particular attention should be paid to the territories near our borders. Their potential has not yet been fully unlocked and we must make them more desirable places in which to live. The government, in conjunction with the Akims, must draw up a range of additional measures to encourage growth in the regions close to our borders.

Fourth, we must modernise our policy regarding the provision of employment and the payment of salaries. The biggest threat to global stability is the rise in unemployment. Real jobs must be provided by all the programmes being implemented in the country – whether state programmes, sector-specific programmes – and not just by some of them, but by all of them. I am therefore ordering the Government and the Akims:

• To integrate all the programmes previously adopted to develop entrepreneurship and support business.

• To draw up mechanisms for the distribution of budget funds to those regions which have the highest percentage of unemployment and to those people on the lowest incomes.

I am making the Prime Minister and the Akims personally responsible for the implementation of this revamped programme.

Six months ago, after the publication of my article, 'Social modernisation: Twenty steps to a society of universal labour', work began on a law concerning professional unions and the regulation of labour activity. Our aim is to form a radically new model of labour relations, combining support for entrepreneurship with a desire to take our employees' interests into account. We must speed up the process of passing this law, so that it can come into force and protect the interests of all those in employment. The government must also devise completely new approaches in relation to the payment of salaries and reduce income imbalances.

A crucial component of our social policy at this new stage is the protection of motherhood and childhood. For the State, and for me personally, motherhood is something that requires particular care. Women are the bedrock on which the family is founded and provide the firm foundations for the State. What our country will be like in the future depends directly on how we bring up our children. Above all, we need to pay particular attention to how we bring up our daughters. It is they who will be the wives of the future, the mothers of the future, and will preserve the family hearth and home.

Kazakhstan is an enlightened state. Whilst ensuring that our citizens are able to enjoy freedom of conscience, the state must nonetheless resist any attempts to impose any form of social norms on the country whatsoever which run counter to our traditions and our laws.

We must create the conditions needed for girls in Kazakhstan to receive a good education, secure a good job and be free. They must have the right to use credit cards, drive cars, build careers for themselves and be modern women, who do not wrap themselves up in clothes which are alien to us and have never traditionally been worn in our country. Our people have their own culture, their own traditions and customs. As the people like to stress: *"Kizdin zholi zhinishke"*. The path open to a girl, a daughter, is a subtle one; it must not be destroyed. Girls and women have always been equal members of our society, whilst mothers have always been held in greater esteem than anyone else. We must re-introduce unconditional respect for women – for mothers, wives and daughters. We must take great care of motherhood itself.

I am concerned by the rise in domestic violence against women and children in the family home. There is no place for a disrespectful attitude towards women in our society. And I wish to underline that violence of this kind must be punished in the strictest possible way. The state must clamp down particularly firmly on the egregious cases of sexual slavery, and cases in which women are treated as a product. There are a large number of single-parent families in our country. The state must assist mothers who are bringing up a child on their own. We must provide women with flexible forms of employment, creating the conditions needed so that they can work from home. The law, the state and I myself will be on the side of our women.

We will continue to create the conditions needed for the expansion of women's role in the life of our country. The modern Kazakhstani woman must be someone who strives to make a career for herself. We should take active steps to get women involved in managerial positions at state level and in society, particularly at the local level in the regions. We must create favourable conditions for women who wish to start businesses and grow them.

A separate area of state policy is the protection of children. It is with regret that we must acknowledge that although we are in a time of peace, there are thousands of orphans in the country: our orphanages and children's homes are full to the brim. This is a global trend and it represents a challenge to globalisation. But we must counteract this trend. Our state and society must encourage people to adopt orphans and build family-style children's homes.

The number of cases of men displaying an extremely irresponsible attitude towards women and children is growing. This is in no way an inherent part of our tradition or culture. Children are the most vulnerable and defenceless section of our society, and they must not be left without rights. As the leader of the nation, I demand that the rights of every child are upheld. Any child born on our land is a Kazakhstani. And the State must take care of that child.

I am against divorce. It is essential to raise young people in a spirit whereby they can see the value of the family and the indeed pernicious nature of divorces, because when a divorce occurs it is the children who suffer more than anyone. "If the father cannot take care of the sheep, the son will not be able to take care of the lambs."

Bringing up children is the job of both parents, not just of the mother. Yet if things do go wrong, the father should be duty-bound to pay maintenance costs. The State must support single mothers and bring in tougher sanctions on fathers who fail to pay maintenance. Bringing up children is a massive investment in the future. We must approach this issue in exactly this way, and strive to give our children the best possible education.

I have put a great deal of effort into giving the new generation greater opportunities to receive the best possible education: the 'Balapan' programme is in operation, there are the Intellectual Schools, there is Nazarbayev University and also the 'Bolashak' programme.

As you know, only children who have been properly prepared or are particularly talented can secure places at these schools. Preparing a child to learn and work is the duty of the child's parents. The slogan "The best we have should be for our children" must be a guiding principle for all parents. I hereby order the Government:

• To re-examine radically the legislation aimed at protecting motherhood and childhood, as well as marriage and the family.

• To bring in tougher punishments for crimes against mothers and children, and also for breaches of the law in this area, however small they may be.

• To reform the system of incentives for increasing the birth rate and supporting large families – through a set of measures, including monetary and non-monetary incentives, such as tax exemptions, medical and social services, the provision of new opportunities in the labour market and so on and so forth. By so doing we must bring an end to parasitic attitudes and help women who adopt an active approach to life, and believe strongly in their strengths and capabilities.

• We must not condone sexual discrimination in our country and must ensure gender equality and equal opportunities for women. I am thinking about employers first and foremost.

One of the priorities in our state policy is the nation's health. This will lay the foundations for a successful future. As part of our long-term modernisation of the national system of healthcare, we must bring in common standards for the quality of medical services throughout the country and improve the technical equipment at our medical institutions. The key tasks in this regard are:

• Providing the population with high-quality, accessible medical services.

• Diagnosing and treating the widest possible range of diseases.

• Turning diagnostic medicine into the key instrument for providing early warning of disease. We must put great emphasis on keeping the population informed and educated.

• We must implement 'smart-medicine' services, remote care and treatment, and 'digital medicine'. These new types of medical services are particularly in demand in a country as territorially large as ours.

• The introduction of new approaches to child health. I propose that it is essential to provide all children under the age of sixteen with the entire spectrum of medical services. We must enshrine this as part of the minimum standard of living under our legislation. This will represent a key contribution to the health of our nation.

• A radical improvement in the system of medical education. Our medical colleges and universities must be strengthened with a network of medium-level specialised educational institutions. Everyday practices must be integrated as fully as possible into the learning process.

• The strengthening of the practical, R&D component of courses at medical universities. It is for our institutes of higher education to bring together the latest knowledge and technological achievements of mankind. As an example, I can point to the university hospitals in the USA, which are significant, highly efficient medical centres. We must develop public-private partnership in this area.

• Create the requisite conditions required for the growth of private medicine. Throughout the developed world, a significant proportion of medical services are provided by the private sector. We must ensure a rapid transition to private hospitals and clinics.

• Enshrining the practice of the international accreditation of medical institutions and establishments into law.

To this day, people are still fairly critical of the medical services provided in the countryside. And people in rural areas account for 43% of our population. Physical exercise and sport must become the state's primary concern. A healthy lifestyle is the key to a healthy nation. Yet the country has a shortage of sports facilities, sports kit and equipment that is accessible to all. In connection, the Government and the local authorities must take measures to develop physical exercise, mass-participation in sport and the construction of physical education and leisure facilities, including projects related to public play areas.

4. Knowledge and professional skills must be the key factors which show us the way towards a modern system of education, training and re-training of workforces.

In order to become a developed and competitive state, we must become a highly educated nation. In the modern world, it is abundantly clear that a bare minimum level of literacy is simply not enough. Our citizens must be constantly prepared to pick up new skills for the workplace, involving the most high-tech equipment and the most state-of-the-art manufacturing methods.

It is also essential to place a strong emphasis on the functional abilities of our children, and of the entire generation currently growing up. This is important if our children are adapt to modern life.

Just like the rest of the world, Kazakhstan must effect a transition towards new methods in nursery education. As you may know, I was the initiator of the 'Balapan' programme, the main objective of which is to provide equal opportunities for our children as they start out in life. Since we began implementing this programme, 3,956 new kindergartens and mini-centres have been opened. Given the high birth rate and our continuing population growth, I have decided to extend the 'Balapan' programme until the year 2020. I have tasked the Government and the Akims to provide nursery education and upbringing to 100% of our children.

Given our new policy course, 'Kazakhstan-2050', I am ordering the Government to ensure the further development of our system of engineering education and our modern technical specialisations, by bringing in certificates based on the international model. Vocational educational and higher education must be oriented primarily towards satisfying the current and future needs of the national economy for particular specialists. To a large extent, this will solve the problem of ensuring near full employment.

Higher education institutions must not be limited to educational functions. It is essential that they create and develop departments for applied science and R&D. The higher education institutions to which we have guaranteed academic autonomy must not confine themselves merely to fine-tuning their academic programmes and actively developing their R&D activity. Social responsibility on the part of private business, non-governmental and charitable organisations and private individuals must be strongly present in the field of education. In the main, this concerns the help given to young people who are not able to pay for their education themselves or secure a decent education. To this end we must:

• Create a network of public-private partnerships for the development of our system of higher and secondary education.

• Develop a multi-phase system of grants for education.

• Create, throughout the country, a system of specialised academic institutions in R&D and applied education, taking into account regional specialisations.

• Enshrine in law mandatory production practices at our firms, starting from the second year of university education.

We must modernise our teaching methods and actively develop the system of online education, creating regional school centres.

• We must intensively introduce innovative methods, solutions and instruments in the national education system, including distance teaching and learning in online mode, which will be accessible to all those who wish to take part.

• It is crucial that we rid ourselves of outdated scientific and educational disciplines or ones that are not in demand, whilst at the same time strengthening areas for which there is demand and which may be needed in the future.

• Change the emphasis and focus of our academic plans for secondary and higher education, including in them programmes for the teaching of practical skills and the obtaining of practical qualifications.

• Create academic curricula, educational courses and institutes that are oriented towards entrepreneurship.

As global practices have shown, attempting to reproduce the entire innovative production cycle in any given country is like trying to re-invent the bicycle. It is a very costly process and one that is not always productive or fruitful. To achieve success, a separate scientific base is required, based on experience gleaned by many generations of academics, many terrabytes of special information and knowledge, and the scientific schools that have emerged over the years. Being on the crest of the new technological wave and creating completely new innovations is something that very few countries can do. This is something we must take into account. We must therefore come up with a strategy that is as realistic and pragmatic as possible. Costly research and development should not be our main focus. What we need is a transfer of the technologies that the country needs and training of specialists so that they know how to use them. 'EXPO-2017' should give a boost to this process and help us to select state-of-the-art technologies for the development of the energy of the future.

We are a young nation, so this will be within our power. Moreover, we are more than capable of getting actively involved in R&D projects of international scale. This will give us the ability to integrate the efforts of our scientists with the foreign R&D community in strategic areas of innovation. Our goal is to become part of the global technological revolution. We must take measures to achieve full-scale cooperation between science and business. I am ordering the Government to unearth inter-industry sectors in which the transfer of technologies is possible, and create demand for them on the part of major users of extractive and national companies.

It is important to draw up clear and precise 'road maps' for the establishment of prospective national clusters. We must also accelerate the process of establishing the legal basis for public-private partnerships. Our task is to bring in the most advanced tools and mechanisms for such partnerships available today.

We also need a review of the laws regulating issues related to copyright and patents. The government must fully analyse all the patents issued in the past and all the copyrights registered to see whether or not they can be commercialised.

I would particularly like to appeal to our young people. The new political and economic course that I am announcing is oriented towards giving them the best possible education, and hence an even better future. I am counting on you – the new generation of Kazakhstanis. You must become the driving force for this new course that we are steering. As the head of state, I have always tried to create all the conditions required for your education and growth. I created a world-class university and special Intellectual Schools, and founded the 'Bolashak' scholarship programme. We are currently devising a new concept for the state's youth policy. All the conditions you require are going to be put in place. The state is doing all it can to open up new opportunities for you. The kinds of opportunities that your parents could never have even dreamed of. Remember: your personal success represents success for your parents, success for your nearest and dearest, success for your whole families, success for all your compatriots and success for our Motherland.

5. Further strengthening of Statehood and the development of democracy in Kazakhstan.

Our goal is to form a new kind of state governance. It must satisfy the new tasks of serving society and strengthening statehood.

Number one. We must continue to perfect our system of state planning and forecasting. I am setting the objective of strengthening the state bodies for the development of plans and programmes, therefore I am ordering the Government:

• To effect a 're-set' of the strategic documents governing the life and work of the country, taking into account my vision for Kazakhstan's development strategy up until 2015.

• To draw up a Concept for the introduction of a state audit in the country, and bring in the relevant draft law in Parliament next year. We need to create a multi-faceted system of state auditing founded on the most advanced practices from around the world.

• In order for our economic strategies to be embodied in life, the state must effectively overcome the effects of the crisis and counteract them. To do so, we must create a multi-level anti-crisis response system.

We must have standard action plans for all possible crisis situations. This is particularly important for the regions. When drawing up this system, we must take into account all the challenges about which I have spoken.

Number two. We must skilfully and competently bring in decentralised government. The essence of the idea of decentralisation consists in transferring the rights and resources necessary for decision-making from the centre to the regional authorities. We must take specific measures to limit the liability and powers between the centre and the regions, and strengthen the local executive bodies. The powers of the local authorities in the regions will be strengthened through funding and additional human resources.

Society and our citizens must be directly involved in the process of decision-making on state matters and their implementation. Through the self-governing bodies, we must provide the population with a genuine ability to solve problems of local scope independently and in a responsible manner. I have approved the Concept for the development of local self-government. It will enable us to enhance the quality of government in the countryside and expand citizens' participation in local issues. We are bestowing additional powers on rural Akims and strengthening their influence on the situation in rural areas. At the same time, we must also strengthen community control and citizens' ability to have an influence on the situation in the regions. I have therefore decided to bring in elected rural Akims, via the Maslikhats.

A total of 2,533 Akims will be elected, including Akims for the rural districts and villages, and also 50 Akims for cities that are of district-wide significance. That represents 91.7% of the total number of Akims at all levels. Thus we will extend the number of elections for all Akims which work directly with citizens and solve problems in the regions. The time has come for our citizens to get actively involved in solving the pressing questions in our regions and monitoring the work of local bodies of power. I am ordering the Government, in conjunction with the President's Administration, to draw up the necessary legislative acts, and ask the Parliament to ensure they are adopted as a priority matter.

We must choose to go down the civilised path, along with the rest of the world, and steer a course towards continuing democratisation of society. We must continue our policy of making Parliament stronger by bestowing more powers on it. At the same time, decentralisation should not be seen solely as a process for creating new bodies of power at local level, to which particular powers can be transferred. Decentralisation is, above all, a qualitiative change to the system of state governance, a change to the system of problem-solving at the local level. At the same time, decentralisation must not lead to a weakening of the top-down power structure, or a reduction in executive discipline and order. This cannot be allowed to happen. The Akims in the regions and the Government must maintain particularly tight control over this.

Number three. We must form a professional state apparatus, for which, in line with the principles I have announced, must primarily be designed to serve the people and the state. We must improve the quality of the staff working in the civil service by bringing in enhanced recruitment methods and professional training.

Managerial decisions at state level must satisfy the following requirements:
• They must take into account not only short-term results but also long-term ones.
• They must take into account the multiplying factor caused by each managerial decision.
• They must provide rules for honest competition and freedom for enterprise.
• They must preclude conflicting interpretations of the official duties of civil servants. Precise legislative regulation of their activities is needed.

Taking these new requirements into account – we have already started the second phase of our administrative reforms.

First and foremost we are going to reform the state apparatus. I have signed a law on a new system of state service. It ensures the strengthening of anti-corruption measures, increased transparency in the recruitment of civil servants and the introduction of meritocratic principles, i.e. promotions for the best personnel.

We will create a national commission on workforce policy. A fundamentally new class of professional managers will be created – corpus 'A' – which is responsible for the implementation of specific areas of state policy. Corpus 'B' will primarily include secretaries in responsible positions and the directors of departments within the regional Akims, and the chairpersons of committees, district Akims and cities. I am ordering the President's Administration to draw up a draft directive on the qualification requirements for those applying to corpus 'A'.

From now on, civil servants must move up the career ladder in a gradual process, moving one rung at a time up the hierarchy of power, honing their skills and increasing their professional qualities as they do so. Exceptions must be made for those who exceed the targets set for them, demonstrate their efficiency and provide high-quality results.

I am ordering the Agency for Civil Service Affairs to ensure that this fundamentally new mechanism for career growth among civil servants is brought in by the end of 2013. Special emphasis must be placed on enhancing the quality of state services. Our task is to move away from a one-sided approach by the authorities in dealings between the state apparatus and the population, towards a quicker and more efficient way of providing state services to citizens. Parliament is currently discussing a draft Law 'On state services'. This law must be passed by the end of the first quarter of 2013.

We must free up the state bodies from having to perform functions which should not properly be theirs, and to ensure a qualitative expansion of state institutes' independence. The Government must bind its implementation to the introduction, from 2014 onwards, of a new mechanism for devising local budgets.

Number four. The state apparatus must build a new system of dialogue with the business community. We must not interfere in business and 'lead everyone by the hand'. We must give business confidence in tomorrow. Entrepreneurs must be able to back themselves and know that the state isn't deceiving them, and will protect them. All they need to do is go about their work honestly. I believe that to this end, we must, firstly, guarantee the de facto right to private ownership of property. Secondly, we must guarantee that contractual obligations will be afforded protection.

The state's duty is to provide its citizens with the best possible opportunities for carrying out business activities. And this means that it must concern itself with creating the infrastructure required for Kazakhstani business. To this end we must begin the next stage of the modernisation of the national legal system.

The legislation should not only protect our national interests, but also be synchronised with the rapidly growing international legal environment. I am ordering the Government to adopt systemic measures to make our legal system more competitive in all its basic forms, both publically and in terms of private rights.

I am also ordering the Government, in conjunction with the President's Administration:

• To commence reforms of the criminal and criminal-processing legislation. The focus must be on futher humanisation, including the decriminalisation of economic infringements.

• Prepare and bring into Parliament four new codes: a criminal-processing code, a criminal code, a criminal-executive code and a code on civil violations. The adoption of these key pieces of legislation will fundamentally modernise the system of criminal legal proceedings and will bring our legal system up to a level whereby we can meet today's challenges in an adequate manner.

Fifth. The state must adopt a principle of zero tolerance towards civil disorder. The starting point for a developed society is discipline and order in all things: clean and tidy entrances to living areas, public areas that are kept in good condition and streets that are free of rubbish. We must not tolerate even the smallest acts of petty crime, hooliganism, or antisocial behaviour, since these things disturb the peace and reduce our quality of life. A sense that there is disorder and an 'anything goes' attitude will pave the way to more serious crimes. An atmosphere of intolerance towards petty crimes is an important step towards strengthening public security and fighting crime. We must overcome nihilist attitudes towards the law and get society involved in protecting civil order. We must ensure that anti-social behaviour has a direct impact on people's ability to find work. We must bring in punishments for acts of hooliganism in public places, which must be compulsorily included on people's case files and CVs and taken into account when hiring people or considering whether or not to give them promotions. All this must become the norm in our communities.

Sixth. The state and society must speak out against corruption, as one. Corruption is not just a breach of the law. It undermines faith in the efficiency of the state and represents a direct threat to national security. We must intensify the battle against corruption, among other things by perfecting anti-corruption legislation so that we can achieve our ultimate goal – rooting out corruption as a phenomenon.

Seventh. We must continue our reforms to the law enforcement bodies and intelligence agencies. Unless we do so, we will not be able to solve the problems of forming a "zero tolerance" approach to disorder and rooting out corruption. Over the last three years, we have brought in a host of important reforms to the law enforcement agencies and the intelligence services. This is an important step in terms of strengthening statehood. The rights basis by which they operate has been improved. Their functions have been clearly defined. No longer is there any duplication in their activities. Our criminal policy has been given a more human face.

We have brought in comprehensive accreditation for the employees in all our security operations. Of more than 100,000 people, 12,500 people did not get through the accreditation tests and were dismissed. We are going to continue this work in the future.

I am ordering the President's Administration, in conjunction with the Security Council and the Government:

• To prepare an action plan for increasing the wages and pensions of employees in the law enforcement agencies. With effect from 2013, I am ordering an increase in the bonuses paid to those in senior positions to the levels paid to senior military officers.

• We must draw up a staffing policy in the law enforcement agencies.

• We must create, at the higher accreditation committee, a continually operating structure for staffing policy in the law enforcement agencies.

• We must form a presidential reserve of directors for the law enforcement and intelligence agencies.

I am ordering the President's Administration and the Security Council, in conjunction with the Government, to form an inter-ministerial working group to draw up a draft programme for continuing the modernisation of the law enforcement system.

A crucial issue in our legal policy is the exercise by citizens of their right to a legal defence in court, which is guaranteed under the Constitution. To this end, we must simplify the process of administering justice, removing any bureaucratic procedures that are surplus to requirements. If we actively bring in new information technologies, this should not be too hard to accomplish.

Meanwhile, in order to free up our courts, we must continue developing institutions for the out-of-court regulation of disputes. We must make plans for a mechanism whereby trivial disputes are resolved by means of out-of-court negotiations. The authority of the judiciary is undermined when the decisions taken by courts are not implemented. In connection with this, measures must be taken so that this situation can be radically corrected. It is vital that we bring in large-scale reforms to our Border service. The task we face is to radically improve its efficiency and activity, and modernise its material and technical basis. To this end I am ordering the Security Council, in conjunction with the President's Administration and the Government, to prepare a special multi-faceted plan for the development of the Border service and the building of infrastructure along our state borders in the medium-term perspective.

6. A foreign policy that is consistent and predictable: promoting our national interests and enhancing regional and global security.

Since it became independent, Kazakhstan has succeeded in becoming a fully-fledged participant in international processes, and we have managed to create favourable conditions in our relations with other countries. Our priorities remain unchanged: developing partnerships with our neighbours – Russia, China, the countries of Central Asia, and also the US, the EU and the countries of Asia.

We will strengthen the Customs Union and the Single economic area. Our goal, in the immediate term, is to create the Eurasian Economic Union and we have made it absolutely clear that all issues will be decided through consensus. Our political sovereignty will not be compromised.

Balance in our foreign policy means the development of amicable, stable and predictable relations with all the states which play a significant role in global affairs and represent a practical interest for Kazakhstan. However, the international situation and the geopolitical environment are subject to fast-paced change, and not always change for the better. A huge arc of instability has made its way from North Africa and the Middle East to North-East Asia.

The balance of power is shifting, both at the global level and in particular regions of the planet. The role played by the regional security mechanisms, such as the UN, the OSCE, NATO, the CSTO (Collective Security Treaty Organisation), the SCO (Shanghai Cooperation Organisation), CICA and others, is thus also growing.

In Central Asia, new threats to national security have reared their heads. In this context, Kazakhstan's foreign policy must be adapted for the modern world, just like our domestic policy. The priorities for the modernisation of our foreign policy must be as follows:

• Take all possible steps to strengthen regional and national security.

• Actively develop our diplomacy on the economy and on trade.

• Intensify our international cooperation in the fields of culture and humanitarian aid, science and education, and related ones.

• Strengthen the legal protection afforded to our citizens and to their personal interests, family interests and business interests, overseas.

In order to implement these priorities, we must abide by the following principles. Firstly, the promotion of our foreign policy interests must be based strictly on pragmatic principles. The tasks we face are to diversify our foreign policy and develop our economic and trade diplomacy, so as to protect and promote our national economic and trade interests.

Secondly, we must continue to be aware of our responsibility for regional security and continue contributing to stability in Central Asia. Our mission is to make as much effort as possible to remove possible causes of conflict in the region.

The best way to achieve stability in Central Asia is to ensure integration within the region. If we do this, we can reduce the potential for conflict in our region, resolve pressing socio-economic problems, and find solutions for disputes related to things such as water and power.

Our voice must be heard all over the world. At the Astana Economic Forum, therefore, I proposed a new format for dialogue, which we decided to call G-Global. There is not a single country in the world that will be capable of overcoming the challenges of the future on its own. The essence of my initiative is to combine everyone's efforts in order to create a secure and just world order.

Thirdly, our country must continue to back all progressive international initiatives and make its contribution to global security. Along with all the other interested parties and our neighbours, Kazakhstan will seek to ensure the regularisation of the political situation in Afghanistan and the restoration of that country. As an authoritative participant in the OIC (Organisation of Islamic Cooperation), Kazakhstan genuinely has a vested interest in the global nature of the process of regularising the Middle East. It is important that the energy of the popular masses in the Arab and Islamic world, now that it has been freed up, should be directed to constructive use and should serve to help resolve the region's socio-economic problems. We must move closer, from an economic perspective, to the countries of the Asia-Pacific region – and we must do so at a rapid rate. By doing so, we will not only reap economic dividends, but also strengthen the balanced nature of our foreign policy.

Fourth, Kazakhstan must enhance its ability to defend itself and focus its military doctrine. Whilst fine-tuning our model for the defence of the nation, we must cooperate with various countries and organisations. Kazakhstan will work closely with its allies in the CSTO thereby enabling us to strengthen the potential and military capability of our rapid-response Collective forces.

7. The new Kazakhstani patriotism is the foundation for the success of our multi-ethnic, multi-faith society.

Our primary objective in this field is clear and simple: we must safeguard and strengthen harmony in our society. This is the immutable condition for our existence as a state, as a society and as a nation. The foundation of Kazakhstani patriotism is the equality of all citizens and their joint responsibility for the honour of the Motherland. At the London Olympics this year, our athletes finished in twelfth place out of 205 national teams. Our team performed as a single squad representing the ethnic diversity of Kazakhstan, as a strong and close-knit family. Our triumph at the Olympics led to even greater cohesion among our people and showed the great power of patriotism. Mass-participation sport and elite sport call for a systemic approach – for only healthy nations can truly be competitive. I am ordering the Government to draw up a programme for the development of mass-participation sport and elite sport, incorporating the most advanced practices from around the world.

Number one. New patriotism in Kazakhstan. You cannot construct a fully-fledged state without confidence in the future. It is vitally important that the aims of the state and the citizen should coincide in all key areas. That is the state's primary objective. Citizens only trust the state when there are strong prospects for the future, opportunities for development and for personal and professional growth. The state and the people must be aware of this and work together.

We must instil a new Kazakhstani patriotism in ourselves and our children. It is primarily about pride in our country and its achievements. Today, though, as we enter a new phase for a state that has found its place in the world, such an understanding is no longer sufficient on its own. We must look at this issue in a pragmatic way. We love our country, we take pride in it, if the state guarantees each and every citizen quality of life, security, equal opportunities and strong prospects. Only an approach such as this will give us a pragmatic and realistic view of the issue of patriotism and the encouragement of it. By 2050, we must build a political system whereby every Kazakhstani citizen can have steadfast confidence in tomorrow and in the future. We should also ensure that our children and grandchildren prefer living in their homeland, because they have things far better here than in a foreign country. Each citizen in our country must have a sense that they belong here on their own land.

Number two. Equal rights between citizens of all ethnicities. We are all Kazakhstanis, and we all have equal rights and equal opportunities. The new Kazakhstani patriotism is what must unite our whole society, regardless of ethnic differences.

We are a multi-ethnic society. On the issue of relations between ethnicities, there must be no double standards. Everyone in the state must be equal. There must be no 'wrong' or 'right' ethnicity, and the same applies to other parameters. I am not just paying lip service to this issue. An infringement against anyone based on their ethnicity should be considered an infringement against all Kazakhstanis. There will not be, and nor should there be, any preferential treatment towards any ethnicities: the rights and responsibilities of all our people are the same. We are building a society of equal opportunities, a society in which all people are equal before the law. We must never again allow people even to entertain the thought that getting a place at university, or getting a job and achieving career growth, are issues which will be decided on the basis of ethnicity.

I demand that the Government and the Akims bring order to our labour policy. We need to have the best people elected to the local government bodies, regardless of their ethnicity. Criterion number one is the highest possible level of ethics and professionalism. It is essential that we correct the one-sidedness that we see when recruiting staff for the ministries and Akims at all levels. There must be no-one in our society who is 'superfluous' or 'alien', no sense of discrimination between those perceived as 'one of us' and those perceived as 'not one of us'. We cannot leave a single citizen of our country behind. Each Kazakhstani citizen must feel the support and strength that the government is providing.

Anyone who tries to drive a wedge into our nation's ethnic tolerance must be punished under the law. And in this regard, there is a particular burden of responsibility on the shoulders of Kazakhstanis. We must realise that the era of multi-nationality states has fallen into oblivion. Kazakhstan is our homeland. It is a land that belonged to our ancestors, since time immemorial. This same land will one day belong to our descendants. And we are directly responsible for ensuring that peace and harmony reign in our land. We must behave like the true proprietors of our land: we must be hospitable, welcoming, generous and tolerant. If we wish to see our country as a strong and powerful state, we must not rock the boat, or destroy the fragile peace and harmony that exists in the world. We must not let anyone sow the seeds of hatred and fear on our cherished land.

You must remember my demand and the demand of our times: that we must live in peace and harmony. There are a large number of forces, both inside the country and outside it, which want to play the card of 'racial division' and are seeking to destroy our peace and harmony from within and interfere with the process of making our state stronger. Don't add any fuel to their fire! We must seek perfection, we must be deserving people, and only then will people respect us and respect our history, culture, traditions and language.

Number three. The Kazakh language and the trinity of languages. A responsible policy towards languages is one of the key consolidating factors for the Kazakhstani nation. The Kazakh language is the spiritual kernel of our culture.

Our task is to develop it, using it actively in all fields of life. We must bestow upon our descendants the legacy of a modern language, in which, to the experience of many generations of our ancestors, we harmoniously add our own significant contribution. This is a task which every self-respecting person should complete in their own right.

The state, for its part, is doing a great deal to strengthen the status of the state language. It is essential that we continue to implement a complex set of measures aimed at making the Kazakh language more widely spoken. It is essential that, from 2025 onwards, we start translating our alphabet into the Latin one. This is an issue of fundamental importance, which our nation must resolve. We made just such a step once before in our history. For the sake of our children's future, we must take this decision, and it is a decision that will create the right conditions for our integration into the world, ensure that our children are better able to learn English and the language of the internet, and, above all – it will give an impetus to the modernisation of the Kazakh language.

We must bring the Kazakh language up to date. We must turn it into a modern language, seek consensus on issues of terminology, and once and for all resolve the issue of translating set phrases from international and foreign words into Kazakh. This issue cannot be solved by some isolated circle of public figures. It is something that the Government must tackle.

There are certain terms which are universally accepted and which enrich any language. As things stand, we are merely making life difficult for ourselves, bringing in causes of confusion and puzzlement, and getting bogged down in archaic language. There are plenty of examples I could point to.

I propose that we draw up a list of at least a hundred contemporary books, written in a contemporary style, and translate them into the version of Kazakh that is spoken today. It may be that we should declare a competition among young people: let them tell us what they think is particularly interesting and useful.

Our policy of developing the Kazakh language must be one that precludes the possibility of the language being rejected – even a potential rejection of it by Kazakhstanis themselves. On the contrary, the language must be a consolidating force for the people of Kazakhstan. To this end, our language policy must be one that is harmonious and consistent, and doesn't impinge on any of the languages spoken by Kazakhstanis.

You are aware of our policy objective: 95% of Kazakhstanis must speak Kazakh by 2025. All the conditions required for this purpose are currently being created. We can already confirm that 60% of our schoolchildren are taught in the state language, it is studied in all our schools. This means that for the children starting school this year, in ten to twelve years we will have a new generation of Kazakhstanis who all speak the Kazakh language fluently. Thus, by 2025, Kazakh will be the primary language in all aspects of life, and the language of day-to-day interaction. This, without question, will represent an extremely important achievement by the state. Our sovereignty, our independence, will finally obtain the factor that binds a nation together and cements it together: its own common language. This will be the jewel in the crown of our state's sovereignty. We are currently taking active steps to create the conditions required so that our children also study Russian and English, as well as Kazakh. Fluency in three languages must be encouraged at state level. We must treat the Russian language and the Cyrillic alphabet with the same care and concern that we show for the Kazakh language. It is clear for all to see that the ability to speak Russian has historically been an advantage to our nation. We cannot afford to ignore the fact that it has been through the Russian language that, over the course of centuries, Kazakhstanis have furthered their knowledge and expanded their horizons and circle of contacts both inside the country and further afield.

We must make a leap forward in the study of English. Fluency in the world's 'lingua franca' will open up new and limitless opportunities in life to each citizen in our country.

Number four. Culture, traditions and authenticity. Traditions and culture are the lifeblood and DNA of any nation. Kazakhs, and the representatives of the other nations which live in our country, in spite of all the hardships and cruelty of the Tsarist era, and the turbulence caused by revolution and totalitarianism, have succeeded in preserving their cultural authenticity. Moreover, since we became independent, our cultural foundations have been strengthened significantly, in spite of the proccesses of globalisation and Westernisation. Kazakhstan is a country like no other. In our society, the most diverse cultural elements have come together and complement one another; it is a truly extraordinary phenomenon.

We must take great care of our national culture and traditions, in all their diversity and magnificence, and assemble our cultural legacy piece by piece. As our history teaches us: the country is only strong when the people are united. Therefore the unity of the Kazakhstanis is the key issue for us. Who, besides us, has a vested interest in the construction of a strong Kazakhstan? The answer to that is self-evident.

We currently face the same problems all nations have faced at different times in their history. Those who managed to overcome them went on to become strong nations and states. As the Leader of the nation, I am troubled by the fact that forces have emerged which are seeking to destroy the unity that exists among the Kazakhstani people. Anyone who falls into this trap, whether consciously or not, starts to discriminate on the basis of various criteria, primarily on the basis of the Kazakhstani family tree, the Shezhire.

We must not forget the profound essence of the tradition of Shezhire itself: it does not end with one particular bloodline or race. Shezhire is a family tree which started from a single, common root. The Shezhire shows and demonstrates that we have shared roots, and that all Kazakhstanis are united. The Shezhire does not break us apart, but rather binds us together.

I am concerned by the fact that our nation is artificially being divided up into 'Nagyz' Kazakhstanis and 'Shala' Kazakhstanis. I feel greatly ashamed of those who are doing this, of those who would break our society apart. And it is dangerous that this is being done under the pretext of sacrosanct notions of love for one's Motherland. Our young people must learn to cherish and love each other, as the children of a common parent, a single people, wherever they are in the world.

Fifth. The role of the nation's intellectual elite. We are entering a period in the development of our statehood, when spiritual issues will be no less important than issues of an economic and material nature. The key role in our spiritual development has always been played by the intelligentsia. Kazakhstan-2050 must be a society of progressive ideals. It is the intellectual elite that must cultivate the foundation for our society's modern outlook and opinions. The intellectual elite must become the leading force in the strengthening of our shared national values, especially at the current state of our nation's development, where we have found our place in the world. We must create the new heroes of our time – those that our young people will revere. The intellectual elite can, and must, play a key role in forming this model, in terms of mentality and outlook, for the country's future, on the basis of my vision for our new political course, 'Kazakhstan-2050'. We must continue the work we have done to create the historical consciousness of our nation. A shared sense of Kazakhstani identity must be at the core of our people's historical consciousness.

Today, Kazakhstanis of all ethnicities or religious beliefs are equal citizens of their countries. The Kazakhstani people and the state language act as the unifying kernel of Kazakhstan's developing civil society. We are creating a just society, in which everyone can say: "I am a citizen of Kazakhstan, and all doors are open to me!"

Today, all doors are open to our citizens, all opportunities and all roads. There are a great many of us, and we are all one country and one people. Being of use to one's country, taking responsibility for the fate of one's Motherland – this is the duty and honour of every responsible politician and every Kazakhstani. We have made the values of unity and harmony the foundation of our society, the basis of our unique Kazakhstani tolerance. We must carefully pass on these values to each future generation of Kazakhstanis.

Sixth. Religion in 21st century Kazakhstan. The question of religious and pseudo-religious movements is one that is felt particularly acutely by our people today. Some of our young people are blindly accepting this alien view of life, because part of our society is not able to immunise itself against alien, pseudo-religious influence. Our Constitution guarantees freedom of religious beliefs – that is a fact. However, as we all know, there is no such thing as unlimited freedom – for that would result in chaos. Everything must be kept within the framework of the Constitution and the laws.

Everyone has the right to make up their own mind. The choice of religious affiliation is something that must be approached in a very responsible manner – after all, it is something on which our lifetime contribution, our everyday existence, and often the entire life of a person depends. Today, in the age of the internet and advanced technologies, when the flow of information has reached colossal proportions, there must be a 'filter' inside each one of us. This inner 'filter' must ask itself: do we think it appropriate that our mothers, sisters and daughters should wear the clothes worn by other peoples, and wrap themselves up in garments from head to toe? That they should not be allowed around the same table as us at mealtimes? That they should not be allowed to drive? These things are the firmly held traditions of other peoples, but on our steppes no such customs have ever existed. Read our classic works of literature, watch some of our films.

Our women feel proud of their country, and have their own traditional style of clothing, but this pride is endowed with a modesty which we men often fail to respect as we should. We are proud of the fact that we are part of the Muslim ummah. This is a part of our tradition. But we mustn't forget that we also have the traditions of an enlightened society, and that Kazakhstan is an enlightened state. We must form a religious consciousness which corresponds to our country's traditions and cultural norms. We must adopt the best possible models to guide our behaviour. The strategy, which I am announcing, will prepare our people for life in the 21st century, rather than life in the dark ages. The state and its citizens must speak out as one against all forms and manifestations of radicalism, extremism and terrorism.

A particularly worrisome threat is the one posed by so-called religious extremism. The spiritual hierarchies share the sense of concern felt by so many. We must not allow genuine faith in the Almighty to be undermined by aggressive and destructive fanaticism. Blind fanaticism is completely alien to the psychology and mentality of our peace-loving people. It goes against the Hanafi Madhhab school of thought to which devout Kazakhstanis adhere. Extremism and terrorism in Kazakhstan have a criminal basis, rather than an ideological one. Pseudo-religious rhetoric is used to hide criminal activity designed to undermine the foundations of society. This represents an attack on peace and stability in our country. It is a test of endurance for our statehood and our civil maturity.

We must perfect our legislation so as to neutralise incidences of religious radicalism and extremism. We must also work to enhance our anti-terrorist legislation. The state must cut out extremism and radicalism, regardless of where it stems from. We must establish new, reliable mechanisms for overcoming social, ethical and religious tension and conflicts. We must curtail the activities of non-traditional sects and dubious, pseudo-religious movements. We must enhance measures taken to cure religious extremism in society, particularly among the younger generation.

It is also essential that we use the advantages which are bestowed on us by the congress of leaders of global and traditional religions. On the basis of this platform for dialogue, we must create a new platform for resolving conflicts on religious grounds. We must be prepared to act as intermediaries wherever conflicts flare up in the region, in the Greater Middle East and even at a more global level, in order to bring an end to religious and ethnic conflicts.

The enlightened nature of our state is an important pre-requisite for the successful development of Kazakhstan. This is something of which current and future Kazakhstani politicians, and all Kazakhs, must have a clear understanding. I am ordering the Government, in conjunction with the President's Administration, to draw up a state programme for countering religious extremism and terrorism. At the same time, I also wish to send a warning to the nation. The battle against extremism must not turn into a witch-hunt and be expanded so that it becomes a battle against religion. We must adopt a thoughtful approach and extreme caution. The state must not interfere in the internal affairs of religious communities. We must hold firm to the principle of freedom of belief and to the traditions of tolerance and respect for others' religion.

In my missive today, I am addressing each and every one of you. The country currently faces some huge challenges. And I firmly believe we will be successful. How do I envisage Kazakhstan in the future?

I firmly believe that in 2050, Kazakhstan will be a society of educated, free people who speak three languages. They will be citizens of the world. They will travel to all corners of the world. They will be open-minded and open to learning new things. They will be hard-working. They will be deeply patriotic.

I am sure that Kazakhstan in 2050 will be a society of universal labour. It will be a state with a strong economy, in which everything a person needs will be available. A country with the best possible education and the best possible healthcare. In which peace and harmony rule. In which citizens are free and equal, and power is exercised in a just manner. In which the rule of law is maintained.

I believe we are moving in the right direction and that nothing can knock us off course. If we are strong, we will be respected. If we rely on some sort of miracle occurring or put our faith in others, we will lose everything we have accomplished. And today, we must make the only true choice we can make. Particular responsibility for the implementation of the new strategic course, 'Kazakhstan-2050', lies primarily with the Kazakhstani people. We mustn't forget that we will only be able to respond appropriately to the challenges of our times if we preserve our cultural code: language, spirituality, traditions, values. Let me put it in clearer terms – terms that the younger generation will understand better than most. When does a computer programme malfunction? When its programming code is damaged. The same thing applies in life. If a nation loses its cultural code, the nation itself is eventually destroyed. Such a thing cannot be allowed to happen!

I believe that our dignified history and the memory of our great forefathers will help us overcome the difficulties we face in the years to come. History is our witness: when the going gets tough, our people have always come together and turned setbacks into brilliant victories.

It was almost 300 years ago, in Anyrakay, where the Kazakhstanis joined forces. Back then, our devotion to our land and good sense prevailed. Each of us has an ancestor who took part in this great feat. The manner in which we emerge from the hardships we face also depends on us, on our unity. It was with good reason that our forefathers used to say: "Otan ottan da istik" (Hotter than fire is the warmth of the Motherland).

I wish to address our older generation. Your wisdom must help our younger generations to walk along the right path and love their Motherland. I wish to address our middle-aged generation. It befell you to live at a time of the collapse of one country and the restoration of an independent state. This was a time of complex and difficult decisions. The experience you gleaned represents invaluable capital, which will help all of us get through the difficulties we face. And finally I wish to address the younger generation. You embody all our hopes for the future. All that we are doing today is being done for your benefit. Most of you are as young as this independent Kazakhstan of ours. And by 2050, you will be mature citizens who are involved in implementing this programme. It is for you to determine the path that the country will take in the future.

You were brought up in an independent country – something that the rest of us never experienced. Your new, independent mindset is the factor that will lead the country to new goals, which seem today to be remote and unobtainable.

I call on all the people to arm themselves with some of life's eternal qualities – passion, hard work and determination, which will help us withstand all challenges and create the future we deserve for our Motherland. I believe in you. I believe that we won't let this new, historic opportunity slip.

Message to the people of Kazakhstan "The 'Kazakhstan-2050' Strategy:
A new political direction for a state that has found its place in the world"
Astana, 14th December 2012

FIFTEEN

FOUNDATIONS FOR SUCCESS

*In this chapter, Nursultan Nazarbayev highlights that the successful
economic, social and political reforms in Kazakhstan have been achieved
through the efforts of a united Kazakhstani people, characterised by
the principles of tolerance, harmony and inter-ethnic concord.
The session adopted the concept of the Assembly of People of Kazakhstan up to 2020.*

The Assembly of the People of Kazakhstan, which was raised in the cradle
of the blessed Kazakhstani land, has now come of age. Today, as it turns
eighteen, it has become both a genuine symbol and a key factor of our unity.
It has demonstrated that it is fit for purpose. It has become an integral part
of our peace-loving society and is the yardstick of our stage of citizenship as
well as a pillar that props up our stability.

We set great store in the theme of this Twentieth Session, 'One people –
one country – one fate'. In its time, Kazakhstan has been a place of refuge
for representatives of all ethnicities, which, through the will of fate, were
thrown together here. Today, all are equal citizens of our country, sharing
its ideals and forming the united Kazakhstani people. They are our citizens,
brought together under a single flag and determined to live, create wealth
and build a common destiny for the good of our native land,. This is why
we have expressed the future of our state using this three-pronged formula:
'One people – one country – one fate'.

Only those countries blessed with close-knit societies can enjoy a happy
existence. Our people, aware of this, hold their unity very dear. As children
of this land since time immemorial, Kazakhstanis have never sought to
differentiate between one another. We clearly and unambiguously set out,
in our Constitution, that all our citizens were to be equal, regardless of
creed, language or faith.

Keen not to rest on our laurels and determined to move forward in our development, we set out, in the 'Kazakhstan-2050' Strategy, what sort of people we wish to become in the long-term. Of the seven priorities set out in the Strategy, the unity of the country has been identified as the key foundation for Kazakhstani patriotism.

A document that is of equal significance is the concept for the development of the Assembly of the People of Kazakhstan up until 2020, which was drawn up on my instructions.

Today we are holding the twentieth session of the Assembly of the People of Kazakhstan. This signifies that we have come a long, long way. In this time, Kazakhstan has become a land that is free of ethnic conflicts. Economic and socio-political reforms have come to fruition thanks to the tranquillity and harmony between our different races. Peace and calm have entered every home. This is the most important outcome of the work we have completed together, the work of the Assembly! Today, we can confidently assert that the Assembly stands for all the people of Kazakhstan! All seventeen million of them! Today, it is a strong, reliable foundation for stability and social harmony. The history of the Assembly is the history of our country and of our people.

The agenda for our session includes an important issue: 'The Kazakhstan-2050 Strategy: One people – one country – one fate'. Why is it that we summarise our theme in this way? Because 'one people' means national interests that are common to all of us. 'One country' means our Motherland, which is shared by us all. 'One fate' stands for the hardships and victories that we have been through together! It is about the prospect we all share – a wealthy, flourishing Kazakhstan! All this, taken together, means that in order to implement the Strategy successfully we require unity in society.

There is currently a 'period of uncertainty' in the global economy. The developed countries are sliding down the charts that measure their wealth, and there is a growing expectation that there will be a new wave of recession. Recent events in Cyprus demonstrated just how high the financial risks that have a direct impact on people's wealth might be. The alarm bell has been sounded. The economic situation in the world also affects the ethnic and cultural situation – one whose trends we have been following closely. The key paradox in today's world is that there are two trends taking shape simultaneously: a movement towards unification and a movement towards greater diversity. The world is not becoming simpler: on the contrary, it is becoming more complicated. Europe alone has faced an influx of millions upon millions of immigrants.

To some, this seems an entirely natural phenomenon, while to others it is seen as a catastrophe. Extremist rhetoric is constantly increasing. It is becoming abundantly clear that the former practice of multiculturalism has run its course. Books are even being written about what some authors see as the prospect of 'self-destruction' among some European states. I firmly believe that the movements towards unity and diversity – as long as there is a clear state strategy and goodwill – are not contradictory, but indeed complement one another. This is precisely the policy we have been following for all twenty sessions of the Assembly of the People of Kazakhstan. And this policy has fully demonstrated its efficacy!

In the years since we gained independence, we have formulated our own model for inter-ethnic unity. We have provided equal rights and opportunities, good living standards and security for our people. Zurab Bobokhidze, from Atyrau, writes the following: *"This is where my home is, my family, my brothers, my three children and five grandchildren. Since we became independent, I have never once felt myself to be excluded from the life of my country due to the fact that I am Georgian."* There are plenty of other people in the country who feel the same way.

Today, the world is changing. All manner of dividing lines are appearing: dividing lines based on where people are from, or on their faith, on social and cultural traditions, on language and on ethnicity. In this new environment, as we start implementing the Strategy that will see us through to 2050, we must use the diversity of our society to our advantage. In these new circumstances, the Assembly must become an institution that is truly representative of all citizens, standing over and above politics and representing the whole nation. Let me emphasise once again: the Assembly's mission in the 21st century is not to become narrower, but to expand!

Unfortunately, not everyone in this country – and that includes civil servants – has come to this realisation. Some still have the old mentality: they see the Assembly as a body designed solely to represent the ethnic minorities. I want to say to all those who don't understand, or don't want to understand, what the Assembly represents today. It has been officially recognised by the UN, the OSCE (Organisation for Security and Co-operation in Europe) and CICA (Conference on Interaction and Confidence Building Measures in Asia). The Assembly represents the whole nation! That's precisely why I became the head of the Assembly! And that is precisely why I declared today that the Assembly represents all seventeen million Kazakhs!

The Assembly's most important mission is to support social harmony in this country. And peace between different ethnicities is merely one aspect of the Assembly's multi-faceted activities. We must recognise, once and for all, that social harmony in Kazakhstan is founded first and foremost on harmony among Kazakhstanis. Peace and stability are essential to Kazakhstanis above all, as a nation state. We will not be able to keep our state intact unless there is internal unity among Kazakhstanis.

"Comrades in misfortune typically become brothers in times of good fortune," as one of our folk sayings would have it. In difficult times, Kazakhstanis have always welcomed people from the most diverse ethnic backgrounds and held them tightly in their embrace. And now they have become our blood-brothers, forming a united people with us.

We are commencing the implementation of the 'Kazakhstan-2050' Strategy. And today, there are strong grounds for composing our strategic vision for inter-ethnic relations until 2050.

What will the shape of Kazakhstan be in 2050? I have every faith that in 2050, Kazakhstan will be a united, closely-knit people, and a model state. Social harmony must become the chief characteristic of the life of our united, poly-ethnic nation, our state and the institutes of our civil society, political parties and religious faiths. Social harmony must become the norm for a society of universal labour. I have had reason on numerous occasions to be convinced, on the basis of my own personal experience, that all forms of labour are only successful when there is mutual understanding and harmony among the workforce. At one of our sessions I awarded a 'Birlik' medal to Khadzhimetova Parakhat. She is sixty seven years old, and she managed to grow a ten hectare orchard and by doing so, helps to feed 156 children at a children's home! There's a true patriot for you! We must help people like that! They set a wonderful example to us all!

In these new times, the level of responsibility resting on the shoulders of the Assembly of the People of Kazakhstan will only grow. Public harmony will be founded on an effective, innovative economy. The middle class will be a stronghold of social harmony. Every citizen of Kazakhstan will have clear prospects, confidence in the future, and every possible opportunity for professional growth. These very issues were reflected in the concept for the development of the Assembly of the People of Kazakhstan up until 2020, which I signed on the eve of this our twentieth anniversary session. It is a new strategic document. The recurring theme being social harmony and national unity.

For the successful implementation of the concept, we require:

Number one. The Akims in the regions to draw up plans for the development of the regional Assemblies, taking into account specific local circumstance and the ethnic and demographic structure of society.

Number two. We must make the work of the House of Friendship as centres for social harmony and social initiative more efficient. Such institutions must exist in all regions. It won't be easy. But I want everyone to be clear about this: for peace and harmony in Kazakhstan, no price is considered too high. I am ordering that a republican, methodical council of directors in Houses of Friendship be created under the auspices of the Assembly, and that the best and most efficient working methods be identified. The ministry of culture and information, together with the Secretariat of the Assembly, must devise a working plan for the Houses of friendship. Their legal status, as regional centres of peace and harmony, must also be defined.

Number three. The 'vertical' and 'horizontal' structures within the Assembly must expand their scope so that they reach every Kazakhstani citizen, particularly every young person in our country. It is crucial that we get young people involved at all levels in the measures brought in by the

Assembly, in terms of shaping harmony in our society.

Number four. Social harmony must become the guiding principle for the life of our nation. Under the aegis of the Assembly, I am instructing that councils for social harmony be formed in all the regions. The eve of this session saw the conclusion of a project entitled 'Road-map for peace and harmony', initiated by me, which demonstrated the ethnic and cultural wealth of our regions and strengthened the unity among our people.

Number five. There is an international aspect to social harmony. Kazakhstan's model for inter-ethnic tolerance and social harmony has become its trademark brand, both among our near neighbours and further afield. The Assembly's project 'Remembering in the name of the future', dedicated to the victims of political persecution, and the civil forum on issues of tolerance both resulted in broad international resonance.

Recently, the Executive Secretariat of CICA launched an initiative to sign a cooperation agreement with the Assembly. I am ordering that this initiative be backed. Let me cite another example. In Ukraine, there is the Kharkov public association of Kazakhs, 'Birlik' . Thanks to this association, hundreds of Kazakhstani families have been able to locate, and visit, the graves of their sons, fathers, brothers, who gave their lives for the freedom of our brother nation, Ukraine, in the battles for Kharkov seventy years ago. I wish to pass on to them the thanks of the Kazakhstani people. I decided to award the gold medal of the Assembly of the People of Kazakhstan, the 'Birlik', to members of the Kharkov group behind this initiative: Makka Karazhanova Sagyngalievna, Tatiana Nikolaevna Krupa and Leonid Mikhailovich Kartseva.

Number six. The preparations for the 'EXPO-2017' exhibition should give powerful impetus to the development of the Assembly. Delegations from dozens of countries from around the world will be taking part in the exhibition, bringing a vast cultural programme with them, including representatives from countries that are home to people of Kazakh ethnicity.

The Assembly and the cross-cultural associations – like living bridges in national diplomacy – must do all they can to ensure the exhibition is a vivid demonstration of the achievements of each ethnic group. The people of Kazakhstan must provide a warm welcome to our guests.

At this new stage of our development strengthening the role of the Kazakhstani people in achieving national unity will be foremost. Firstly, the Kazakh people are the powerful historic kernel of our nation-state representing all Kazakhstan's ethnic and social groups. We are aware that the Kazakhstani world has never historically been a narrow state with a single ethnicity and a single culture. We have never been on the sidelines of the global process of civilisation. What's more, our forefathers were the ones who formed this global process.

It should be stressed that in terms of Eurasia as a whole, all the different creeds in Kazakhstan have lived alongside one another for several centuries. Our ancestors gave the world some inspirational examples of culture and spirituality. Our task is to continue the good work that they started. Modern-day Kazakhs, following the traditions of their ancestors, must set an example of unity, tolerance and patriotism, and an example of selfless service to the state and society.

Secondly, we require a common national historical consciousness. Our perception of history must be one that is all-embracing, positive and has a unifying effect on our society, rather than a divisive effect. If we are to raise our national mindset to the heights required, we must clearly understand the true nature of our history, culture and religion. The national history of Kazakhstanis and their ethnicity must be seen as a single, uninterrupted process that has been taking place for millennia. In this context, modern-day Kazakhstan is rightly becoming one of the key natural inheritors of the great civilisations of the steppes.

As I have already observed: Kazakhstan has never been an isolated country. The academic discipline of history must, therefore, accurately reflect the processes of cultural and economic cooperation between Kazakhstanis and other peoples, and the contribution made by various ethnicities to the country's history. As a result, the Kazakhstani people's historical consciousness must work towards bringing us closer together, towards building a patriotic view of our past, our present and our future.

Thirdly, we must make every possible effort to strengthen the internal unity among Kazakhstanis. We are living in the 21st century now, a time of innovation, and Kazakhstani society cannot be the same as it was in centuries gone by. Kazakhstan's intellectual elite must take heed of what I am saying. Kazakhstan is our native land, we are the children of this land. To put it simply: without the active involvement of the Kazakhstanis themselves, no long-term social harmony in Kazakhstan will be possible. Kazakstan is a land which always belonged to our forefathers, and which will one day belong to our descendants. And we must bear direct responsibility for peace in our land.

Tolerance is a national value and a great achievement of the people of Kazakhstan. It was formed on the basis of centuries-old traditions and cultural mores among the Kazakhstani people.

'El-zhurt,' (Citizenry) 'Zheti Ata,' (Heritage) 'Konakzhailik,' (Hospitality) 'Asar,' (Unity) 'Soyalistik,' (Respect) 'Sabirlilik' (Tolerance) – these concepts are at the heart of our world-view and the vital contribution made by Kazakhstanis. Thanks to these values, we've succeeded in preserving peace and harmony in our home country. We must therefore look to the original socio-cultural norms, customs and traditions of the Kazakhstani people, which have shaped this tolerance, as a non-material cultural legacy of significance for the whole of humanity. It would be useful to recognise this experience as one of the areas of work to be completed by the Kazakhstani representative office at UNESCO (United Nations Educational, Scientific and Cultural Organization).

Number four, in the years since we became independent, the ethnic polyphony of our languages, cultures and traditions has acquired a strong voice, a wealth of many distinctive hues and great beauty. In today's world, ten to twenty-five oral languages are disappearing every year (estimates of the actual figure vary), and entire cultures are vanishing from the face of the planet. One of the last speakers of the Chamikuro language, Natalia Sangama, said: *"I dream in Chamikuro, but I can't tell anyone about my dreams because there's no-one left who speaks it any more. It's a lonely feeling when you're the last one left."*

The last speaker of the Erk language, Mary Smith, who passed away in 2008, had this to say: *"It's sad to be the last person left who speaks a particular language. Please go back to your roots and learn your native language, so that you're never as lonely as I have been."*

Since Kazakhstan became an independent country, not a single ethnicity has lost its native tongue. We've carefully looked after our languages and we are creating every opportunity needed to develop the culture of even the smallest ethnic groups: Assyrians, Rutuls, Laks and many others.

Kazakhstan incorporates more than 100 different ethnicities. Of course, if all this ethnic diversity is to become a united nation, some high-quality cement is needed. And today the most important factor that is binding our nation is the Kazakh language – the language of our state.

Number five, we must form a mental model and template for the future of a country based on our new political strategy, 'Kazakhstan-2050'. This template must be realistic, attractive and inspirational. Given the global challenges that we face, we will only be able to provide an adequate response if we preserve our cultural DNA: our language, our traditions and our values. Love of our Motherland is something of special significance to all Kazakhs, along with love of our native soil, our ancestors and our shared and indivisible history. Our ideals are independence, unity and harmony, and they are flourishing. They were formed by the people of Kazakhstan themselves.

Of particular importance in strengthening the unity of the nation is the activity of the intellectual elite. Our intellectual elite include those who are capable of leading the process of bringing our society even closer together. Our capital must become the centre of this work. This is why we built a world-class theatre for opera and ballet in Astana – the Astana Opera – and it is why we are building a new museum dedicated to the history of Kazakhstan.

Number six, our formula for unity is being built around concrete issues. We are implementing a programme of inclusive industrialisation combined with social modernisation. This is the most durable, material basis for our unity. I am convinced that social harmony will be at its best when everyone is an owner of property. That is why I am ordering the Government to implement a programme for a national IPO. The Assembly is playing an active role in helping to explain this programme. It is a crucially important matter of nationwide scope. It must be continued.

Today, we can confidently state that unity and tolerance are our assets, our non-monetary investments in the modernisation of our country! Today, it is clear for all to see: the policy of peace and harmony has a direct economic effect. Domestic stability enables the strengthening of trust among investors and the development of economic cooperation. That is why Kazakhstan is a leader in terms of attracting the investments that peace and harmony represent in our country.

Number seven: we must, taking account of global trends, find an effective model for interaction between the state, society and religion. The historic choice we have made is in favour of an enlightened state and an enlightened society. But by 'enlightened', we don't mean 'atheist'. By 'enlightened', we mean a progressive, peaceful, tolerant and open model.

We support traditional religions, but are categorically against all forms of extremism. I firmly believe: young people must be shielded from radical religious movements which have no place in our country. Our great steppe was a place of tolerance for thousands of years. What is more, I wish to emphasise that a tolerant society is by no means the same thing as a permissive society, as some people would have you believe. Tolerance is the moral norm for our society, which we will strengthen, protect and instil in every future generation.

Over the course of two decades, the path taken by Kazakhstan has set the standard for national success in other newly independent countries. This is the result of the hard work and togetherness of all Kazakhs! Their genuine passion has led to a huge surge forward by our nation! This is a great characteristic that is found only among strong nations. We have become just such a nation, and we must make sure our standards remain high! Kazakhstan is a single land, with a single people and a single future.

This landmark session represents a good starting point for new work in the interests of all Kazakhstanis. We have big plans for the future. These will be implemented against the backdrop of some fairly complex global transformations. We must be ready for this from this point on, and make every effort to ensure that our people remain united. Because we are one people – one country – one destiny!

I wish to congratulate all Kazakhstanis on the forthcoming Day of the unity of the people of Kazakhstan!

I wish all delegates, all our people and all our friends throughout the world great success!

The speech at the XX Session of the Assembly of People of Kazakhstan
"Strategy Kazakhstan-2050: One nation – one country – one destiny"
Astana, 24th April, 2013

SIXTEEN

DEVELOPING DOMESTIC MEDIA

The Eurasian Media Forum, established in 2001, is a special
platform for international dialogue and discussion on global and
regional socio-economic and geopolitical developments.
During his speech at the XI Eurasian Media Forum, Nursultan
Nazarbayev shared his vision for the development of domestic media
within the framework of the Strategy "Kazakhstan-2050".

Since the new Kazakhstani media centre in which we are now gathered opened its doors, Kazakhstan's capital has become one of the important hubs for the communication of information in Eurasia. Over the course of its eleven year history, the Eurasian media forum has become a unique platform for the exchange of opinions between politicians, experts and the media community. I would particularly like to stress the contribution the forum has made to the enhancement of Eurasian integration. Three countries – Kazakhstan, Russia and Belarus – created the Customs Union and the Single Economic Area, and are carrying out productive work on the formation of a Eurasian Economic Union.

In the 21st century, the significance of the media sector is growing dramatically. The media sector is becoming more than merely a system for passing on information about the events taking place in the world around us: in many ways it is becoming one of the leading factors which determine the course of events in particular countries and in the world as a whole. Undoubtedly, mass online journalism represents a new phase in the development of the mass media. It is providing almost limitless opportunities for the development of the media.

Firstly, according to experts' assessments, in the foreseeable future communications and the media will account for a substantial portion of gross domestic product in developed countries. In spite of the downturns and stagnant periods endured by other economic spheres, the media market is growing steadily and consistently, a result of increasing demand from consumers. Secondly, in the next five years annual growth in global consumer costs for internet access, and consequently the cost of using and creating its content, is forecast to rise by more than nine per cent.

Thirdly, the media is entering an era where content is organised directly by the person consuming the information. This is creating a new scenario for both the digital and the printed media. I feel that talk of the imminent disappearance of the print media, or, as they say, the *'end of the Gutenberg era'*, is premature. Newspapers and the publishing industry will survive the decades to come. Just as the theatre survived the advent of the silver screen, radio survived the advent of television, and TV has survived the rise of the internet.

Information and communications networks are now an integral part of contemporary culture. In Kazakhstan we view the prospects for mass media as important for strengthening the unity of our society and ensuring our country continues to progress. It says a great deal that the first document to be approved, following the publication last December of the 'Kazakhstan-2050' Strategy, was the State programme 'A Kazakhstan of Information – 2020'. This sets out large-scale tasks for the technical modernisation of Kazakhstan's media sector, and its transformation into an important mechanism in our society's ability to compete in the world of the 21st century.

The increasing role played by the media sector is causing new media to be born, mass innovation enabling the development of the economy, politics, social life and the spiritual and moral state of society. I see this as the most important mission both for the national and the global mass media in the 21st century.

Central Asia, like the world as a whole, is entering a period of change. Problems of regional security and how it is assessed globally over the coming decade, are extremely topical. I'll say this right away: I do not accept the "disaster theories". I don't feel there is an inherent countdown towards a regional Armageddon, when the active phase of operations by the coalition forces in Afghanistan comes to an end. I am confident that nothing of the kind will happen, although there are certainly those who would like it to, and scaremongers who predict such scenarios.

To be frank, the inertia of the past plays a powerful role in the way Central Asia is perceived by the outside world. I believe this is due to the stereotypical archaic mentalities which we have not yet overcome, and which are inherent in certain circles of the mass media, analysts and, on occasion, politicians.

Firstly, there are some who cannot see, or refuse to see, the changing realities of this new region. No longer is Central Asia a 'God-forsaken' territory or some sort of 'No-man's land': instead, it is a dynamic sub-region within the whole of Eurasia and the world. Kazakhstan and other states in Central Asia have demonstrated their capacity for dignified development and development as sovereign states. Secondly, treating the countries of Central Asia as objects of foreign influence, without taking their national interests into account, is nothing short of geopolitical short-sightedness. Thirdly, Central Asia is a civilised community of peoples with a great history, deserving of genuine prospects – vast prospects – in the future.

The peculiarity of our countries rests on the fact they are not just states which are experiencing a period of regeneration. They are completely new states with forward looking people, a dynamic economic model, a restored culture, a new national spirit and new opportunities. They were, and will remain, an integral part of a globalised world. The organic combination of Turkic passion, Slavic spirituality and European reason will give the world, I am sure of it, some extremely important templates for growth.

Fourthly, we need to see the difference between the situation in the region at the turn of the 21st century and the situation we have today.

There is a system of security in Central Asia that has multiple levels and multiple aspects, and is oriented along key geopolitical vectors. Its key components – CICA (Conference on Interaction and Confidence Building Measures in Asia), the SCO (Shanghai Cooperation Organisation), the CSTO (Collective Security Treaty Organisation) and the OSCE (Organisation for Security and Co-operation in Europe) – are balanced, and this makes the system, as a whole, dependable and sound. The capacity of these bodies to react to crises at the regional level is high. And this is something that must be taken into account.

Fifth, I do not agree with those who claim that the international coalition in Afghanistan failed to achieve its objectives. Direct threats to security have been significantly reduced and localised. Admittedly, there have been problems in the process of regulating the situation inside Afghanistan, but positive changes have been achieved.

I have always stressed how important it is for the global community to take measures aimed at building peace post-conflict, and helping to grow the Afghan economy. Unfortunately, the results achieved to date in this regard have been fairly modest, and this means that it is the right time to enhance international humanitarian aid and investment aid to Afghanistan. Kazakhstan is willing to offer its services to arrange a new international platform for resolving this problem effectively. In connection, I would like to draw your attention to the following problem. This is the third year in a row in which we have seen a host of states 'falling out' of a state of stability, despite having previously enjoyed rapid economic and social growth. I am referring to a whole host of countries in the Middle East and North Africa. The threat of instability is very real for several Asian states as well. The list of countries which currently need post-conflict restoration is already lengthy, and it may get longer over time.

The fact that certain countries are 'chronically' dependent on global aid represents a serious burden to the global economic system. And this could have the effect of slowing down development for a long time to come. I therefore believe that a 'frivolous geopolitical attitude' represents a serious global economic problem, which will cost mankind dearly. Given the way technologies are progressing and becoming more expensive, this could result in the global economy being backed into a corner. Against this backdrop, the promotion of innovation and responsibility to positions of prime importance for global economic growth and sustainable development seems very much the right approach.

Firstly, innovative approaches are needed not only in geoeconomics, but also in geopolitics. Secondly, responsibility must lie not only with states, but also on the regions. Kazakhstan has a responsible attitude towards issues of regional development. This is precisely the reason why we, together with the Russian Federation and the Republic of Belarus, are carrying out preparatory work with a view to creating a Eurasian Economic Union. There are politicians and experts in the world today who look on Eurasian integration through the dark prism of the 'Cold War' era. This outdated perspective has the effect of distorting reality. These three countries' attempts to unite their markets for goods, services and manpower will work to benefit the entire global economy. A vast region, geographically located at the intersection between Asia and Europe, East and West, will be united by an area with shared, predictable, transparent rules governing business activity. A stable economic arena will be created with secure, trans-Eurasian highways providing reliable, high-speed transport. By this, finally, members of the future Eurasian Economic Union will not be shut off from the world, but will instead cooperate actively with everyone else.

We can already see that a host of countries are showing an appetite for being part of the Eurasian Economic Union, and therefore it is only likely to expand in the future. It goes without saying that integration is not an instantaneous process. We must learn by observing the European Union, and the issues it's currently experiencing, and will continue to experience. We are carefully studying what is happening in Europe, and the mistakes Europe has made. It is therefore the responsibility of our media to talk about these issues boldly and fearlessly, to uncover and convey all the different aspects of this issue, and to propose possible solutions. In this spirit, I call on journalists to shine a light on the process of Eurasian integration. The importance of Central Asia as one of the active players in global politics is gaining ground.

Kazakhstan, as you know, has become a key location for negotiations on some of the most complex problems facing the modern world. In Almaty, meetings are being held in the format 'five+one', where we are searching for potential avenues for resolving the issues around the Iranian nuclear programme.

I would like to call on the community of journalists and experts to undertake balanced, objective assessments of the situation and processes at work in Central Asia. We must overcome our habit of looking at the region through old prisms and take into account the striking changes which have taken place in little more than a few decades.

Today, Kazakhstan is more confident in its abilities than ever before. Our optimism is embodied in the 'Kazakhstan-2050' Strategy. In it, we have set out our most important objective – to become one of the thirty most developed countries in the world. We plan to achieve this goal by adopting the role to which we are logically suited given global economic and political trends. We will coordinate our own objectives and capabilities with the practices and trends developing around the world. As you know, Kazakhstan's capital, Astana, has been chosen as the venue for the International exhibition 'EXPO' in 2017, the theme for which will be 'The Energy of the Future'. We have already set to work on preparing for the exhibition. I invite all countries, business groups and media outlets to play an active part in the planning and staging of 'EXPO-2017'.

It is important at this stage to begin the search for global economic solutions, within the framework of the G20, in which Kazakhstan has been invited to take part.

In our view, the key feature of the current phase in global development is the transition to a new state. I came up with the idea of G-Global, which I suggested could serve as a basis for the formation of a new world order in the 21st century. My idea is primarily to invite the entire global community to take part in common dialogue on all the problems facing the world economy and global politics. The G-Global communications platform is now established on the internet, and has already attracted several million hits. As part of the project, a discussion is taking place on the five principles I put forward for a G-Global world order with a multi-polar approach. I shall run through these principles in brief. Number one, evolution and the rejection of revolutionary changes in politics; number two, justice, equality and consensus; number three, global tolerance and trust; number four, global transparency; number five, a constructive, multi-polar system. On the basis of these principles, it will be possible to have successful dialogue on any global problem and find solutions which will be acceptable to all parties.

The main logic behind the G-Global idea is to offer a positive alternative to the chaotic pace of change in the global paradigm of the world's development. I firmly believe that our unique world deserves to exist in a state of constructive multipolarity.

Against the backdrop of globalisation, wide-ranging discussions of the pressing problems in Eurasia, and the world as a whole, are becoming increasingly important and beneficial. Dialogue in the 21st century is an important instrument in globalisation, which experts have christened 'mega-diplomacy'.

Speech at the 11th Eurasian Media Forum
Astana, 25th April 2013

SEVENTEEN

STABILIZING AFGHANISTAN

*The 2013 Conference for Foreign Ministers focused on stabilising Afghanistan
in the context of the planned withdrawal of the international coalition.
Nursultan Nazarbayev underlined the importance of a speedy economic
recovery in Afghanistan and its integration into regional economic activity.
The President stressed that Kazakhstan actively supports Afghanistan
in implementing economic projects and is providing access for Afghan
specialists at leading universities in Kazakhstan.*

Our task today is to discuss issues related to the future of Afghanistan.
This problem is currently high on the agenda for the global community. I
therefore hope that the decisions we take during this conference will enable
us to sort out the process of putting Afghanistan back on the road towards
peace. It is important that we jointly look for ways to stabilise the political
situation in Afghan society and restore its economy.

Afghanistan is entering an important historical period. The mission
of the international security forces is reaching its conclusion. Most of the
country's territory is already under the control of the Afghan Government.
We welcome the efforts made by the country's government and the
international community to strengthen this trend. However, the withdrawal
of the international coalition forces, in my opinion, must not be seen as
a sign that the world's focus on Afghanistan will diminish. It must send a
signal to all the progressive forces in the country that a transition to a new,
peaceful phase of development is occurring. Our main task is to achieve
harmony between nations and lay the foundations for long-term peace.
The key to solving Afghanistan's problems is primarily in the hands of the
Afghan people themselves, and of the Government, as the people's lawful
representative. It is important that the global community should encourage
the development of dialogue within Afghanistan in every possible way.

Support must be given to those forces which demonstrate their readiness to establish peace and order in Afghanistan. In addition, it is extremely important that properly planned presidential elections should be held in Afghanistan in 2014. I hope that the elected head of state will enjoy the full support of all sections of Afghan society.

The element at the heart of the international cooperation programme is the economic rehabilitation of Afghanistan. It is essential that we force through an expansion of economic cooperation in the region and take active steps to integrate Afghanistan into these processes. Kazakhstan is a firm supporter of regional integration. Our country is actively investing in the creation of regional transport infrastructure. The 'Western Europe to Western China' transit corridor; the 'Kazakhstan – Turkmenistan – Iran' railway line; the transport infrastructure in Kazakhstan within the Northern distribution network for the withdrawal from Afghanistan of the international coalition forces; fresh ideas within the context of the 'New Silk Road' programme – these initiatives represent the important contribution of Kazakhstan to regional integration.

We are supporting major regional projects which are under development. These include 'TAPI' (the 'Turkmenistan-Afghanistan-Pakistan-India' gas pipeline), 'CASA-1000' (the high-tech 'Central Asia-South Asia-1000' electricity cable), and the expansion of the rail network around and inside Afghanistan.

In my view, the opportunities offered by the city of Almaty could also help to solve some of the issues related to Afghanistan's development. Our southern capital is a powerful transport hub offering extensive opportunities and located fairly close to Afghanistan. Almaty is home to a variety of international agencies, including a number of UN bodies. For this reason, the proposal that an international centre should be created for the UN in Almaty remains especially relevant. Its activities would be focused, among other things, on post-conflict rehabilitation in Afghanistan. Such a body is essential to coordinate the financial and economic aid given to the country via the regional and sub-regional representative offices of the UN and other international and regional organisations. This will make it possible to implement the current programmes and objectives of our multilateral cooperation in the future.

Kazakhstan's role with regard to Afghanistan goes back a long way. In 1996, when the situation in the north of Afghanistan deteriorated drastically, an emergency meeting was held in Almaty for the Heads of State of the countries of Central Asia and Russia. At the suggestion of those attending, an emergency meeting of the UN Security Council was convened. It was at that point, on 22 October 1996, that the first separate resolution of the UN Security Council on Afghanistan – resolution 1076 – was unanimously adopted. Kazakhstan put in considerable effort to help solve the problems in Afghanistan during its chairmanship of the OSCE. The same approach was taken during our tenure at the helm of the Council of Foreign Ministers of the Organisation of Islamic Cooperation.

Our country actively participates in initiatives to resolve Afghanistan's problems via the Shanghai organisation for cooperation and the Organisation of the Agreement on collective security. The range of challenges related to Afghanistan is one of the important areas of cooperation between the Republic of Kazakhstan and the North Atlantic Alliance.

We are committed to fulfilling our obligations regarding the restoration of Afghanistan. Since the start of operations by the international security forces, Kazakhstan has provided assistance to the coalition troops as part of the implementation of agreements on the transit of goods with the Alliance, and also under bilateral agreements with the USA, Germany, France, Spain and the United Kingdom. We are now preparing to expand our transit assistance for NATO deliveries with the help of the Caspian Sea port of Aktau.

Kazakhstan is also actively involved in the international community's humanitarian efforts aimed at restoring Afghanistan. Since 2007, our country has been implementing a special plan of assistance for Afghanistan. Under this plan, we are training Afghan citizens in peace-time professions with a team of a thousand specialists. Every year, Kazakhstan provides technical and humanitarian aid to Afghanistan, free of charge. It was thanks to Kazakhstani funding that the 'Talukan – Kunduz – Sherkhan-Bandar' highway was renovated. Schools and a hospital have also been built thanks to aid provided by Kazakhstan.

Currently, the National agency for the provision of official aid in development and technical support, 'KazAID', is being created. One of the priority areas of its activity will be the implementation of projects in Afghanistan.

Kazakhstan will continue to help restore peacetime existence in Afghanistan – with an emphasis on social and educational programmes and projects, and the provision of humanitarian aid in the form of supplies of food and petroleum products. Kazakhstan is willing, via the mechanisms of the UN, FAO and the UN World Food Programme, to increase supplies of grain, flour and other foodstuffs to the country. We call on international donors to make more active use of Kazakhstan's potential in the process of restoring Afghanistan.

It is important to note that today, the problems of drug production and the drug trade are among the major challenges to the region's development. I hereby call for joint and coordinated efforts in the battle against this global problem. Without a full-scale solution, it will be hard to secure peace and stability in Afghanistan after 2014.

In our view, an important role should be played by the Central Asian regional information coordination centre in the battle against illegal profits from narcotics, psychotropic substances and the forerunners of these substances. This unique body, created in Almaty under the auspices of the UN, has already shown itself to be an effective mechanism in the battle against cross-border drug-related crime in the region.

Another significant regional problem is the threat of international terrorism and religious extremism. Afghanistan continues to be a source of, and exporter of, terrorist and extremist activity to its neighbouring countries and elsewhere. It seems to me that we must not forget this issue when planning our joint efforts in Afghanistan.

Clear approaches, a constructive policy, a rejection of the geopolitical strategies which have damaged the stable development of the region – these are the core components of our theory concerning a "platform for regional interests". We must publicise the unity of intent among Eurasian countries regarding Afghanistan, in the name of securing peace in the region. I hope that this approach will also be supported by countries outside the region.

The document that we draw up at the end of this meeting – the Almaty declaration – must contain clear signals to Afghan society, and to the political forces in the country and beyond its borders, that the international community's strategy of continuing support for Afghanistan as a responsible and equal partner remains undiminished.

I am sure that all the states taking part in the Istanbul process will continue to remain committed to a policy of openness, constructive dialogue and cooperation.

Speech at the Conference for Foreign Ministers
of the member states of the Istanbul process
Almaty, 26th April 2013

EIGHTEEN

GLOBAL CHALLENGES AND THREATS

*In this speech, Nursultan Nazarbayev discusses the main outcomes
of the Astana Economic Forum during its five-year history and shared
his views on contemporary global challenges and threats.*

The Astana Economic Forum has been held regularly over the last five years. It has now become a significant forum for the exchange of opinions, both in terms of its format and in terms of its content. Why do I hold that view? Firstly, the efforts made by the forum to devise an all-encompassing plan for countering the global crisis was approved by the sixty seventh session of the UN General Assembly. At the same time as this sixth Astana Economic Forum, we are also hosting a Conference on solutions to the global crisis, which is taking place under the auspices of the UN for the first time. There are more than a hundred states taking part.

Secondly, over the five years in which the forum has existed, the number of delegates has risen dramatically. The total number attending the Astana Forum and the Conference on the global crisis is more than 10,000 delegates, including around 3,000 foreign guests from 132 countries around the world. Thirdly, I would like to thank the great scientists of today, including several Nobel prize winners, who, by creating the Eurasian Economic Scientists' Club in Astana, are actively taking part in the Astana Economic Forum and thereby lending it the kind of support that carries great weight and prestige. Fourth, the Astana Economic Forum has triggered a wide-ranging debate on the internet, involving more than 120 permanent users of the worldwide web. Fifth, there are other reasons which point to the growing influence of the Astana Economic Forum. For example, a year ago I spoke from this same platform and proposed the creation of G-Global. Today, the Google search engine alone has recorded around a billion searches for this term. In the light of the above, I have every reason to hope that the conclusions drawn by the sixth Astana Economic Forum and the Conference on the global crisis will be in great demand at both the regional and global levels.

I would like to share with you my vision of the current problems that are up for discussion by those attending this forum.

First and foremost, I would like to mention the potential anti-crisis approaches. Whilst getting started on the process of drawing up a global anti-crisis plan, it is essential that we take into account a number of important lessons learned in recent years.

At the end of last year, almost everyone in the world was certain we had already 'turned the page' on the first ever universal crisis to hit the global economy in the 21st century. Many financial institutes were at pains to convince us that this was the case. As it turned out, there was to be no euphoria. The collapse of the financial system in Cyprus left many feeling that the age of universal economic stability was still some way off. I know there are analysts who deny there is a link between the 'Cyprus incident' and the global crisis. But the fact remains: even those with little understanding of economics could easily note similarities between the problems suffered by the banks in Cyprus and the collapse of the US mortgage agencies five years ago. It is first and foremost about the artificial 'collapse' of financial bubbles and a hunger for 'easy money', a failure to show the kind of responsibility required on the part of the national financial institutes, and the weakness of global financial management.

In essence, these reasons, and the other fundamental causes of the global crisis, have not yet been fully addressed. And therefore we cannot afford to imagine that the global crisis is over. Moreover, it appears that the crisis is moving into a new phase, which will be accompanied by painful 'explosions' in a host of local financial systems. I believe that this is the first lesson we should learn, and that we should take it into account when drawing up a Global Anti-Crisis Plan. The second lesson is that people are attempting to solve a global recession using anti-crisis measures taken at the national level, however paradoxical that may seem. Without question, during any crisis, action is better than inaction. Kazakhstan has implemented a successful anti-crisis programme which has enabled us to save jobs and maintain positive economic growth.

Not all of the anti-crisis recommendations drawn up within the G20 Group were implemented – far from it. A large number of states took protectionist measures. This led to a slowing of the growth rate in global trade, and a fall in prices in global and regional markets. The amount of cross-border lending and investment fell – it currently stands at just 60% of its pre-crisis level.

Another aspect of the problem is the sharp reverse in people's sense of social well-being. Unemployment is rising around the world. The International Labour Organisation has predicted that there will be more than 200 million people out of work globally, this year alone. At the start of this year there were more than twenty six million people without a job in Europe, a figure which is 1.5 times higher than five years ago.

Many states are cutting expenditure on education, medicine and developing human potential. These things are clear signs of a global social crisis, which threatens a reduction in the quality of life even in developed societies. According to calculations made by experts from Oxford University, half of all the under-privileged people on the planet live in countries that are part of the G20. 250 million people have had no choice but to emigrate in search of a better life, and this, too, has engendered significant social problems.

The social inequality that we see today in many countries is the direct consequence of financial and economic inefficiency. National anti-crisis plans helped to soften the blow caused by the consequences of the crisis, but required effective radical measures at the global level. In my article 'The keys to the crisis', published four years ago, I described the flaws in the global currency system as a major cause of the current global economic storm. I would like to remind readers that I called for a change to the way global currencies are issued and circulated, which are currently neither lawful, democratic, effectively monitored nor responsible. To date, no effective global anti-crisis mechanisms have been created, nor is there a reliable global currency reserve or groups of regional currencies. The kind of resolve and accountability required to adopt these radical solutions is lacking.

The third lesson to take into account when working on the global anti-crisis plan is overcoming mistrust. I share the opinion of those who say that the global crisis was a crisis of trust, first and foremost. There is little trust between the global financial institutions and nation states, between the financial sector and the real economy, between different countries, and so on. I firmly believe that unless there is trust on all sides, any anti-crisis plan will only 'paper over the cracks'.

In the 21st century, the world needs a new economic model. It must be based primarily on a global financial system that is honest and fair, in which there is no deceit, no failure of responsibility and no wastefulness. Where mankind has achieved good things, they will be directed towards creative work and progress in the name of the happiness and development of every society.

The fourth lesson concerns our attempts to gain a sense of proportion. Firstly, the financial sector cannot, and must not, develop in isolation from real manufacturing at both global and national levels. The pre-crisis situation, when the turnover from derivatives was eight times higher than the total GDP of the entire planet, represented a suicidal state of affairs for the global economy. Particular emphasis, in the reform of global financial management, must therefore be placed on creating an effective model for regulating the derivatives market.

Secondly, it is important to monitor off-shore companies on a global scale. The amount taken from national economies and diverted to off-shore zones stands at some thirty trillion dollars. Essentially, this is a time bomb which could detonate at any moment. And the situation regarding Cyprus is the kind of warning that cannot be ignored. The fifth lesson concerns the fact that the current global crisis is a multi-dimensional one. It is with good reason that I described it as the first universal crisis to hit the globalised world. The course and dynamics of the crisis are determined not just by economic factors, but also by political and humanitarian causes and issues related to our morals and values.

Today, for example, one cannot fail to see the problems related to the growing number of countries which have become 'chronic recipients' of international aid. The domestic conflicts in the Middle East and North

Africa are placing a heavy burden on the world economy. But it will not be possible to stop the "global economic fire" by means of a "worldwide flood" of political instability. A new global economy will not be possible without a new, just world order.

I would like to stress how important it is to take these five lessons into account, all of which have become apparent during the global crisis, in order to establish the right anti-crisis measures for global development this century. It is pleasing to see the role played by the United Nations in seeking global anti-crisis solutions is increasing.

In September 2011, speaking at the sixty sixth session of the UN General Assembly, I called on the world community to start work, without delay, on a pact on global regulation. This document could become a genuine instrument for achieving agreement on key aspects of international economic policy. It concerns the establishment of structures to ensure the proper functioning of the new global financial system, and the creation of a global regulator to determine the rules of the game for everyone. It is vitally important today that we expand the debate about global anti-crisis management within the framework of the G8 and the G20. Kazakhstan, as a country which has been invited to the upcoming G20 summit in St Petersburg, will be highlighting the proposals and recommendations of the Astana Economic Forum and the Global Anti-crisis Conference, to the attention of the delegates at the G20.

If we look towards the future with trepidation, the future will look back at us in the same way. All crises represent, first and foremost, opportunities for radical change. A year ago I put forward the idea of G-Global. I am grateful to all those who have praised my suggestion. The main rationale of G-Global represents a positive alternative to the chaotic way in which the global paradigms for worldwide development are changing. It is based on the potential of five clear and simple principles to bring people together. I wish to remind you what those principles are: Number one, evolutionary change and the rejection of revolutionary change in politics; number two, justice, equality and consensus; number three, global tolerance and trust; number four, global transparency; number five, constructive multipolarity.

On the basis of these things, successful debate on any global challenge will be possible in the 21st century, and we will arrive at solutions which are acceptable to all parties.

Today, the world needs a new global financial and economic system and effective global security structures, including nuclear ones. There is vast potential in continuing the global debate, so that it leads to the strengthening of tolerance and harmony. Given the global transformation that is taking place, there is a greater need now for political will, decisiveness, agreement, openness and trust than ever before. I sincerely hope that the supporters of G-Global will continue to grow. In order to develop this idea further, I propose that a Board of Trustees be created for G-Global, along the same lines as the Rome Club or the Madrid Club. The Board of Trustees would be responsible for organising research into the fundamental aspects of the idea.

Kazakhstan first appeared on the political map of the world just two decades ago. We started from scratch, and today our economic successes have received universal acclaim. In 2012, in the World Bank's ratings of the best countries in which to do business, Kazakhstan came forty ninth, while in the 'investor protection' category we came tenth. In the competitiveness index compiled by the World Economic Forum, Kazakhstan was in fifty first place. We are already on the brink of achieving the target I set a few years ago – that of making it into the top fifty most competitive countries in the world. We have drawn up the 'Kazakhstan-2050' Strategy. Its main goal is to transform Kazakhstan into one of the thirty most developed countries, making progress on the basis of innovative economic and social principles. The most important of these is the harmonious development of the triad 'economy – energy – ecology'. And this is by no means some utopia hidden beyond the clouds, but rather a genuine requirement of humanity.

The world's emergence from the crisis, which is on the horizon, will inevitably lead to a large-scale increase in production and consumption. In today's world, one in five people have no access to electricity. It would therefore be unjust to postpone the solving of problems related to energy and the environment to a later date. At last year's summit in Rio de Janeiro, my initiatives on a global energy and environmental strategy and the 'Green Bridge' programme received backing from the global community. The transition to 'green energy' and the introduction of 'green technologies' is a growing trend in the global economy. Kazakhstan, in spite of our vast reserves of natural riches, including hydrocarbons, intends to develop renewable sources of energy. These tasks have been set out in the 'Kazakhstan-2050' Strategy. We will invest two per cent of the nation's GDP in 'green modernisation' every year. This is reflected in the concept that we have adopted for the transition to a 'green economy'. In four years' time, the international exhibition 'EXPO-2017' will take place in Astana. There is a good reason why we proposed that the theme of the exhibition should be 'The Energy of the Future'.

The 21st century is moving on apace, 'compressing' time and distance as it does so. A new type of global economy is emerging, new principles are being established in international relations and new values are emerging in our societies. It is therefore important that we find the right solutions to global problems.

Speech at the 6th Astana Economic Forum
Astana, 23rd May 2013

NINETEEN

G-GLOBAL AND A NEW WORLD ORDER

*At the 2013 G20 summit, Nursultan Nazarbayev highlighted the
concept of "G-Global", the global internet communication platform
designed to encourage a new world order. He shared these views
with the aim of reaching solutions to a range of global issues.*

There is a pressing need now to encourage more states to seek anti-crisis solutions. G20 summits have become one of the modern world's responses to the challenges it faces. Yet the views of most developing countries are only indirectly reflected in the results of these summits. In order to ensure that the voices of smaller countries such as Kazakhstan are heard, I initiated the G-Global project two years ago. It is not an alternative to the G8 or the G20, but rather an additional forum for global debate. The proposed cooperation will be founded on clear and simple principles: evolutionary change, justice, trust and global transparency. Its effectiveness is founded on a three-pronged partnership between science, pragmatism and politics. G-Global is already being implemented as a discussion club for the dissemination of information. It has brought together three million internet users from 160 countries. Its working platform is the Astana Economic Forum, which this year was added to the list of outreach events at the G20 summit.

Another of our initiatives was the proposal to create a high-level global anti-crisis conference. It was held in Astana with support from the UN General Assembly. It was attended by the directors of economic institutes from 104 countries.

Whilst presenting these innovative global formats for dialogue, I would like to share our vision of how the world's most pressing problems could be solved. First of all, gradual, evolutionary changes must be made to the global currency and financial architecture, so that it meets the needs of all countries. Ideally, a new global currency would be instituted, which would be: lawful and democratic, i.e. adopted with the consent of all countries; reliable, i.e. an instrument for measuring true value and controllable profit-making; balanced, i.e. oriented towards the long-term tasks and values of development.

The simplest response to the current conditions would be to adopt a number of currencies as reserve currencies. At the same time, we must increase accountability among those who issue them. At the same time, we must also strengthen coordination between currency policies. To do so, we need a strong body for global currency regulation.

Secondly, the world's financial system must be reformed. We need a system of regulation which levels out risks and incorporates both restrictions and incentives. The issue of taxing international financial operations has already been raised, and it is one that must be solved. These resources must constitute stabilisation funds. Thirdly, we must balance our debt relations. The proposal is that new arrangements should be proposed for regulating and controlling the amount of borrowing, both by states and by corporations.

I touched on the global financial architecture as the most pressing problem in the current crisis. Yet it is a multi-faceted problem. The search for ways to overcome this problem must therefore cover all areas of activity in the global economy. Trade and investment, energy and food security, migration and income – all these issues have deep and interconnected problems and achievements. This search will not end with the G-Global forum.

The crisis – unprecedented in its sheer scale – shattered people's trust in the path of globalisation. But we firmly believe it would be wrong to resort to isolation as a means of salvation. Regional integration, founded on principles of equality and mutual interest, is a reliable method for restoring sustainable growth.

In the name of its partners, Russia and Belarus, Kazakhstan is representing the interests of the Single Economic Area at this summit. This association is already up and running and has consolidated the success enjoyed by the Customs Union. A common market between the three states has been created and has started working. This market contains 170 million people and a combined GDP of around USD 2 trillion. The next step will be the creation of the Eurasian Economic Union. I would particularly like to stress that this association is not pursuing any political objectives and is open to membership applications from other countries.

Kazakhstan is rich in natural resources, and this brings with it certain responsibilities. We are backing the G20's initiative concerning a 'Green Climate Fund'. For our part, we have initiated the 'Green Bridge' Partnership programme, which was approved by the 'Rio+20' summit. It is my belief that the leading countries must help developing countries access new technologies and stimulate their dissemination.

Kazakhstan became the first country in the post-Soviet area to step firmly down the path of 'green modernisation' and actively promote the principles behind it. Evidence of this can be seen in the decision to make Astana the venue for the International exhibition 'EXPO-2017', on the theme of 'The Energy of the Future'. We would be delighted to see the states of the G20 being among the most active participants in the 'EXPO'.

Speech at the G20 Summit
St Petersburg, Russian Federation, 5th September 2013

TWENTY

BECOMING A TOP THIRTY NATION

The Eurasian forum of emerging markets entitled "Eurasia in the 21ˢᵗ century: leadership through renewal" was held for the first time in a CIS country. The main theme of the forum was the strategy "Kazakhstan – 2050" and Kazakhstan's objective of becoming one of the world's top thirty developed countries.

By 2050, Kazakhstan must become one of the top thirty most developed countries in the world and has every chance of achieving this. The crisis of the collapsed Soviet economy was comparable in scale, for us, to the Great Depression in America. Doubts were expressed about our ability to survive as an independent state, and to preserve and protect our borders. We overcame these difficulties, and despite the new regional and global crises, have pressed ahead confidently along the path of modernising our country.

We started to create our own future, independently and in a balanced, decisive manner. And now that a strong foundation has been created in Kazakhstan for new achievements, we are expanding the horizons of our capabilities. We have a precise understanding of our competitive advantages and know how to turn these into economic and social advantages. We have a vast land mass, rich in natural resources, extensive arable land and significant potential for developing wind and solar power. We have provided macro-economic resilience. Our high economic growth has become more stable.

We are implementing an effective policy for managing the profits made from oil. The country has a total of USD 90 billion of gold and currency reserves. That represents around 30% of our country's economy. We have built the basic institutions required to form a full-scale market economy and a democratic society. We are leaders in the region in terms of the investment and business climate. Kazakhstan's population is growing. Quality of life is improving as is the health of our citizens, while life expectancy has risen to seventy.

The proportion of highly qualified experts in the country is increasing. We have created special academic schools, a holding company for the development of professional and technical education and a world-class university. We are steadily and determinedly moving closer to the best educational standards in developed countries. Today, the world knows Kazakhstan as a peaceful country, which speaks out in favour of mutually beneficial cooperation and integration. We are also well aware of the barriers which could impede the country's development.

We have a low population density: almost half of all Kazakhstanis live in rural areas. Many populated areas are a long way from the centres of economic growth. This is restricting the opportunities for universal access to high-quality education, the provision of high-qualified medical aid, employment in manufacturing and infrastructure. We are still in the risk zone in terms of developing the 'Dutch disease'. The country's economy is still in the process of diversifying its manufacturing and export base. The bulk of direct foreign investment is going towards the economy's mining sector. We inherited an economy based on energy, with a relatively low level of labour productivity. The transport, utilities and communication/information infrastructure is in need of modernisation. The barriers we experience are not a reason to stop growing, but rather a good reason to fine-tune our approach. We need to ensure that we can transform these obstacles into opportunities for growth.

Today, the question is often asked: "How do you define a developed country?" It seems to me that the concept of a developed country is one that is both complex and multi-faceted. The developed countries that are in the world's top thirty today are the countries with the highest level of GDP per head of the population. But this is nothing more than a quantitative indicator, criticised by many experts given that it does not reflect the qualitative changes to the country's development.

All developed countries have a high volume of scientific activity, with a dominant service sector and high labour productivity. Scientific knowledge and the high-tech sectors of industry play a key role in ensuring economic growth. Based on current notions of the definition of a developed country, Kazakhstan must not only make a substantial breakthrough in its development, but also requires a burgeoning and all-encompassing process of modernisation.

According to expert assessments, the impact of global trends over the next fifteen to twenty years will be favourable for Kazakhstan. This will give us a 'window of opportunity' in fifteen to twenty years' time to achieve the best possible results in a short space of time. Kazakhstan's path towards becoming a developed country must stem from the desire of each and every citizen to change themselves, to change Kazakhstan and to make it part of the global world. The desire for new, high-quality development: this must be the main focus of our nation over the coming decade.

We must be prepared for all manner of diverse development scenarios around the world, and form a flexible policy to achieve the goal of getting into the world's top thirty most developed countries. The key to success, in an uncertain world, lies in our ability to react quickly and in the right way to the changes taking place and to change as quickly as the world itself is changing. No-one can say with certainty what sort of world we will be living in by 2050. Events which might seem insignificant could lead to influential trends developing, while other trends might appear suddenly, out of nowhere. In the 1970s, no-one could have imagined that in forty years' time, China would be the world's second largest economy. No-one could have foreseen the collapse of the Soviet Union, or Japan's "two lost decades". It is exactly the same today. The real picture of the world in the future may look utterly different from how we expect it to look.

As the experiences of the most developed countries show, the transition to a science-heavy economy provides flexibility, dynamism and sustainable growth in the economy, contributing to the wealth of the country as a whole. Kazakhstan's accession to the top thirty most developed countries must therefore be founded on the formation of a science-rich economy.

The principles for establishing a science-rich economy must be an open market economy, a meritocracy, partnership and pragmatism, the rule of law, inclusiveness, as well as exposure to constant structural change through innovation. These principles are creating the incentives required for citizens to achieve fulfilment and undertake business initiatives. They provide each citizen with equal rights and equal opportunities. They establish equal rules of the game for everyone, without exception, and create an atmosphere of freedom, honest competition and justice. They create incentives for constant striving towards new knowledge and higher levels of professionalism. Our entire policy, and all the measures we take, must be subordinate and clearly in line with these objectives.

The basis for our new economic policy must be the two most important priorities. These are, firstly, the creation of the right conditions for the development of the individual – the main driver of innovation. Secondly, we must perfect the institutional environment, providing the necessary conditions to grow businesses and develop entrepreneurial initiatives.

Number one. The development of our human capital. Education, as the key instrument for building a science-rich economy, must be oriented towards creating higher standards at all levels of the education system. This means making nursery education and teaching accessible to all children, including those under three, regardless of their parents' social status and material wealth. It means providing high-quality secondary, vocational and tertiary education. The education system must provide not only knowledge but also the skills required to put this knowledge into practice; modern teaching methods must be introduced, and information and communications technology must be actively used. It is important for us to construct an effective system of vocational education. We plan to construct at least two world-class colleges in Astana and Almaty. We must react without delay to the structural changes taking place in the labour market, introducing a practice of life-long learning. In order to adapt higher education so that it meets the needs of a science-rich economy, we must integrate universities, science and business.

We must ensure that every level of the education system gives students the knowledge and skills they need both in the economy and in life. One of the important areas of the development of education, for us, is the training of teaching staff who are ready for the modern world. We are taking wide-ranging measures to improve teachers' qualifications, create incentives for further professional growth and make the teaching profession more prestigious in the eyes of society.

The development of our human capital depends on many ways on the conditions for enhancing quality of life – the quality of the healthcare system and a healthy way of life. Each citizen must be given access to clean water, clean air and proper bio resources. To improve the quality of the healthcare system, we are placing our bets, first and foremost, on prophylactic treatment and early-stage diagnosis of diseases. Primary stage medical care must be available to all urban and rural populated areas and form the basis of our healthcare system. We must introduce the principles of joint responsibility on the part of the state, the employer and the employee, for our people's health. From 2015 onwards, a fund for social medical insurance will commence in Kazakhstan.

Number two. Perfecting our institutional environment. We must construct a flexible, effective system of economic and socio-political institutes. Their primary task must be to ensure that a favourable environment is maintained for the development of entrepreneurialism, the self-fulfilment of every citizen and the safeguarding of his or her rights. The crisis of 2008 forced the government to play a more active role in regulating economic processes. It is clear that for long-term and sustainable growth, reducing the role of the state and strengthening market mechanisms is the only possible way to go. We plan to reduce the shares owned by the state in industrial and infrastructural entities. A new phase of privatisation, the 'National IPO' programme, and regular additional issuances of securities will be the key measures in reducing the State's role.

We must continue to improve the conditions for doing business and enable the development of entrepreneurial initiatives. To do so, we must continue to implement a policy of reducing red tape. Above all, we must remove the barriers to international trade, fine-tune our system of customs administration and regulate our foreign trade activity. The structural changes in the economy and the transition to a science-rich economy are making it all the more important to protect intellectual property. In this regard, it is important that we simplify and speed up the registration process for the documentation protecting intellectual property.

Efficiency in the market economy, and partnership and pragmatism in society, are being achieved via decentralisation. A precise distribution of power between the levels of state management, the strengthening of local budgets and the development of local self-regulation will resolve issues of regional differences in quality of life. There should also be increasing autonomy in the activities of schools, hospitals and higher education institutes. We plan to expand the practice of creating boards of trustees. We intend to develop the provision of corporate governance within state sector organisations, providing them with greater independence. Yet at the same time it is important to have strategic control over the results of these organisations' activities.

The rule of law is guaranteed by the effectiveness of state governance, transparency in the judicial system and awareness that everyone is equal before the law. The judicial system must be accessible and transparent, and allow the quick and straightforward resolution of disputes – not just in theory, but in practice. The pursuit by judges of their professional duties, honestly and in good faith, and their independence when taking court decisions, shall guarantee compensation when rights are violated. This serves to strengthen society's confidence in justice and in the neutrality and independence of the courts. And this is what we must achieve. The rooting out of corruption is one key precondition to encourage an increase in entrepreneurial initiatives and creative development on the part of every citizen in the country. We will conduct wide-ranging institutional reform of the system of law enforcement, create new institutes and a system of relations whereby people are motivated to fulfil their obligations honestly. All of these objectives will be resolved in the new criminal and criminal procedure codes, which the Government will be passing through Parliament in the near future.

We must build an efficient system of state governance. In the civil service, it is of the utmost importance that we deepen the principles of meritocracy, create 'social lifts' and strengthen levels of professionalism, among other things by training effective managers in the 'A' corpus. This year, elections were held for the Akims in almost 2,500 district towns, rural boroughs and villages. This is a huge step on the path of providing further democracy in our society. We will continue to gradually deepen democratic reforms and strengthen the institutions of local self-governance. I am sure that by perfecting the institutional environment and the development of our human capital, this will enable our country to lay a firm foundation for the formation of a science-rich economy and competitiveness in the long-term. These two main priorities must be key over the decades to come. Strong institutions and human capital will form the basis on which, in the long-term, Kazakhstan can make large-scale changes and withstand the global changes taking place.

Now a few words about our territorial development. This is an important issue, given our huge land mass and low population density. The choice we have made is to develop urban conglomerations – the points of economic growth along with satellite towns adjoining them. The country's long-term objective will be to form four competitive, world-class metropolises and a host of 'smart', 'green' towns which will be comfortable and safe places to live. This will provide the physical framework for the formation of a science-rich economy. The experience of other countries tell us this: innovation happens in big cities.

High population density and the diverse and developed nature of infrastructure and human capital strengthen the exchange and spread of knowledge. This encourages the process of change and innovation and gives rise to new areas of activity in the economy. The centres of these conglomerations could be our biggest cities, Astana and Almaty. Other cities could also join them. In these cities, it is the small and medium-sized businesses that are growing fastest: they have a high share of employment and boast the most developed infrastructure. We must now turn them into major centres of research and development and the focus of innovation and entrepreneurship, and create a network of intellectual and innovative clusters or so-called science parks.

The first intellectual and innovation cluster is now being established in Astana, at Nazarbayev University. In the future, this practice must also be translated to other conglomerations. They must become focal points for the country's population by providing high-quality services in education, information and transport, intensive competition, and attractive conditions for investment. At these centres of growth, it is essential that we introduce modern infrastructure: develop high-speed bus routes, tram networks and underground lines, and expand the use of information and communication technologies. We must improve the efficiency of our institutions focused on the development and support of science and innovation. To this end we must fine-tune our legislation on venture financing, protect intellectual property, support research and development, and also foster the commercialisation of scientific inventions.

To effect this transition to a knowledge-based economy we must balance and coordinate our strategies in the management of energy resources, develop renewable sources of energy and provide energy-efficient, industrial development. Number one; a change in our approach to the management of hydrocarbon resources. Reserves of raw materials and, in particular, energy resources must not be a basic source of income for the state, but must support growth in the multi-sector national economy. This is the key task the Government faces. Likewise, our energy policy must be re-oriented towards the consistent, sustainable and environmentally friendly use of energy resources. It is essential that we preserve the long-term export potential of our oil resources, develop renewable sources of energy and also ensure energy efficiency.

We must thoroughly examine the various approaches to our policy in the management and extraction of oil resources, from an aggressive to a conservative scenario. Of the three types of asset – oil reserves in the oilfields, the financial assets of the National Fund and social infrastructure – the untapped oil resources will have a positive effect on profitability in the long-term. It is crucial to determine the level of resource extraction sufficient for our economy – and stop once we reach it. With a conservative approach, we will be able to provide sustainability in our extraction and export of oil resources up until 2050 as well as stable levels of profitability for the National Fund. In the more aggressive scenario, we could rapidly lose our ability to export oil resources, significantly strengthening the risk of developing the 'Dutch disease'.

Number two; develop alternative sources of energy and increase energy efficiency. Kazakhstan has significant potential for developing alternative sources of energy to provide 50% of the total amount of electricity consumed, while simultaneously reducing power consumption in the economy. To achieve this we must make the country's economy as energy-efficient as the Chinese economy by 2050. This means that up to 2020, the annual fall in energy consumption must be at least 2.5%, and after 2020 – at least 3.5%. To do this we must devise a complex, institutional approach, including the creation of an agency for the development of clean energy, a fund for supporting projects in the field of alternative sources of energy, energy services companies and the roll-out of the 'Leader in energy efficiency' programme.

Number three; adjustments to our industrial policy. We must optimise the current priorities in industrialisation and reject 'fading' areas of manufacturing. We must limit the number of priority sectors to create a competitive industrial and innovation policy. Should we fail to do so, it will lead to the disintegration of our resources and poor results. In order to be competitive in the future, we must take action now to ensure we specialise in high-tech areas of manufacturing. It is essential that we strengthen our research potential in areas of manufacturing such as 'clean energy', robotic technologies, nanotechnology, genetic engineering in agriculture, and the technological niches in aerospace. We must also form a high-tech services sector, primary geological surveys and engineering services, information and communication services, and wide-ranging services in the production and servicing of reactors and nuclear power stations.

Without question, the agricultural sector has huge potential for development in the long-term. The growing global demand for foodstuffs, the rise in population numbers in developing countries, and global climate change are creating powerful drivers for the development of this sector. It is crucial that we introduce new technologies and incorporate, into agricultural production, land which was previously barren, in dry or semi-arid regions. It is important to activate scientific research in the field of agriculture, create the conditions needed to increase the sector's investment appeal and expand access to financing. It is important to move towards a rational use of resources, among other things by developing genetically modified products.

These new approaches to our economic policy must be in harmony with the principles of a 'green economy'. These are sustainable development, low power consumption in the economy, the development of alternative sources of energy and the rational use of resources. They are also innovative development, with minimal impact on the environment.

And finally, issues of integration. The vast dimensions of our country's land mass, our low population, and the fact that we lack a coastline mean that Kazakhstan must adopt an open, active integration policy and become a country which is an active member of the global community. This is not the only reason why we must do so. Countries' openness to international trade has been one of the causes of sustainable growth in all rapidly growing countries. This was the path taken by the developed countries of today's world, in the post-war period. We can use our geographical position to our advantage, as a country located at the crossroads between Europe and Asia. Our transit potential brings massive potential for development. Openness and pragmatism must be deep-rooted within all areas of our trade relations with other states. This concerns the Customs Union, the WTO (World Trade Organisation) and the Central Asian region. Supporting stable economic growth and improving the wealth of our neighbours will have a positive impact on Kazakhstan's own development. The prosperity of these countries will also enable us to minimise the potential risks of a rise in drug trafficking, the threat of terrorism, religious extremism and the intensifying of ethnic conflicts.

I have set out my vision and approach to Kazakhstan's long-term development in a concise format. A detailed plan of action is currently being drawn up and will be published imminently. I am confident that this will enable Kazakhstan to take its place in the top thirty most developed states and lay the foundations for reaching new milestones even beyond 2050. We have commenced this work. Last year, the Government was ordered to draw up a conceptual plan on how to get Kazakhstan into the top thirty most developed countries.

Over the course of more than twenty years, we have moved together, through our concerted efforts, to the situation we have now: a prosperous society and a strong, rapidly growing economy. This is a sound basis for new beginnings. By implementing the 'Kazakhstan-2030' Strategy, we became a fully-fledged state, capable of solving the more complex tasks that lie ahead for our country's continuing development. To achieve a worthy and certain future for our younger generations, however, we must now achieve much more. Our surroundings have changed. They will continue to change, just as we ourselves will. Time is moving on apace. And the period that lies ahead until the year 2050, which at this point seems nothing more than an abstraction, is just a small interval in historical terms. Thus far, time has been on our side; I hope this will continue to be the case in the future. We must therefore take action today so as to ensure that we achieve the goals we have set to the best of our ability in the future. When we have set ourselves a goal, we always end up achieving it. I would like our future generations to live in a free, peaceful Kazakhstan which has preserved its culture and traditions, a country of great opportunities, in a country in which the laws encourage private initiative and operate in the interests of the public. In a society of mutual accountability and partnership. I would like to see Kazakhstani scientists and researchers being acclaimed as world leaders in chemistry, genetics, physics and technology, and to see our businessmen being leaders in the application of new technologies. I hope that the Kazakhstani people will be one of the healthiest nations in the world, with high standards of living. As Kazakhstan develops and flourishes, remaining a peace-loving country and a reliable partner, it is our country's destiny to become one of the leading countries in the world. I have no doubt about this whatsoever!

As I pondered what a fully developed Kazakhstan might look like in the year 2050, I tried to imagine how a historian might evaluate the progress our country has made. At the start of 2050, the Government will summarise the results of the progress we have achieved, and one of our historians (still a student today) will write:

"In December 2012, the then President announced the goal of securing a place in the top thirty most developed countries in the world. We have achieved that goal.

In just four short decades, we have gone from being a country in which the average annual income is USD 12,000 per capita to a level whereby we have been ranked in the world's top thirty most developed states. We have created institutes which support private initiative and provide effective protection for vulnerable sections of society. We have used our natural resources in such a way that they support our development, rather than slowing it down. Most of our economic success has been achieved through rapid industrialisation and the development of aspects of the service sector. We have completed the transition to a 'green economy'. Kazakhstan has achieved the greatest possible successes in the development of its labour resource base. We have one of the most advanced education systems in the world. Our country is the leader in satisfying its citizens' healthcare needs. We are a peaceful country. Kazakhstan, which does not pose a threat to any countries whatsoever and is a friend to all, has taken up its place among the world's leading states. We must now continue to consolidate the strong position we have attained. It would be nice to see the new generation taking up this challenge with enthusiasm, confident that they will succeed."

Speech at the Eurasian forum for emerging markets
Astana, 10th September 2013

TWENTY-ONE

THE ROLE OF NUR OTAN

The "Nur Otan" party was founded in 1999 on the initiative of President Nursultan Nazarbayev. The discussion at the 2013 Party Congress, highlighted fifteen years of work by the "Nur Otan" party. The Congress delegates adopted its political doctrine.

In the history of our party and country, this congress has a special significance. At this congress we must examine the results of the party's activity over the last fifteen years and adopt a programme for its further development.

Looking far into the future, we are setting ourselves ambitious goals. After clearly defining the main areas of our development in the long-term, we immediately set about the task of making them a reality. As for the mission of mobilising the Kazakhstani nation in order to implement the tasks in the Strategy, this rests on the most capable political force in our society: the Nur Otan party.

Any journey, no matter how long, must begin with just a few small steps. I recall how, fourteen years ago, there were some 400 delegates in attendance at the founding congress of our party. In just a short space of time, however, Nur Otan transformed into a powerful organisation which boasts 250 branches and 6,300 primary organisations. The party has taken a key position within the structure of the executive and representative branches of power. It is actively involved in all matters of importance to the state and, whilst supporting all my initiatives, is allowing them to come to fruition with great enthusiasm. Thanks to this, the party has accumulated a solid level of practical experience.

It is in man's nature not only to see phenomena, but also to recognise their essence. In this sense, Nur Otan, by showing itself to be the party of concrete steps and measures, has managed to earn society's trust. As the old folk saying goes: *"If your country is strong, long will be your happiness."*

Making the country strong so that we have better lives is the duty we share as the children of our country. Ensuring that Kazakhstan joins the top thirty most developed states in the world is our great objective. For Nur Otan, this must be our guiding star, pointing the way ahead to the future. This is also what the party's new political doctrine, which we are to adopt at today's congress, is oriented towards. We are a society that has managed to turn distinctive characteristics into its strengths. We have made our diversity our great wealth, and our unity – the source of our success. Society's intellectual elite must always be aware of this and set an example of this kind of consolidation to our young people. It is also very important that the party's doctrine indicates that the state language is a unifying factor for the country. On this issue, the time for a qualitative, positive change has come. Knowledge of the Kazakhstani language is not only each person's civil duty, but also a manifestation of respect for the nation. Love of the Motherland begins first and foremost with one's own family. Each one of our citizens must remember this.

This year, we are celebrating the twenty second anniversary of our independence. Independence was the cherished dream of our ancestors. Their struggle for freedom over many centuries is something that was brought to a triumphant conclusion by us all: for many of those present here today are my long-time peers, colleagues, comrades, members of the Government, deputies in Parliament, and kin of all levels. I wish to express to you my deep gratitude for this.

Today's forum is taking place at a decisive moment in Kazakhstan's modern history. Our society has made a confident start in its bid to meet the great new objective which was announced in the 'Kazakhstan-2050' Strategy. It has been set out clearly and precisely that Kazakhstan will attain a historical apotheosis in the middle of the 21st century. We know what sort of goal we wish to achieve, and we know what must be done to achieve it, and how. History, for its part, always makes its own corrections and adjustments: circumstances change, and we too will need to change. Nonetheless, this objective has been clearly outlined for us and for future generations. This is something that inspires us, just as we were inspired when we implemented the 'Kazakhstan-2030' Strategy ahead of time. I am sure that we will once again succeed in implementing the new Strategy, thereby providing prosperity for our people and stability in the country.

At the core of the new Strategy is the idea that we must become one of the top thirty most developed countries in the world. The epic scale of our goal is clear for all to see. Never before in our history have our people attained the kind of economic and social standards that they enjoy today. It was only thanks to the efforts of the current generation of Kazakhstanis that we were able to achieve this. By declaring our independence and developing this country of ours, we once and for all ceased to be on the fringes of development, and became a new and worthy state in Eurasia. And now we must progress with the same rhythm as the rest of the global community.

The 'Kazakhstan-2050' Strategy is our great, historic chance to join the family of the most famous nations in the world, once and for all. At present, work is being finalised on drawing up the specific tasks which must be solved if we are to reach a new phase in the development of the economy, our society and the state. There is a big and complex job ahead of us. In the 'Kazakhstan-2050' Strategy, I outlined ten global challenges in the 21st century. Last year showed just how accurate this forecast was.

The dramatic nature of global development is abundantly clear. At the start of the year, the 'Cyprus crisis' was quelled with great difficulty. The economy of the EU is going through a difficult stage of development as it balances on the brink of the lowest macro-indicators imaginable. The social crisis remains as acute as ever, unemployment is high and there is discontent among the people. The rate of growth among most of the BRIC countries has also slowed considerably.

Recently, the General Secretary of the UN, Ban Ki Moon, published a report by UN experts which states that by 2050, 50% of the Earth's population will be suffering from an acute shortage of water. The Middle East is currently suffering the effects of what we might call the 'Arab anti-spring'. In Egypt and Tunisia it has taken just a little over a year of rule by the Islamists for broad sections of the population to become convinced that such a policy will lead nowhere. The civil war in Syria has led to the use of chemical weapons of mass destruction against innocent and defenceless civilians. My political intuition and experience tell me that the next stage of the world's development is going to be extremely complicated. In these circumstances, all Kazakhstanis must cherish stability and the fact that our Motherland is able to develop along a predictable path.

Against the backdrop of the difficulties and crises set out above, our country is developing in a stable manner. According to forecasts, this year's growth will be around six per cent in GDP. This is higher than last year, and I would emphasise that this is despite the volatile state of the global markets. Our farmers gathered an outstanding harvest – 20 million tonnes of grain. The country's combined gold and currency reserves are multiplying. This year, they passed the USD 90 billion mark, taking account of assets in the National Fund. This is our response to any hardships and cataclysms which may occur in the global economy. Consumer goods made in Kazakhstan are being exported to 111 countries around the world! Goods exported from Kazakhstan include batteries, transformers, metal pipes, fertilisers, foodstuffs and many other ready goods. We now have completely new sectors in our economy. Never before has there been such a scale of manufacturing in our country – of cars, railway engines, railway coaches and helicopters.

A total of more than 250 new types of product are now being produced as part of our industrial programme. These include high-tech products in engineering, pharmaceuticals and the chemicals industry. For example, we now produce more than 100 different types of medicine. Today, there is every reason to expect that the year will end with success in all the major performance indicators. As we implement the 'Kazakhstan-2050' Strategy, our country must make a decisive change for the better. These changes will be profound and all-encompassing. They will cover every aspect of the life of our society. It is for the Nur Otan party to take charge of this epic mission! The central task of this congress is to determine the role and political significance of the Nur Otan party in terms of achieving all our goals by the middle of the 21st century.

In a few short months, in March of next year, our party will be fifteen years old! It was created on the basis of a national coalition in support of my reform path – a coalition which was formed on the eve of the first ever presidential elections in Kazakhstan's history.

It was then that a union of fellow thinkers came into being and became a major political force through the will of the people. It was then that our fledgling democracy began operating at full power. Together with the progressive, leading party Nur Otan, democracy took root here, just as it had occurred at various times in other advanced countries – Singapore, South Korea, and Japan. The story of Nur Otan is an integral part of the global experience of democracy.

The atmosphere at that first congress will live long in our memories. At that stage our bold dreams were considerably more modest than the achievements to which we can point today. I wish to echo the words that I spoke at that congress, words which have lost none of their relevance fifteen years later: *"A huge thank you to you, my dear comrades, for your hearts, which beat in the name of the Motherland. For the fact that you care about our nation's honour, for the fact that you have all come together on the path towards preserving and strengthening our statehood, like children of the same family!"*

I am grateful to all those Kazakhstanis who have built our new country together with me, for their hard work and patience! Particular thanks must go to my fellow politicians who created our party together with me. To all those who have contributed to the growth of the Nur Otan party! Right from the start, our party has been held together by the enthusiasm and belief of my fellow thinkers. Present here today are Sergei Aleksandrovich Tereshchenko, Kairzhan Shaikhievich Takuov and others. They continue to contribute to the work of the party, preserving our glorious traditions.

The parliamentary elections of 1999 represented the first test for us. Over the course of one and a half decades, the party has had to pass through the filter of election campaigns on several occasions, and has always emerged victorious during an honest and competitive struggle. We have always been inspired by the support of the people, which has grown with every new election. The Nur Otan party never made promises that it knew it wouldn't be able to keep. It has always been a party that gets things done, a party of real issues. Thanks to the efforts of hundreds of thousands of its members and the determined, hard work of each Kazakhstani citizen, the 'Kazakhstan-2030' Strategy was implemented well ahead of schedule.

I see my peers of every age, nationality and profession, all of whom represent our vast Motherland. I am sure that each of you can share the latest news about the achievements of your nearest and dearest, your towns and villages, and indeed the entire country. A massive amount of work has been completed to improve the living conditions of each and every family. Hundreds of new firms and roads have been built and hundreds of thousands of new jobs have been created. New nurseries, schools and hospitals have been opened. New universities, libraries, theatres, concert halls, stadia and sports halls have been opened. Above all, the spirit of our people has been reborn.

Today, the Nur Otan party has around 900,000 members and the party's deputies have a majority in the Majilis (Lower house of parliament). This is an important indication that Nur Otan enjoys the support of the nation. We have picked up a colossal amount of experience in parliamentary law-making. In the fifth session of Parliament alone, more than 140 laws were passed! The Nur Otan party drew up twelve draft laws on healthcare, agriculture and state services of social significance. The party has raised a plethora of parliamentarians and Majilikhat deputies, who defend our national interests. Our party forms the Government and has ensured that all the branches of the executive work together harmoniously.

I would particularly like to comment on the activities of the party's community wings: the Council for the struggle against corruption, the Legal council and others. The activity of the party's youth wing, Zhas Otan, is growing more prominent. Our young party members are actively implementing the resolutions adopted at their second congress. Nur Otan is cooperating with other parliamentary parties, federal professional unions, the civil alliance, veterans' and women's organisations and other NGOs. Of particular note is the active and fruitful work being done by the Ak Zhol wing of the party and the Communist People's Party of Kazakhstan, who have been setting out their opinion and taking up positions on fundamental issues and standing up for ordinary people.

Our party is the binding force in the National democratic coalition, 'Kazakhstan-2050'. Today, Nur Otan is the primary mechanism for political leadership, providing Kazakhstan with successful progress forward in the 21st century! We now have everything in order to lead our people to new victories. Above all, this is the great trust and support that we enjoy from all Kazakhstanis. This is the primary source of Nur Otan's political leadership in the 21st century. And the party's resources must now be distributed in the correct manner. It is essential that we strengthen party accountability for each member of Nur Otan. We must triple the energy with which we carry out the party's work.

The 'Kazakhstan-2050' Strategy is the basis of our party's political programme. I have no doubt whatsoever that its implementation will only be possible if Nur Otan retains its political leadership. The party must act in such a way that it can generate a single political will and take charge of the Kazakhstani people at every turn along the way. This is primarily a collective responsibility that we bear for the country's fate. Nur Otan brings together an extremely diverse range of people. In essence, the party reflects the whole of our society. For the party to be the conduit for our people's interests, we must have effective control on the part of the deputies over the work done by the executive. Today, we need systemic renewal. We are therefore adopting a political doctrine which enshrines our ideals, values and principles.

Our party must always be on the crest of change, following the global trends for successful parties, reacting quickly and flexibly to any risks and challenges that society faces. We must be able to see clearly that in the modern world, success is only achieved by those political forces that have clearly defined strategies. Success only occurs where long-term political leadership is provided as a durable guarantee of stability in development and unity among all our people. Not only have such dynamic countries as Turkey, Japan, India, Singapore and Malaysia taken this path, but so have a host of countries in Northern Europe: Sweden, Norway, Finland and Denmark. And at the same time, wherever political leadership has been weakened at moments of great responsibility in history, society has slipped into the chaos of turbulence and conflict. Therefore every member of Nur Otan – from the ministers to the ordinary party members – must clearly understand what leadership of the party means in the 21st century.

Number one. Nur Otan must be the main patriotic force in the country. The party's most important mission is to become a nationwide centre for the formation of the New Kazakhstani patriotism declared in the 'Kazakhstan-2050' Strategy. The children's organisations Zhas Kyran and Zhas Ulan must take part in this work, along with the youth associations led by Zhas Otan, the Republican council of veterans, and all the patriotic media and NGOs.

Number two. The party must always be the central link in the national chain of unity. Firstly, Nur Otan is the party of unity of the people. We must take pride in the fact that we have been able to turn the centuries-old dream of independence, harboured by our ancestors, into a reality. The new chapter in our nation's history is being written as a great manuscript describing the construction of a strong and successful independent state. Over these years, our people have demonstrated a model of genuine courage and unity. Our people have come to understand how difficult independence can be to obtain and to see that it is even harder to preserve. I am sincerely grateful to my people, who, having grasped these ideas, have proved capable of coming together to form a united front at a difficult time.

Everything is gradually taking shape and solutions are being found to all problems. We must not frighten away the bird of happiness that has perched on our hand. We must transform this favourable time into a golden age of rebirth for our native tongue, our national culture and the traditions of our forefathers. The Nur Otan party must devise an effective system for its social and political work aimed at strengthening the status of the state language and restoring Kazakhstani culture and traditions.

Secondly, the party has a great responsibility for providing unity among our multi-ethnic population. In this regard, it is essential that we have an integrated system of action by party organisations of various levels including the Assembly of the People of Kazakhstan, the parliamentary faction of Nur Otan and the Majilis deputies from the Assembly. Our slogan, 'One country – one people – one destiny', is also a crucial principle to which we adhere in real life.

Thirdly, the party must bring together the regions of the country and strengthen inter-regional ties. The process of creating a new regional politics in the state is currently under way. Elections have been held throughout the country for Akims in towns and villages, and local government has undergone a decisive overhaul. Real powers have been devolved from central government to the regions. Staff are being rotated from the regions to the centre, and also in the other direction. The system for hiring and promoting staff in the civil service has changed radically, and must be based only on merit and be run on competitive lines. The cadre of senior managers schooled in governance has also undergone a serious process of renewal. The party must once and for all overcome the archaic forms of regionalism which still exist in the minds of some segments of the population, and be a binding force for the interests of all Kazakhstanis.

Number three. Nur Otan must always be the leader of civil society. The party must develop cooperation with the civil alliance, as we have always done, and be a political conduit for the interests of all patriotic NGOs which are solving people's individual problems, helping them and relying on their support. We must consistently strengthen and expand the national coalition 'Kazakhstan-2050'. There must be no slowing down in this work, because our party is at the core of the movement forming our country's future.

Number four. One of the key issues facing the party's leaders is the aim of becoming the national epicentre of economic and social innovation. Our party must feed society and state with bold, innovative ideas about development. Today, the world's economy is working towards growth by creating innovative companies and high-quality jobs. It is therefore essential that we train suitable specialists. We adopted a programme of industrial and innovative development at the right time, and other countries have followed suit preparing similar industrial programmes. We must use it as the kernel of the development of our country's entire economy.

Both of these issues must be resolved on the basis of innovation and scientific invention. In the 21st century, scientific discoveries will be of the utmost importance in finding solutions. The key areas of innovation will be at the intersection of biology, nanotechnology and mathematics. They are already in operation. The search is on for completely new types of energy, as yet undiscovered by mankind. I wish to stress that an important condition for success in the 21st century is creativity. Nur Otan must therefore be a creative party. We must strengthen our work with the creative intelligentsia. Nur Otan's members must be ever-present in the online debate on issues of key importance for Kazakhstan's development.

Number five. The leading party in the 21st century is the main instrument for national oversight. First and foremost, Nur Otan must make wider use of its ability to provide parliamentary and social control over the implementation of the work plan in the 'Kazakhstan-2050' Strategy. In the fifth session of the Majilis alone, Nur Otan deputies have submitted around 300 requests to the state bodies on all aspects of the implementation of the party's pre-election platform. These requests must be examined carefully, so that a report can be made to the people on the implementation of the pre-election platform, as this is our common task.

An important instrument for national control during drafting of laws is the consultative and advisory boards attached to the Nur Otan parliamentary party. They are composed of experts and take account of the opinions of broad sections of society on important draft laws. I would particularly like to note the principled position adopted by Nur Otan on issues of taxation. I consider it entirely right that the deputies from our party have decided it is not permissible to increase the tax burden on the middle class. Just over 20% of our production is generated by SMEs, whereas in developed countries, among whose number we wish to be, this figure stands at 60-70%. We must increase the share provided by SMEs to 50%. It is therefore essential that we do all we can to help entrepreneurship, which forms the basis of the middle class. As I decreed five years ago, we must bring in indirect taxes on luxury goods, elite property and expensive cars. The same also goes for alcohol and tobacco. This is a civil and patriotic stance. The Government must take heed of what the parliamentarians are saying.

On the other hand, we understand that we must add to the budget, and we have the lowest rates of corporate and income tax – and we have created a class of well-off citizens. This is entirely right. It is a carefully targeted policy. There must be more wealthy people, and they must direct some of their wealth towards the development of the country which has enabled them to create their wealth. Now, as the affluent class expands, they can, and must, make their contribution to the common task of social responsibility. This is how things work all over the world. Yet here, both millionaires and ordinary workers pay the same rate – 10% – in income tax. It is worth taking time to reflect on this. I am therefore backing the initiative of my colleagues, the deputies in the Majilis. It is important to expand the practice of having consultative and advisory bodies, and apply it to the work of the Majilikhats as well.

Nur Otan is a parliamentary party. A crucial aspect of the strengthening of its work is therefore the activity of the group in the Majilis. Each draft law initiated by our deputies, each decision, must be based on a clear understanding of the country's long-term interests, and must be in line with the provisions of the doctrine. Nur Otan must show by example what it means to be an open, transparent, effective and responsible political force. We are open and we have nothing to hide. We are working honestly and talking openly to the people about all the flaws, providing support and realising that there are still some problems.

We must always work in the name of our people's prosperity. The party must systematically enhance the work of its public reception offices. This year alone, the public reception offices have processed around 100,000 messages from citizens. The other day we launched our 'Digital party' project. Now, any citizen with internet access can contact Nur Otan from the comfort of their own home. We need to maintain a constant dialogue with our citizens. This is the main source of the widespread popular support enjoyed by Nur Otan!

A fundamental issue in political leadership is our tireless anti-corruption strategy. The party must be a highly principled watchman guarding the civil honour of our party members. People in the regions are well aware of who takes bribes, and that means that rank and file party members know who the culprits are too. They must be the first to sound the alarm and to expose corrupt officials. The task of the party and the law enforcement agencies is to protect those who are fighting against corruption and to help them. Not a single KZT from the state coffers must be left unsupervised. Only then will the battle against embezzlement of public funds be successful.

Number six. In the 21st century, the only party fit to lead will be the one that actively supports young people. I am therefore highlighting youth policy as an important instrument for social modernisation. Zhas Otan has more than 200,000 members. A year ago, at the second congress of Zhas Otan, I put forward a full-scale programme for strengthening the work we do with young people. Let me say quite frankly, however, that thus far my orders have been implemented in a hap-hazard manner. Let's take an example: the Government approved the concept for youth policy up until 2020. Yet in the plan of measures for its implementation, the Government failed to determine the amount of financing. Everything is left in the hands of the programme administrators, based on "the limits allocated". But as to whether or not these limits are made known to the beneficiaries, one might well wonder.

Here's another example. On my orders, the Ministry of Education and Science founded the science and research centre 'Youth'. Yet the centre is not fully operational due to a lack of funding. This is despite the fact that the amounts in question are not large sums, and could be raised in the regions through sponsorship, and the Government could also allocate funds. The creation of resource centres for young people in the region is also suffering from delays. At present there are around ninety six centres in ten regions. In the cities of Astana and Almaty, and in the Aktybinsk, West Kazakhstan, Kysylordinsk and North Kazakhstan regions, this work hasn't even started.

As you are all aware, on my orders the 'Zhasil El' (Green Country) project is being implemented throughout the country. We have the ninth largest territory of all the world's nations, the bulk of which is desert and semi-desert, while forests account for less than 10%. The issue of planting trees in the country is therefore a significant one for the environment and for the health of our people. This is a great and noble task. This project must continue, and the party must support it.

This year, over KZT 429 million was set aside for projects initiated by the ministry for environmental protection. Here is an example of the kind of thing that has happened: the regional headquarters of the youth working brigades in the South Kazakhstan region only received its funding in August, just before the start of the academic year. Due to this, the majority of the students had to pull out of the programme. This is a failing on the part of the directors. The students were in no way at fault. Those at fault are specific civil servants, who fail to implement my orders. This sort of attitude towards youth policy is unacceptable.

The leadership of the party and the Government, in conjunction with the Akims, must rectify the situation and engage in targeted work to implement all of the orders I issued at the second Zhas Otan congress. Young people are our golden fund. The support of young Kazakhstanis for the course taken by the party, and their widespread participation in implementing the 'Kazakhstan-2050' Strategy, is of vast significance, both historically and as a stabilising factor.

From the floor of the party congress I wish to address all the young people of Kazakhstan once again. All that has been done in our country has been done first and foremost for you! For you, all doors in Kazakhstan are open! Take good care of the unity of the people! Cherish the hard work of your parents and the older generations in making Kazakhstan what it is today for you! Study hard and work selflessly and with dignity, in the name of the great future of our Motherland! You are the hope of the whole of Kazakhstan!

Number seven. Nur Otan must actively defend and promote our state's key foreign policy values. These values are well known. Kazakhstan's growing international authority is based on them. We speak in favour of a balanced and secure, multipolar and tolerant world. The party is going to introduce these values into its inter-parliamentary and international activity, expanding contact with political parties from other countries which are similar to us in terms of their spirit and views. These are the tasks facing the long-term leadership of Nur Otan in the 21st century.

The Party congress must now adopt its political doctrine. The draft version was widely discussed both within Nur Otan and in society as a whole. The documents which set out Nur Otan's programme have been successful because they have always referred to specific issues. We never had our heads in the clouds. We never set abstract goals or made empty promises. We have always backed up every utterance with genuine efforts and specific action. I am certain that things will remain like this forever! For Nur Otan is a party whose role is to lead!

The main party slogan that conveys our brand is 'Kazakhstan, ever onwards!' As we implement the 'Kazakhstan-2050' Strategy, this slogan is taking on an increasingly tangible meaning. Onwards towards a new, innovative and industrial economy! Onwards towards a new quality of life for Kazakhs, as a united and close-knit nation! Onwards towards new heights in Kazakhstan's international prestige as a dynamic and responsible state in the 21st century!

This is the three-pronged course of action that we must adhere to until the middle of the 21st century. It incorporates the historic significance of the work that lies ahead for the party and the state. It is the profound essence of our shared dream for Kazakhstan. Onwards, Nur Otan! Kazakhstan, ever onwards!

Speech at the 15th Congress of the Nur Otan party
Astana, 18th October 2013

TWENTY-TWO

THE ROLE OF THE JUDICIAL SYSTEM

In this speech, the President dicusses the implementation of the
objectives at the VI Congress of Judges of Kazakhstan along with
new priorities to modernise Kazakhstan's judicial system.

One year ago to the day, I announced the Strategy for the development of the country until 2050. We are defining the priorities and tasks for all aspects of our new political course. All of these are subordinate to our strategic objective: to become one of the world's top thirty most developed countries by that time.

In the 21st century, the most important criterion for judging a nation's development is that it has a flawless and effective national legal system. Courts that are independent and just are at the core of any state's activities. Without this, not a single country in the world – particularly among the most developed states – can have a favourable investment climate, a high level of wealth among its citizens, or a society which develops successfully.

In the four years that have passed since the previous Congress of Judges was held, our judicial system has risen twenty-three places in the index which measures the 'independence of judges' in the global competitiveness ratings. This is welcome news. Nevertheless, it still leaves us in eighty eighth place for the time being. This means that in order for us to be in the top thirty, we must move up another sixty places. It is therefore essential that we re-double our efforts to reform the legal system and particularly its core – the justice system.

Increasing the competiveness of our legal system in all its basic areas, in both public and private law, is one of the key tasks within the 'Kazakhstan-2050' Strategy. And it is important that we define the priority areas and specific mechanisms for large-scale work designed to increase the authority, independence and effectiveness of the judiciary. I see this as the central task facing the sixth Congress of Judges.

Today, Kazakhstan has a justice system that is fit for the modern world, with a professional body of judges. There are 378 courts in the country, in the general, administrative, economic, criminal, juvenile and financial jurisdictions. There are 2,214 judges recruited through a strict process. Criminal cases involving the most serious crimes are subject to trial by jury. In order to enhance the protection of our citizens' rights and freedoms, the institution of court sanctioning for arrests was introduced and is now in operation.

The judicial reforms introduced in Kazakhstan have brought our justice system closer to the demands and interests of citizens, and significantly enhanced the quality of court proceedings. The level of confidence that Kazakhstanis have in the courts has risen and this can be seen in the increase in the number of cases which are tried in court. This figure stands at over one million each year, since 2000. Secondly, the qualitative changes to the court system have been confirmed by sociological studies conducted under the aegis of the UN.

In order to make our courts more independent, powers designed to examine their disciplinary responsibility have been bestowed exclusively on the court jury. This had reduced the possibility of pressure being exerted on judges and has strengthened the courts' independence. In the last four years, the number of judges who have been subject to disciplinary measures and relieved of their duties for negative reasons has fallen almost four-fold.

Since 2009, the annual figures for court verdicts, which have been annulled or overturned, has on average become more stable, reaching 0.5% and 0.9% of all verdicts, respectively. This also points to the increased level of fairness in the dispensation of justice in our country. The national judicial system must work quickly and fairly. This is being enabled by strengthening the role of the regional courts and the cancelling the practice of returning cases to the courts of first instance. Work is continuing on introducing specialist courts.

The activities of all the structures within Kazakhstan's judicial system have become more transparent. It is now possible to read the courts' decisions in digital format, on the website of the Supreme Court and the sites of the local courts. On my orders in 2010, the courts were relieved of functions which should not properly be theirs. The execution of court acts has been assigned to the bodies of justice, and an independent department has been formed at the Supreme Court. The courts' administrative bodies are focused on helping the judges carry out their duties.

In Kazakhstan, an institute has been founded for mediation – the process of reconciling the parties with the help of a mediator not attached to the courts. This is creating the conditions needed to relieve the courts of the burden of having to try cases in which mutually acceptable settlements are possible. This institute must be developed and brought in line with international standards.

Increasing the efficiency of the judicial system has always been a concern of the state and one of my own personal preoccupations. The cost to the Republic's budget of providing for the activities of judges has risen 2.6 times since 2006, from KZT 11.2 billion to KZT 30 billion. We have made the material basis for the judicial system much stronger and Kazakhstan's courts have suitable technical equipment and are located in buildings which satisfy modern standards for the dispensation of justice. And this work is set to continue. The construction of new buildings for courts in Astana and the Almaty and Kostanay regions has already been completed. In just four years, the pay packets for those who work in the Kazakhstani justice system have risen by 60%. The salaries of judges, at all levels, are among the highest in our region.

Recognition of our achievements in reforming the judicial system is demonstrated by the fact that the Union of Judges of the Republic of Kazakhstan was accepted as a full member of the International Association of Judges. This is an important step towards integrating the Kazakhstani justice system into the international legal community as well as recognising the achievements of our judiciary. Generally speaking, Kazakhstani justice has become a self-sufficient, accountable and dynamic branch of the unified state executive. I see this as a huge accomplishment on the part of judges at all levels. I am grateful to you for serving the law, for staying true to the honour of your judges' gowns, and for the good work you do on a daily basis in the name of the triumph of justice and law and order in our country.

The renewal of the field of law and order must be an integral part of the country's step-by-step development, the course of which is set out in the 'Kazakhstan-2050' Strategy. As time has gone by, significant changes have occurred in the economy. In particular, there is now a market economy in the country, a new financial system has been established, and the interaction between employers and their staff has changed. Therefore, when we talk about judges' qualifications, they would be well advised to examine all these issues. For everything that happens in economic and political life must be subject to the law.

Today, it is important, first and foremost, to see the potential for growth in the judiciary, and uncover and quickly resolve any problems in a self-critical manner. Firstly, the dispensation of justice in Kazakhstan is still unnecessarily long-winded and formal. Procedure and rules for the dispensation of justice are required to ensure a thorough modernisation. Insufficient use is currently made of information technology in the dispensation of justice and the problems arising with the mass media are due to judges and their employees providing inadequate information about their activities and their decisions.

Secondly, as regards the development of court specialisations, we are only just starting out. The introduction of the Institute of Investigative Judges is enhancing the role of the courts in monitoring pre-trial procedures. In the new codes – the criminal procedure code and others – we are resolving this issue. Moreover, we are also expanding the role of investigative powers that the courts can sanction. It is also important to build up practical experience in the trial by jury system.

Thirdly, it is important to solve the problem of the growing burden placed on the judges. In the courts of first instance, it has risen on average from thirty eight cases a month to fifty eight cases a month, per judge, in the last four years. In some regions this indicator is even higher. I am aware of this, and that is why an order has been issued to allow, in the republic's budget for 2014, for an increase in the number of judges by 450, i.e. a rise of 25%, and also to provide additional resources for 450 new members of staff and sixty court bailiffs. As a result, the total workforce in the judicial and the court apparatus will be increased by 960 people.

Fourthly, the Kazakhstani justice system is still encountering errors by the courts, violations of the law and of judicial ethics. Such cases cause acute public grievance and give rise to all kinds of negative assessments of the entire judicial system. Some judges allow too much bureaucracy and red tape to get in the way, thereby dragging out the claims process. The staffing policy in the judicial system has not yet been perfected. The barriers to prevent unscrupulous individuals from becoming judges are not yet sufficient.

Each year in Kazakhstan, two or three judges, on average, are charged with offences related to corruption. Thirty nine judges have faced disciplinary measures, including eight who were relieved of their positions. There have been cases when, at regional level, even those judges who have committed violations are afforded protection. I realise that we must protect judges, but we must also clean out our ranks and be strict as regards our colleagues.

There are a number of questions in the judicial system that demand adequate responses.

Our 'Kazakhstan-2050' Strategy not only provides a new, large-scale objective. It provides for an accelerating pace in the dynamics of economic and social relations in the decades to come. This, without question, will increase the role and responsibility of the national judicial system in terms of providing law and order, enhancing stability in society, and maintaining the citizens' legal culture. The Kazakhstani justice system must be fully prepared for the striking changes which will take place in the economy in the period to come.

The community of the judiciary in Kazakhstan must be able to match all the challenges of our times. It must be open and willing to accept legal and judicial innovations, which are already taking place in global jurisprudence and, without doubt, will continue to take place in the future. Only by clearly sticking to the spirit and the letter of the law, improving our professionalism, and developing and perfecting our approach, will the national judicial system be able to provide a sustainable legal basis for the implementation of our Strategy.

The most crucial areas in the development of our national justice system are set out in our concept for legal policy up until 2020. Today, however, it is important to look further into the future. We must take into account how the global legal field will evolve. It is from this viewpoint that we must clearly define the prospects for the development of our national judicial system. In this connection, I wish to share my vision of the key priorities of the Kazakhstani judiciary.

Number one. It is important that we perfect the legislative and procedural norms for judges' behaviour, in a comprehensive manner. A draft version of a new Criminal Code, a new Criminal Procedure Code and a Criminal Executive Code have already been prepared, along with a code on civil infringements. The work that went into these codes was painstaking and extensive, and they have been examined by all of us, including me. They provide the courts with new areas of competency, including a new, simplified procedure for the dispensation of justice. The framework of judicial control has been expanded, as have judges' powers during the course of court proceedings. The courts will be more accessible and 'humanised', but this is not an end in itself: the main aim is that we should not allow the rule of law to be weakened. The imminent adoption of these codes will open up new opportunities to increase the quality and speed of criminal justice.

We must also modernise the procedure for the dispensation of civil justice. I am ordering the Government, in conjunction with the Supreme Court, to begin developing a draft of a new Civil Procedure Code. The procedure for trying civil cases must be simple and quick for the parties involved, and oriented towards reconciliation of the parties with the extensive use of modern technology. We should draw up and introduce a methodology, with a basis in law, for restricting the number of cases in which a review of the court's verdict is required. All judges must be prepared to work within the new legislation, trying cases promptly, lawfully and in a fair and just manner. Both judges and court chairmen must take personal responsibility for this.

Number two. We must continue to perfect the way justice is dispensed. The issue of an effective system of civil justice is linked to this. This task is outlined in the concept for reform of the legal system up until 2020. The system of civil justice must be part of the administrative reforms which we are bringing in to improve the work of the entire state apparatus. This system must be introduced gradually, without being too hasty. In the light of our legal culture, we would be well advised to study the practices of other countries and introduce them in our procedures. Within the jurisdiction of this important area of judicial power should be issues related to resolving disputes arising between citizens and the state. The restrictions on the jurisdiction to try cases which are subject to oversight by the Supreme Court must be enshrined in law.

Number three. The significant potential for the development of Kazakhstan's legal system is to be found in the introduction of alternative methods of resolving disputes and conflicts, particularly in the social domain. The flaws in the legislation on mediation are holding back the development in our country of non-judicial institutes for regulating dispute situations. This year, only one per cent of the total number of cases involved the use of mediation tools. It is essential that we bring the Kazakhstani laws on mediation into line with international standards and this will have a positive impact on the judicial system in Kazakhstan and enable us to reduce the workload on the courts. At the same time, it will help to strengthen business activity and create a favourable investment climate in the country.

I often find myself talking about the investment climate in the country, at all my meetings with law enforcement agencies, and Kazakhstan, like any other country, requires investment, whether it is from within or from the outside. We must not restrict business by bringing in all sorts of checks and putting up obstacles. In the codes we have considered for economic crimes, provisions are made for the use of financial sanctions; thus, we will avoid having to increase the population of our country's prisons as a result of economic violations. In this regard, pre-trial solutions are of great significance.

Number four. It is vital that we make justice accessible to broad sections of our citizens. Digital recordings of court procedures should be brought in throughout the country, as a mechanism for guaranteeing that trials take place in full adherence to protocol. We must ensure that all courts of first instance have access to video conferencing technology, so that they can dispense justice remotely. Those who appeal to the courts should not have to face obstacles of a territorial or administrative nature as they seek to have their rights asserted.

It is important to expand the practice of having alternative jurisdictions for trying cases, at the decision of the parties, and remove all formal requirements as to the claims brought to court. This is particularly pertinent for cases concerning socially vulnerable sections of the population, including minors. The courts are not entitled to find loopholes in the legislation so as to refuse claims on the pretext that formal requirements have not been satisfied. Judges are servants of the people, like all civil servants. Their primary duty consists in doing everything in their power to protect the rights and interests of citizens.

Number five. It is important that we raise the level of professionalism throughout Kazakhstan's body of judges. No-one can ever guarantee that they won't make any mistakes, of course. But mistakes by judges come at a cost that is too high for society and individuals. Judges are entrusted with acting for the good of justice in the name of the law; as such, there is a dual responsibility on their shoulders. Achieving this task requires, above all, modernisation of the education system for judges.

We must also continue working to improve the social and material conditions for judges' activities, while toughening the requirements as to the quality of their work and their accountability. We must ensure that our judges and our courts are provided with everything they need to work successfully. At the same time, a positive and respectful attitude towards the judicial system should be ingrained in society, with the mass media enlisted to help get this message across.

Regrettably, a fair amount of pressure is sometimes exerted on judges, and we must face up to the fact that this occurs. I once said that if a deputy manager or the manager of one section of a state body admits his guilt over something, then the director in overall charge must also be considered responsible. This practice began to take root, and in order to find out whether regional judges were corrupt, people began examining the behaviour of district judges. This is not the right approach. Each judge must be evaluated separately, and his guilt or innocence determined.

The national judicial system must be a reliable guarantee of stability in society, the rule of law, unstinting adherence to the interests of society and the state, and the protection of the rights and freedoms of the Kazakhstani people. In this lies the great purpose of serving the people by the judging community in Kazakhstan. In this lies the main obligation of Kazakhstan's judges in the complex work required to implement the 'Kazakhstan-2050' Strategy. I firmly believe that the body of judges in Kazakhstan, which contains more than two thousand members, will make a worthy contribution to the implementation of our objective and of the tasks of renewing and strengthening our Motherland.

There is a popular saying among Kazakhs: *"It's easy to judge, but it's not so easy to reason."* Managing his court in a just and fair way is the sacred duty of every judge. To achieve this, it is not enough simply to know the laws like the back of your hand. The key thing is this: a judge must be someone who is honest and fair. A judge is the conscience of the people. If his verdicts are impartial and objective, the parties to the case will be left with no lingering doubts as to whether or not the sentence is the right one, and the guilty party will know that violations of the law will inevitably lead to punishment.

We are a people which has set itself the goal of building a civilised, highly developed society. The just nature of the verdicts reached by the courts, taken together with how rigorously and fully they are implemented, is an indication of the maturity of any state. The development of the judicial system is not something that can happen overnight, and it therefore requires constant adjustments and improvements. What we require from you, our judges, meanwhile, is a high level of qualification and complete honesty.

A society in which the people respect the laws and trust the courts is the most highly developed society there can be. Our goal is to build precisely such a society. This is one of the key priorities of the 'Kazakhstan-2050' Strategy. And that means that your mission is clearly defined and the course you are following is true. I hope you will live up to the trust that has been placed in you and continue to work with honesty. May justice and devotion to your duty to serve remain your companions. I wish you every success!

Speech at the 6th Congress of Judges in the Republic of Kazakhstan 'The tasks facing the national judicial system in the context of the 'Kazakhstan-2050' Strategy' Astana, 20th November 2013

TWENTY-THREE

THE ROLE OF THE 'BOLASHAK' PROGRAMME

"Bolashak" is the international educational scholarship programme
initiated by the President of Kazakhstan on 5 November 1993.
In this speech, Nursultan Nazarbayev outlines the vital role that
the "Bolashak" programme plays in creating a new generation of
managers and specialists with advanced professional skills, who
are contributing to the modern development of Kazakhstan.

Today marks a shared celebration for us all. From the bottom of my heart I congratulate you on the 20th anniversary of the 'Bolashak' programme! This is one of the golden chapters in our history as an independent nation.

I welcome all the experts who have been able to receive an education overseas under the presidential programme! All those who, today, as they fulfil their patriotic duty, are working in various sectors of our economy, society and state. I welcome all the recipients of bursaries, who are currently studying at institutes of higher education in thirty three countries around the world!

Twenty years ago, in the difficult time during our first few years of independence, not everyone was able to envisage the bright future awaiting us. The economy had collapsed; almost all the major manufacturing plants had come to a halt. People were unable to get their wages, pensions or benefits on time. Inflation had exceeded all sensible limits and unemployment was on the rise. The country was stuck in a period of 'wild capitalism'. Back then, we had only just begun the transition to a market economy. Few people really understood what that meant. Even many of the most experienced managers only had vague notions about how to manage the new economic and social processes, and how to create a sovereign state. Independent Kazakhstan was in dire need of a professional workforce with a high-quality, international-class education.

By adopting the 'Bolashak' programme, we effectively put an 'equals' sign between the quality of the education received by Kazakhstanis and the successful future of our country. It was the right strategic decision to make! We have been abiding by it for two decades now. Along the way, we have also drawn up and successfully implemented – earlier than anticipated (in just fifteen years) – the 'Kazakhstan-2030' Strategy. Having started from scratch, we have created an effective economy with a growing sector of small and medium-sized businesses and dynamic growth.

Major changes have occurred in the social sector, and the living standards of the Kazakhstani people have become many times better than before. Systemic changes are being successfully introduced in the fields of science and education, where we are actively bringing in international level teaching and research. A professional cohort of civil servants and senior managers for national and private companies have been trained in Kazakhstan. Kazakhstan has become one of the top fifty most competitive countries in the world.

A year ago, I put forward the 'Kazakhstan-2050' Strategy. We now have a new goal: to be included in the top thirty most developed countries in the world. Our economy has moved onto a path of innovative industrialisation. All of these things represent historic achievements. And a valuable contribution has been made by the beneficiaries of the 'Bolashak' programme.

In 1994, I personally accompanied the first 187 recipients of grants under the 'Bolashak' programme before they set off to study abroad. Today, the number of people who have benefited from the programme already stands at more than 10,000. The 'Bolashak' programme has played a huge role in the country's development. Firstly, it is predominantly about providing a new workforce for the economy, education, science, healthcare, national culture and art. One in two beneficiaries of the programme now works for a public or private Kazakhstani company, or a company part-owned by the state. 19% of them are managers of national companies. Around 4% are working for international organisations, or for Kazakhstani NGOs.

In total, three quarters of the beneficiaries are working in the real sector of the economy and in civil society. Around 24% of the 'Bolashakovites' are working for state institutions and organisations, including some who are involved in state governance – around 19% of the recipients of the award. To date, around 2000 engineers and technical specialists have received training under 'Bolashak'. They include people working in the fields of innovation, technology, metallurgy, telecommunications and energy. On the whole, a balance has been achieved between specialisations in the humanities and in engineering and technical subjects.

Secondly, almost two thirds of the recipients of bursaries under the programme are the children of people from outside the state structures, and pensioners. In 8% of the cases, their parents were unemployed at the time they were awarded their bursaries. More than 200 of the recipients of the award are talented young people who for one reason or another were left without parents.

Thirdly, workforces for all regions of Kazakhstan are being trained under the 'Bolashak' programme. Five years ago, at a forum dedicated to the fifteenth anniversary of the programme, I set the goal of expanding access to the bursaries for young people living in the regions. Today, almost half of all the beneficiaries come from Kazakhstan's regions and after completing their education, most of them find work in their home towns.

Fourthly, all of the recipients of the award study at leading universities around the world, which are among the leaders in the 'Shanghai Ranking'. All this points to the high level of results achieved by the 'Bolashak' programme. Thanks to the programme, a 'social lift' has been created for talented young Kazakhstanis, and they have been able to study at world-class academic and educational centres. A creative cadre of young scientists, teachers and managers is being created.

'Bolashak' has served as a driving force for our education system. On the one hand, we have created a main arterial route for the transfer of global technologies to Kazakhstan's economic and social space. On the other hand, the world has been able to learn more about Kazakhstan through interaction with the beneficiaries of our award, about its people, culture and traditions, and the opportunities and potential our country offers. Thanks to the 'Bolashak' programme, we have found our place in the worldwide system for the teaching of the global elite. This is an important part of my plan for the formation of a new generation of Kazakhstanis for the era of independence.

The opening of a world-class higher education institute in 2010 – Nazarbayev University – marked the start of Kazakhstan's transformation into a regional exporter of knowledge. Today, there are more than 200 beneficiaries of the 'Bolashak' award working at Nazarbayev University. The Association of beneficiaries of the 'Bolashak' programme is in operation. It has implemented sixty projects which have affected broad sections of Kazakhstan's younger generation. The association also has a charitable fund attached to it, and a consulting group. The 'Baikonyr' social award has been established and awarded. The association helps the beneficiaries of the bursaries in the employment market, organises rallies and meetings for them, and provides administrative support in the countries in which they study. Today, it is important not to lose sight of the new tasks facing our people in the context of the development of the entire world, and in the context of our 'Kazakhstan-2050' Strategy.

The speech at the Forum of fellows and alumni of the International "Bolashak" scholarship programme, initiated by the President of the Republic of Kazakhstan, on the occasion of the 20th anniversary of the programme's establishment Astana, 29th November 2013

TWENTY-FOUR

NEW APPROACHES FOR KAZAKHSTAN

A solemn meeting was held on the eve of 16th December 2013 –
the Independence Day of the Republic of Kazakhstan.
Speaking at the meeting, Nursultan Nazarbayev highlighted the country's
successes and outlined new approaches for the independent Kazakhstani State.

Twenty two years ago, we took our first step towards becoming 'Mangilik El' ('Eternal Country'). We declared to the whole world that we were now independent. This was a sacred day when the dreams of many generations of our ancestors came true and we acquired our long-awaited freedom. This was a triumphant day which gave our descendants the joy of being born into, and being the children of, a free nation. A great day which marked the start of the period when we set about restoring our native tongue, returning to our centuries-old faith and resurrecting our national history; when we decided for ourselves what our destiny was to be.

Independence is the happy lot enjoyed only by those who are strong of spirit. It was on this day that the 'Kazakhstan-2050' Strategy saw the light of day – a programme of modernisation and development for our sovereign state, in the new century.

On 16 December 1991, a new star was born in the galaxy of the world's nations – the Republic of Kazakhstan. On this day, we began our journey as Kazakhstan. We carried out a great mission: we became the trailblazers of independence. It is amazing how time flies. Today, the events which occurred immediately after the birth of independent Kazakhstan are now a distant part of history. We can form judgements about that time by comparing it to our current achievements. Twenty two years ago, we could only dream about one day resurrecting our economy. Yet this year, Kazakhstan has become one of the top fifty most competitive countries in the world. At the dawn of our independence, we didn't feature in any global ratings or indices. Our international rating was effectively zero. When, in 1996, I set the objective of becoming one of the world's top fifty most competitive countries, a large number of people in the country and elsewhere were sceptical about this step. Yet the fact remains: in just seven years, we have completed this task!

On the first morning of independence, we had no finances of our own to speak of, with which to support our fledgling currency. This year marks the twentieth anniversary of the introduction of the Kazakhstani tenge. We have a stable financial system which is operating successfully. The country's total international reserves are growing. Their levels have now reached an all-time high of USD 100 billion.

Over these years, we have built an effective regional policy and balanced the pace of development in all areas. This year, elections to the local Akims were held for the first time ever. In the elections, in which there were more than 7,000 candidates, the majilikhaty elected almost 2,500 Akims for cities in the districts, villages and towns. That amounts to 91% of the total number of Akims in the country.

In the first few days of independence, many found it hard to imagine when, or how, we would be able to solve the painful social problems of which, at the time, there seemed to be no end. In Kazakhstan today, the nation's wealth is growing, and people's incomes are far higher than they used to be. Between 2000 and 2013, Kazakhstanis carried out around sixty one million foreign trips on business or tourist visas throughout the world. In the same period, our country was visited by about forty six million foreign visitors. This indicates, first and foremost, that there is a growing level of prosperity among our citizens, and also highlights the growing interest in our homeland around the world.

Today, Kazakhstani students are studying at some of the world's best universities, in thirty three different countries, under the 'Bolashak' programme. More than 10,000 people have already received bursaries under the programme. According to data from the Organisation for Economic Cooperation and Development, in 2012, 65,000 Kazakhstanis were studying at various universities around the world. In addition to the 'Bolashakovites', these include tens of thousands of young Kazakhstanis whose studies were paid for by their parents. All of this has become possible thanks to increasing prosperity and opportunities for Kazakhstanis.

Over the last four years, which have been crisis years for the world's economy, we have almost doubled the average monthly salary paid to teachers. In twenty two years, a real revolution has taken place in terms of the cars we drive! Whereas in 1992 there were 885,000 privately owned cars, by 2013 that figure had shot up to 3.6 million. That represents growth of more than 400%. Twenty two years ago, it was predicted that Kazakhstan would suffer a crisis in population numbers. But this prediction, like so many other gloomy ones, did not come true. In the years since we achieved independence, 6,736,000 children have been born in Kazakhstan!

Thanks to our focus on doctor training, in the first nine months of this year alone, 40,000 heart operations of various kinds were carried out in Kazakhstan. Around 10,000 of these were cases of open-heart surgery! This is all being delivered free of charge, and thus the state is covering the cost. Such an approach is unheard of in many other countries around the world. Over the course of these years, 560 highly qualified doctors have received training under the 'Bolashak' programme. And each one is now treating people, providing consultations or offering work experience to medical students. All of this represents the specific results of two decades of the implementation of our plan to develop healthcare, our concern for young mothers and children, and for the elderly.

The most important outcome is that average life expectancy is rising, the death rate is falling and the country's population is on the increase. This is the key and the most important statistic in which we can take pride. Twenty two years ago, we chose the right path for our future development. We set down our plans for a great country in the 'Kazakhstan-2030' Strategy and implemented this more quickly than expected, in just fifteen years. Independence has given us the ability to look confidently towards the future, and clearly see the prospects ahead. This magnificent gift is something that we are making full use of today, as we attempt to complete the historic tasks set out in the 'Kazakhstan-2050' Strategy. The year 2050, which is still thirty seven years away, seems distant and remote, but in the grand scheme of things it is a relatively short period of time. We have overcome a considerable number of difficulties, and time has always been on our side. I have every faith that this will always remain the case.

Our people have always attached a special significance to the number seven. The 'seven blessings', 'seventh heaven', the 'seven treasures'; there seems to be an endless number of sacred concepts such as this. The most important programme of development for our country in the new century – the 'Kazakhstan-2050' Strategy – also consists of seven priorities. Thanks to our independence, our people have acquired seven invaluable treasures.

The first of these treasures is our Motherland, which stretches from the Altai to the Atyrau, from Saryarka to Alatau. Having delineated our country's borders and created a protective belt of peace and security around us, having established amicable relations with our neighbours and ties of mutual respect with more distant countries, we began to restore the edifice of our statehood successfully. Our supreme goal is to restore our 'Mangilik El' with love and care and make it one of the glories of the 21st century.

Our second treasure is the unity among our people. We have transformed our country into a genuine cradle for peace. Through peace and tranquillity, we have ensured stability; through harmony, we have preserved unity. All of the ethnicities living in Kazakhstan have come together as one around the state-forming Kazakhstani nation. In spite of the diversity of our ethnic origins, we have become a single people with shared ideals and shared ambitions. Unity and mutual understanding represent our greatest form of wealth – a priceless treasure with no alternative. If we have peace as our foundation, stability as the rock on which we stand and harmony as the goal we strive for, our country is destined to take up its rightful place in world civilisation. Independence has brought our people together under the Shanyrak of the Assembly – the preserver of peace and harmony. Our spiritual unity is the cornerstone of our enlightened state and society.

Our third treasure is our primordial culture and native tongue, which were roused to new life by our independence. When we gained our freedom, our national spirit was made stronger, and our culture once again acquired its true dignity. The status once enjoyed by our native tongue and our centuries-old faith has now been restored. The Kazakh language is not only the official language of our country, but has also gradually become one of the leading languages in the Turkic world. On one of my trips through the country's regions, one of the members of the Assembly, who speaks fluent Kazakh, said to me: *"By learning the official state language, I opened the door to the national culture of more than twenty five peoples which speak Turkic languages."* The Kazakh language is currently taught – if you exclude the countries which are our neighbours – in academic institutions in Azerbaijan, Armenia, Belarus, Poland, Hungary, South Korea, Germany, the UK and the USA. The number of such states is increasing year on year. A special course in the Kazakh language, history and culture is now taught at the world-famous Cambridge University. All this testifies to the fact that there is a respectful attitude towards the Kazakh language, and that the social demand is steadily growing. The state's carefully targeted policy has created the conditions necessary to strengthen the status of the Kazakh language and expand its areas of application. It has become the language of the Kazakhstani media, the civil service, the internet, science and education. The vast majority of schoolchildren and students are taught in Kazakh. At present, as many as 70% of Kazakhstanis speak the state language. Thanks to independence, our national culture is undergoing a renaissance. When we implemented the 'cultural legacy' programme, we undertook a colossal amount of work as we restored our culture and history and filled the missing links. As a result, the culture and art of the Kazakhstani people have been added to the treasure trove of world culture.

The fourth treasure is our innovative, industrial economy. The programme of industrialisation represents the future of our economy. Today, the wealth of our land belongs to and serves all our people, and they create the conditions necessary for ensuring a continuous increase in our national prosperity. International experts suggest that this year, Kazakhstan came nineteenth in the world in terms of the management of mineral resources. We have mastered the lessons that the global crises have taught us. In the 21st century, the path of all successful nations has been determined by industrial might and innovation. The impressive results we have achieved in our industrial and innovative development are therefore the key to the economic sustainability of independent Kazakhstan. As we implemented the first five-year plan in the industrialisation process, we built 700 completely new enterprises, creating 200,000 new jobs in the process. We spent KZT 2.1 trillion, but these firms have already made profits of KZT 2.3 trillion. Thus we are seeing a return on the money that was invested.

Our fifth treasure is a society of universal labour – the foundation of our national wealth, social prosperity and economic flourishing. A society of universal labour is the fundamental requirement for our national wealth. Through painstaking work, we have achieved all the things that Kazakhstan and its people are now able to enjoy. Hard work is the thing that makes every person noble and makes countries great. A society of universal labour is our national Kazakhstani ideal, which was developed as part of the difficult work we undertook to strengthen our independence.

Our sixth treasure is the heart of our Motherland and the symbol of our independence: our beautiful capital, Astana. Today, Astana is the artchitectural embodiment of the strength of the state. In its new districts, squares, parks and architectural gems, the great history of our independence is reflected, as in a mirror. The love we feel for Astana is thus the love felt by each Kazakhstani citizen for our shared Motherland – the Republic of Kazakhstan. It is the alpha and omega of our new Kazakhstani patriotism.

Our seventh treasure consists of the creative initiatives that Kazakhstan is implementing, which have brought it global acclaim. Since the first days of independence, our country has shown the world that it is a responsible sovereign power. The international community has praised our initiatives aimed at strengthening global nuclear security and dialogue between different cultures and religions. This year, Kazakhstan contributed to the achievement of a breakthrough in the negotiations over Iran's nuclear programme. The two rounds of multilateral negotiations which took place in Almaty in many ways helped to break the ice of distrust, leading ultimately to the Geneva agreements. Astana is leading the preparations as host of the International exhibition 'EXPO-2017'. All these things represent the eternal values of our independence, its genuine results and prospects.

Every so often, days come along which are as valuable as years, and years come along which are as valuable as centuries. For us, the past twenty two years have been just such a time. We have gone from being a pupil-nation to a teacher-nation, which strives neither to vanquish others nor, indeed, to be vanquished. It is on the basis of that which we must accomplish today that we will be judged by our descendants tomorrow. And if we prove capable of looking after and multiplying these seven treasures, we will have a clear conscience about how they will judge us. We have commenced implementing the 'Kazakhstan-2050' Strategy, by taking the first steps towards our goal: to be among the world's top thirty most highly developed states. And nothing will knock us off course as we move along this thorny path: our guiding star – independence – will make sure of it. Independence is our life force, which lends strength and creative power to our people and lights up their souls. We are proud of our country, in which the wisdom and far-sightedness, unity and determination of our people have been woven together so harmoniously. Time chose us, by giving us the honour of being able to fly the flag of independence.

We have laid the foundation of 'Mangilik El'. Its heart is the capital city, Astana, which we built, and its backbone is our competitive economy. All of this amounts to the sacred gift of independence, the precious treasure of our freedom. May our independence be durable and our statehood filled with vitality! May our beloved 'Mangilik El' be ever beautiful and may our business affairs be productive. I wish all our fellow citizens a happy life, in a time of peace and prosperity!

Speech at the Assembly marking Independence Day of the Republic of Kazahkstan
Astana, 14th December 2013

TWENTY-FIVE

IMPLEMENTING THE DEVELOPMENT STRATEGY

*In this address, the President of Kazakhstan proposes new priorities
for the successful implementation of the Development Strategy
of Kazakhstan until 2050, with the overall aim of propelling
Kazakhstan into the world's thirty most developed countries.*

21st century Kazakhstan is a country that was created 'from scratch' in just two decades by a talented, assiduous, and tolerant people! The country is like a much-loved child to us all, in whom we take great pride! It is our great creation, which we love with a passion!

We have adopted the 'Kazakhstan-2050' Strategy so that Kazakhstanis can feel they are firmly at the helm as our country determines its future. Many successful countries are currently operating on the basis of long-term plans. Strategic planning is rule number one in the 21st century. For no winds will be favourable if the country doesn't know the route or the port to which it is headed. The Strategy-2050, like a beacon guiding the way, is enabling us to tackle the issues people are facing in their everyday lives, without losing sight of our overriding goal. This means that we intend to improve people's lives every single year, not just in thirty to fifty years.

The Strategy is a programme of specific practical measures which, from one day to the next and from one year to the next, will make the country and the lives of its people better. Yet each of us must recognise that in a market economy, one cannot sit back and expect miracles, but instead work as effectively as possible. The task of the state is to create all the conditions necessary to allow this to happen. I firmly believe that a bright future for our homeland, among the world's most advanced countries, is the very thing that will unite all Kazakhstanis for centuries.

Today, I want to present our plan on how we are going to become one of the world's top thirty most developed countries. On my orders, the Government has drawn up a draft version of the detailed concept behind this plan. I have given this document my overall approval; once it has been amended in accordance with my instructions, as set out in this message, it will receive final approval. According to my forecasts, the next fifteen to seventeen years will represent a 'window of opportunity' for Kazakhstan. In this period, the favourable external environment from which we have benefited will remain in place, we will see a continuing rise in the consumption of resources, energy and foodstuffs, and the Third Industrial Revolution will come of age. We must use this period to our advantage.

We will face challenging global competition as we move towards our goal in 2050. The next few decades will bring plenty of challenges that we know about, and also a great many unforeseen situations, new crises in the global markets and in world politics. There will be no easy route through the 21st century. The middle of the century is already looming on the horizon. The world's developed countries are drawing up concrete strategies in which they use this date as a benchmark. The second third of the 21st century will without doubt be more complicated, and only a few countries will have a realistic chance of making it into the world's top 30 most developed states. I have said several times in the past that the concept of a 'developed country' is one that changes with the time. In developed countries, one finds a dramatically improved quality of life among the population.

At present, the fundamental indicators of development are demonstrated by the member states of the Organisation for Economic Cooperation and Development (OECD). The OECD contains thirty four countries, which together produce over 60% of global GDP. Another six countries are candidates to join the OECD: Brazil, China, India, Indonesia, Russia and South Africa. All of the member states have undertaken intensive modernisation programmes, and boast high indicators in terms of investment, scientific inventions, labour productivity, business development and standard of living. The indicators of the OECD states, taking their long-term future trends into account, must serve as markers for our journey to the top thirty most developed states on the planet.

I am setting the task of introducing a number of OECD principles and standards in Kazakhstan. These are reflected in the draft version of the concept. There are plans to achieve annual growth of at least 4% in GDP. We must ensure that the volume of investment increases from the current figure of 18% to 30% of the total volume of GDP. The introduction of a science-rich model for the economy will help achieve the goal of increasing the share of raw material products in Kazakhstan's exports.

The creation of new high-tech sectors in the economy will demand an increase in funding for science to at least 3% of GDP. It is important that we increase to half the amount contributed by the energy sector to our gross domestic product. By 2050, SMEs will account for at least 50% of Kazakhstan's GDP, as opposed to the current level of 20%. There must be a five-fold increase in labour productivity, from the current level of USD 24,500 to USD 126,000.

The key targets to guide our development in the social sector up to 2050 are set out in the specific indicator figures. We must have a four and a half fold increase in the figure for the volume of GDP per capita, from USD 13,000 to USD 60,000. Kazakhstan is to be a country in which the middle class constitutes the biggest section of society. In line with the global trend for urbanisation, the proportion of people living in the cities will rise from the current level of 55% of the population to around 70% of the population. Our cities and towns will be connected by high-quality roads and high-speed routes for all modes of transport.

The promotion of a healthy lifestyle and advances in medicine will lead to an increase in average life expectancy among Kazakhstanis, to eighty or more. Kazakhstan will become one of the leading Eurasian centres for medical tourism. We will finish building a leading national education system. Kazakhstan must become one of the world's most secure and pleasant places to live. Peace and stability, a fair and unbiased judiciary and the rule of law – these are the foundations of a developed country.

The concept for Kazakhstan's bid to become one of the thirty most developed countries in the world sets out our long-term priorities for the work that lies ahead. We must tackle a series of challenges related to the following key areas.

Number one. It is important that we consolidate the trend towards innovative industrialisation, and fine-tune it where necessary. I have given the Government a series of orders concerning the production of a draft plan for the second five-year period of industrial and innovative development for 2016-2019. We must focus the number of priorities in our process of industrialisation.

We must make the traditional mining sector more efficient. We have a natural competitive strength in this sector. We need new approaches to the way hydrocarbons are managed, extracted and processed, as we safeguard the export potential of our oil and gas sector. We must determine, once and for all, which of the possible scenarios will unfold regarding the extraction of oil and gas. It is important that we increase processing of rare earth metals, taking into account their significance for the science-rich sectors: electronics, laser technology, communication and medical equipment.

Kazakhstan must move into the global market of geological prospecting. We should attract investment from foreign engineering companies to this industry, and simplify the legislation. We should have separate plans for the development of all the traditional sectors. Each five-year plan must aim to create new sectors in the economy. In the context of the first five-year plan, new capabilities have been created for car manufacturing, aircraft manufacturing and the production of rail coaches for passengers and goods. These must be expanded and exported into foreign markets.

The time remaining until 2050 can be divided into seven five-year periods, each of which must be designed to help achieve the same objective: to become one of the top thirty most developed countries in the world. As part of the second five-year plan and subsequent ones due to come after it, we must establish mobile and multimedia sectors, and the sectors for nanotechnology, space technology, robot technology, genetic engineering, and the search for and discovery of the energy of the future. The work undertaken by the state should create the most favourable possible conditions for the development of Kazakhstani business, predominantly small and medium-sized businesses. Over the coming ten to fifteen years we must create a science-rich economic basis, for without this we will not be able to join the ranks of the world's developed countries. This will be achieved through a highly-developed science base.

Number two. It is important to ensure that the agricultural and industrial complex is shifted onto innovative lines. Global demand for foodstuffs is set to rise and there will be increasing investment going into this sector. Today's farmers must therefore concern themselves with increasing production, rather than being satisfied with short-term achievements linked to weather conditions. Competition in global agricultural production is only going to grow. Those tilling the ground must include, first and foremost, those who are introducing new technologies and constantly increasing productivity, and those working to the best international standards.

First and foremost, we must create an effective market for land, by means of transparent pricing mechanisms, among other things. By leasing farmland in a way that takes account of investment and the introduction of advanced technologies, we will be able to increase competition. All the barriers which are hindering business development in agriculture, agricultural cooperation and effective land use, must be removed.

The future lies in safeguarding the network of new manufacturing firms in the agricultural sector, chiefly in the form of SMEs. In this field we must support businesses by giving them loans. Farmers must have direct access to long-term funding and to sales markets, without the need for middlemen. A pressing issue is the creation of an effective system for guaranteeing and insuring loans to agricultural manufacturers. Kazakhstan must become one of the biggest exporters of meat, dairy and other farm products in the region. In crop production, we must reduce the proportion of water-rich cultivation which is not very profitable and replace this with vegetable, oilseed and feed products. We need a set of measures to enlarge the efficient use of agricultural chemicals, to expand modern technologies, avoid cultivation in dry soils, and other innovations.

In line with the concept that has been adopted for the transition to a 'green' economy, 15% of the land available for crops will be transferred to water-saving technologies by 2030. We must develop the agricultural science base and create experimental agricultural and innovative clusters.

It is important that we do not fall behind the times, and in addition to producing natural foodstuffs, produce genetically modified cultivations which are resistant to drought. In the light of the tasks I have set out, I am ordering the Government to amend the plans for the development of the agricultural-industrial complex accordingly.

Number three. The creation of a science-rich economy is first and foremost about increasing the potential of Kazakhstani science. In this area, we must amend the legislation on venture financing, the protection of intellectual property, the support of research and innovation, and also the commercialisation of scientific inventions. I am ordering the Government to draw up and bring before Parliament a package of applicable draft laws by 1 September. We must have a specific plan to increase funding for science and for specific inventions and discoveries working in the country. This funding should be brought into line with the figures for developed countries.

Attracting foreign investment is a policy which also involves the transfer of knowledge and new technologies into our country. It is essential that we create project and engineering centres in conjunction with foreign companies. We must call on leading transnational corporations, which operate major oil and gas and mining and metals facilities, to create production sites here to meet their own needs and provide services. I know that some major companies are willing to do this. The government must work on this issue and, if necessary, create the conditions required. We should not bring in equipment from overseas when we are capable of manufacturing it here at home.

It is important that we make the national innovation system, and its basic institutions, more efficient. Their activity must be aimed at supporting startups and the early stages of venture deals. We must activate the work of technological parks, particularly in major urban conglomerations, primarily in Astana and Almaty. The first intellectual and innovation cluster is already operating successfully in Astana, based at Nazarbayev University. In Almaty, there is the 'Alatau' Park for information technologies. It is important that we develop measures to stimulate the additional creation of manufacturing facilities for Kazakhstani companies in technology parks.

Number four. We must ensure dynamic growth in the infrastructural triad: conglomerations, transport and energy. Conglomerations are the framework for Kazakhstan's science-rich economy. The creation and development of these is an important issue, given the country's vast land-mass and low population density. Kazakhstan's first modern urban centres will be its major cities, Astana and Almaty, and thereafter: Shymkent and Aktobe. These cities must also be centres of science and attract investment and people, and provide high-quality educational, medical and socio-cultural services.

Transport infrastructure is the lifeblood of our industrial economy and society. I have said many times before that one cannot be a developed country without high-quality modern arterial transport routes. In order to create a network of roads inside the country, we are building road highways 'Astana-Karaganda-Almaty', 'Astana-Pavlodar-Ust Kamenogorsk', and 'Almaty-Kapchagai-Ust Kamenogorsk'. High-speed trains are already running along the railway lines covering these same routes.

It is essential that we develop our logistics services sector. First and foremost, it is a matter of making the best possible use of the Customs Union to transport cargo. Construction of the 'Western Europe-Western China' corridor is nearing completion, and a railway has been built to Turkmenistan and Iran, which leads to the Persian Gulf. In the long-run, Kazakhstan must invest in the creation of logistics centres in those countries which have a coastline. We must reduce the time taken for processing cargos by the customs authorities, increase the through-flow capacity of border crossings, strengthen the capacity of the port of Aktau, and simplify the procedures involved in export and import operations.

We are building a new 1,200 km railway, 'Zhezkazgan-Shalkar-Beiney'. It will provide a direct link between the country's East and West, thereby regenerating a host of regions in the centre of the country. This epic construction project will be completed in 2015. This new mainline will then give us access to Europe, via the Caspian Sea and the Caucasus. In the east, meanwhile, it will give provide access to the port of Lianyungang in the Pacific Ocean, an agreement which is in place with China.

We will develop energy in its traditional forms. It is essential that we support research and discoveries to reduce emissions from TPPs and savings in electricity based on cutting-edge technologies in manufacturing and sales. Not long ago, the first ten major companies in the European Union publicly spoke out against the EU's energy strategy, which was adopted on the basis of the well-known concept of a green economy. In four years, the EU has lost 51 gigawatts of energy capacity. As we work on our programme for a green economy, we must take these mistakes into account.

The preparations for the Global exhibition 'EXPO-2017' in Astana must be used to create a centre for the study and implementation of the best global practices to reach for and creating the energy of the future as well as a green economy. The group of specialists working under the auspices of Nazarbayev University must set to work on these tasks. We must ensure that our public transport uses environmentally friendly forms of fuel, that electric vehicles are introduced, and that appropriate infrastructure is established. The country needs large volumes of petrol, diesel fuel and aviation kerosene requiring a new oil refinery.

At the same time, we must not forget about our potential in the nuclear power sector. In the foreseeable future, the demand for cheap nuclear power is only going to grow. Kazakhstan is a world leader in the mining of uranium and we must develop our own fuel production for nuclear power plants and build nuclear power plants of our own.

Number five. The development of small and medium-sized businesses is a key tool for the industrial and social modernisation of Kazakhstan in the 21st century. In this regard my position, as you know, is unambiguous, and I have made it clear on many occasions. The higher the proportion of SMEs in our economy, the more sustainable Kazakhstan's development will be. There are more than 800,000 SMEs operating in the country, employing 2.4 million Kazakhstanis. The volume of production in this sector has risen by 160% in four years, and now amounts to more than KZT 8.3 billion.

According to global ratings, Kazakhstan is now among the countries with the most favourable conditions for doing business, and we must continue to build on this trend. SMEs provide a sound economic basis for our society of universal labour. In order to help them grow, we need multi

A visit to the Czech Republic, 23rd October 2012

President Nursultan Nazarbayev with Austrian President Heinz Fischer, 22nd October 2012

President Nursultan Nazarbayev meets Korean President Park Geun-hye, 6th September 2013

17

Above: President Nursultan Nazarbayev and President of Azerbaijan Ilham Aliyev, 16th August 2013

Below: David Cameron, Prime Minister of the United Kingdom and President Nursultan Nazarbayev

18

Above: President Nursultan Nazarbayev and José Manuel Barroso, 9th October 2014

Below: President Nursultan Nazarbayev and President Barack Obama

21

Left: President Nursultan Nazarbayev with Chinese President Xi Jinping

Below: President Nursultan Nazarbayev and Finnish President Sauli Niinisto, 24th March 2014

Bottom: President Nursultan Nazarbayev with French President François Hollande, 21st November 2012

22

23

**President Nursultan Nazarbayev with the King of Spain,
Juan Carlos, 6th February 2013**

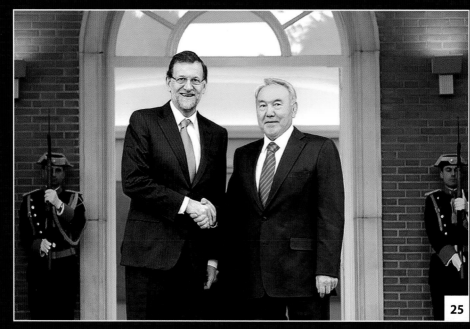

**President Nursultan Nazarbayev and Spanish Prime Minister Mariano Rajoy,
6th February 2013**

Left: President
Nursultan Nazarbayev
with Iranian President
Hassan Rouhani,
12th September 2013

Right: President
Nursultan Nazarbayev
and the Prime Minister
of the Netherlands
Mark Rutte

Above: President Nursultan Nazarbayev with Kyrgyz President Almazbek Atambayev

Below: President Nursultan Nazarbayev and Turkish President Recep Tayyip Erdoğan, 11th October 2012

30

President Nursultan Nazarbayev with Russian President Vladimir Putin

31

dimensional solutions to give stronger legal protection to private property. We must cancel all legal impediments to the development of business. Small businesses must become family traditions which are handed down from one generation to the next.

It is crucial that we take measures to make small businesses more specialised, giving them the support to become medium-sized businesses. We must bring in clearly-defined bankruptcy systems for companies in this sector. SMEs must be encouraged to spring up around new innovative firms. I have ordered the Government to incorporate a plan for the second five-year period of industrialisation into the 'Business-2020' road-map. The Government, in conjunction with the National Chamber of Entrepreneurs, must create effective mechanisms for providing support to businessmen who are just starting out.

Number six. Our path to the future is linked to new opportunities for unlocking Kazakhstani citizens' potential. A developed country in the 21st century is one whose citizens are active, well-educated and lead a healthy lifestyle. What must be done to achieve this? First of all, all developed countries have high quality education systems. We must improve the quality of every aspect of the national education system. We plan to ensure that 100% of Kazakhstani children between the ages of three and six are in nursery education by 2020. It is therefore important that we provide modern curricula and teaching methods, and highly qualified teachers. In secondary education, we must bring standards up to the level of teaching seen at the Nazarbayev Intellectual Schools. Those attending our schools must speak Kazakh, Russian and English fluently by the time they leave. On leaving school, our pupils must possess the skills of critical thinking and the ability to search for information independently and analyse it in detail.

Over the next three years, until 2017, we must resolve the problem of the school place shortages and bring in double shift teaching at all schools where this is required. The Government and the Akims must set aside the budgetary funds required to achieve this. In the next two to three years, we must develop the core of the national system of dual vocational education. In the long run, we must prepare for a shift towards a system whereby the state guarantees that young people will receive a vocational education.

It is essential that we start work on a gradual transition by the leading universities towards autonomy, both on academic issues and in the way they are governed. It is essential to create an effective system for supporting students and schoolchildren who are performing well at school. I am ordering the Government to increase the size of grants by 25% as of 1 January 2016.

Secondly, our main priority in healthcare must be the development of primary medical and sanitary assistance. We must look into the introduction of mandatory medical insurance. Joint liability on the part of the state, the employer and the employee for health must be the fundamental principle behind the entire system of medical services. Taking part in sport, a balanced diet and regular health check-ups – these are the basic requirements when it comes to early prevention of diseases.

Thirdly, we must bring new impetus to the development of culture throughout the whole of Kazakhstan. We must draw up a long-term concept for our cultural policy. It should incorporate measures aimed at forming a competitive cultural mentality among Kazakhstanis, and the development of modern clusters of cultural facilities.

Fourthly, we should review the social benefits packages paid to those working in education, healthcare and social welfare. I am ordering the Government to devise and introduce, with effect from 1 July 2015, a new model for paying salaries to civil servants. It must stipulate salary increases of up to 28% for those working in healthcare, up to 29% for those in education and up to 40% for those in social welfare.

Fifthly, we must have a greater focus on those citizens who have disabilities. Kazakhstan must become a barrier-free zone in this regard. Showing concern for these people, who make up a sizeable section of society, is something that we owe ourselves and our society. This is an area in which people throughout the world are taking active steps. People with disabilities are capable of working in firms which provide everyday services, in the food industry and in agriculture. Once again I wish to address the whole of our business community and ask it to lend its assistance to getting people into work. We could also look at the possibility of a special quota system.

We will get this group involved in an active life, and they will not only receive benefits but also be able to fulfil themselves as members of society and useful employees. All our social institutions and NGOs, and the Nur Otan party, must play a part in this work. If necessary, the Government must be involved in this issue in cooperation with the corporate sector. I am ordering the Government to introduce a 25% increase in social benefit payments for those with disabilities and those who have no one to provide for them. The legal basis for the activities of associations for the disabled must also be enhanced. It is important that we strengthen the work of all state bodies – from the Government to the local Akims. We should continue to reduce the level of poverty and hold back the rise in unemployment. It is also important that we do not permit any increase in parasitic behaviour. A rule should be brought in whereby all those receiving benefits and aid must take part in employment programmes and social adaptation programmes.

Number seven. The adjustment of the work by state institutes. If we are to move into the top thirty most developed countries in the world, there must be an atmosphere of honest competition, fairness, the rule of law and an advanced legal culture. We need updated tools for interaction between the state and the non-governmental sector and business. The notion that all are equal in the eyes of the law must become the genuine basis of law and order. The judicial system must become transparent and accessible, with all disputes settled quickly and straightforwardly. We must increase the quality of the work by the whole law enforcement system. Those with epaulettes on their shoulders, entrusted with great powers, must evince flawless behaviour and a high level of professionalism.

A critical task is to continue to implement a new anti-corruption strategy. Administrative reforms must not become a cumbersome process of needless paperwork and form-filling. We must give local government bodies more independence in the regions, simultaneously making them take on more responsibility for results and making them more accountable to the people.

We must continue to introduce the principles of a meritocracy to the staffing policy of state enterprises, national companies and state-funded organisations. I am ordering the Government to increase the salaries of civil servants in corpus 'B' by 15% from 1 July 2015, and by another 15% from 1 July 2016.

These are the specific tasks that our state and society face as we seek to become one of the thirty most developed countries in the world. We must ensure they are embodied in the letter of the law and in specific solutions.

Our progress towards the thirty most developed states in the world must be conducted in two phases. The first phase will cover the period up to 2030, when we will need to make a leap forward in the modernisation process, using this 'window of opportunity' in the 21st century. In this period, Kazakhstan must replicate the work of the world's developed countries during the industrial boom in the last century. This is certainly within our power. South Korea and Singapore have both made similar journeys. At this stage, we are ensuring dynamic growth in the traditional sectors of the economy and creating a strong manufacturing and industrial sector.

In the second stage, from 2030 to 2050, we must ensure sustainable development in the country, based on the principles of a science-rich economy and will form a powerful manufacturing industry. In the traditional sectors, there will be a transition to value added products and engineering services will be developed as the basis for a science-rich economy. I am giving the Government and the National Bank specific instructions for the current year.

Number one. The Government must provide growth in economy of 6-7% this year. GDP per capita must be at least USD 14,500 by the end of this year.

Number two. I am ordering the National bank and the Government to draw up a set of measures to cut inflation by 3-4% in the medium-term.

Number three. The Government, in conjunction with the National Bank must draw up a full-scale Programme for the development of the financial sector up until 2030.

Number four. The Government, in conjunction with the Samruk-Kazyna Fund, must analyse all companies in which the state owns assets and draw up a list of companies which should be transferred to the private sector. The same work must be done throughout the rest of the state sector. In the first quarter of this year, a multi-faceted privatisation programme for 2014-2016 must be adopted.

Number five. By the end of this year, the Government must draw up drafts of strategies for creating conglomerations in the cities of Astana and Almaty in the period until 2030.

Number six. The Government must draw up a programme of development for Kazakhstan's transit potential through 2030, containing measures designed to remove barriers to international trade.

Number seven. By the end of the first quarter of this year, the Government must tackle issues related to the location, sources of investment and time-frame for constructing a fourth oil refinery and nuclear power plant.

All of the steps we are taking to achieve the key goal set out in the 'Kazakhstan-2050' Strategy must adhere to clear principles. Firstly, all the decisions taken must reflect the principles of pragmatism and evolutionary change. We must not allow any leaps forward, ill-thought-through experiments or adventurism in economics, politics or social life. Our country and society must change as rapidly as the world around us. Secondly, the principle of mutual openness. We will attract wide-ranging economic investment, technologies and innovations to our economy. We will create favourable conditions for our work with investors. We can clearly see that an important mechanism for getting into the top thirty most developed countries is to deepen the extent that our economy is integrated into the regional and global economic systems. This is related above all to our involvement in the formation of the Eurasian Economic Union and our accession to the World Trade Organisation. Thirdly, the principle of strengthening the Kazakhstani people's prosperity. The social well-being of ordinary people must be seen as a crucial indicator of how much progress we have made towards our main objective. Fourthly, the principle of nationwide support is extremely important. My message to the people is itself the key document in terms of clarifying our goals and objectives. Every minister, Akim and company director must take charge of disseminating the message and get everyone involved in this work. Specific measures to implement the goals and objectives set out in the message must be brought to the attention of every Kazakhstani citizen. I am confident that this will become one of the key issues of the Nur Otan party. For this to occur, civil servants themselves, first and foremost, must be aware of, and have a strong grasp of, the ideas set out in our Strategy. The work done by the President's Administration and the Government and Akimats at all levels must be oriented towards the fulfilment of these tasks. On the whole, the structure of the state bodies must be appropriate for meeting the tasks we face and ensuring that the objectives set out in the 'Kazakhstan-2050' Strategy are met.

We, the people of Kazakhstan, are a united people! The fate that we all share is our 'Mangilik El', our great and dignified Kazakhstan! 'Mangilik El' is a national idea for our shared Kazakhstani home, the dream of our ancestors. In twenty two years of sovereign development, we have created the key values which unite all Kazakhstanis and provide the foundations for our country's future. They are not taken from abstract theories, these values represent the experience accumulated in Kazakhstan's journey, as the country withstands the tests of our times.

Number one, there is the independence that Kazakhstan and Astana enjoy. Number two, there is the national unity, peace and harmony that we have in our society. Number three, there is the enlightened society and high level of spirituality that we have. Number four, there is the value of economic growth founded on industrialisation and innovation. Number five, we have a society of universal labour. Number six, we have a shared history, culture and language. Number seven, we have our national security and our country's global participation in solving global and regional problems. Thanks to these values, we have always triumphed, strengthened our country and seen our great successes multiply. These state-building, shared national values embody the ideological foundations for the new Kazakhstani patriotism.

I am ordering the President's Administration, the Government and the Assembly of the People of Kazakhstan, in conjunction with the National movement 'Kazakhstan-2050' to organise the compilation and adoption of the Patriotic act 'Mangilik El'. We are setting great objectives for the good of our people, and I am therefore calling on all political parties, charities, and all Kazakhstanis to take part actively in the work required to achieve the main objective in the 'Kazakhstan-2050' Strategy! I would like to appeal particularly to our young people. This Strategy is for you. It is for you to get involved in its implementation, and it is for you to enjoy the fruits of its success. I call on all of you to get involved in it, each from your own particular place of work. Do not be indifferent. Help create the destiny of your country, together with all the people!

The Address to the Nation "Kazakhstan's way –
2050: a single goal, common interests, common future"
Astana, 17th January 2014

TWENTY-SIX

FOREIGN POLICY PRIORITIES

*President Nursultan Nazarbayev outlines Kazakhstan's foreign
policy priorities for 2014 and the implementation of Kazakhstan's
policy of political and economic modernistion in accordance
with the principles deployed by the developed nations.*

We are meeting on the eve of an important event for the world: the twenty
second Winter Olympic Games in Sochi. The Games are being held in the
CIS for the first time ever. I would like to wish the host country for the
Games and our strategic partner, the Russian Federation, every success in
hosting the Olympic mission. May all of your countries' national teams
enjoy eye-catching sporting successes and triumphs!

Our meeting is taking place against the backdrop of the start of a new
phase in Kazakhstan's development. We have begun the countdown towards
a new period in our country's sovereign history. In my message to the people,
the key areas and concrete tasks on Kazakhstan's path towards joining the
top thirty developed countries were set out. We firmly believe that we will
achieve our goal in the first half of the 21st century.

Our 'Kazakhstan-2050' Strategy calls for the development of wide-
ranging debate and mutually beneficial cooperation with all states that have
a vested interest in friendship with Kazakhstan. First and foremost, this
concerns cooperation on investment, exchange of technologies, importing
of innovations and experience, and increasing exports of Kazakhstani goods.
I call on the foreign business community to invest actively in Kazakhstan,
open up new manufacturing sites here, and sign mutually beneficial deals
with us on the mining and deep processing of minerals, infrastructure
development, agricultural production and many other things. As part of our
industrial policy, Kazakhstan will continue to create the conditions required
for business to operate in a mutually beneficial way. We are hoping for

understanding and support on the part of your governments and are keen to cooperate with you in this area.

I would particularly like to stress that establishing the goal of becoming one of the top thirty developed states in the world is very important for our country. Firstly, Kazakhstan finds the path followed by today's leading nations attractive. Between 2000 and 2013, Kazakhstanis made around 61 million foreign trips, for business or tourist purposes, all over the world. Tens of thousands of young Kazakhstanis have received an overseas education or are currently studying in one of a number of developed countries. It is therefore entirely understandable that Kazakhstani citizens are keen to see good living standards, high-quality education, healthcare and social services and professional employment here in our own country. We are committed to the principles and standards on which the member states of the Organisation for Economic Cooperation and Development base their development.

Secondly, we see dynamic growth rates as a firm guarantee of our independence in the 21st century. Therefore our national idea is 'Mangilik El', with a blessed, united and amicable multi-ethnic people. Today, this idea unites all Kazakhstanis, regardless of creed or religion. It provides monumental vital strength, and strengthens our people's belief in their great abilities and in the future we deserve.

Number three, we look upon the next fifteen to seventeen years as a 'window of opportunity' in which our country can make large-scale advances. Our experience in strategic planning indicates that at present, the geopolitical and geo-economic environment is relatively favourable. At the same time, we can clearly see, and are accounting for, the global challenges which face our world and each individual country in this century. We therefore owe it to ourselves to use and expand our regional competitive strengths. We intend to transform these strengths into incentives to ensure further success as we seek to develop the country.

Number four, Kazakhstan has always seen itself, and continues to see itself, as a valid element of a lawful and just world. Our path towards inclusion in the top thirty leading states includes the task of becoming actively involved in tackling all issues, at both the regional and global level. This represents the practical essence of the idea of G-Global, which Kazakhstan proposed in 2012. As you know, it involves expanding the global dialogue about the formation of a new, constructive, multi-polar world order in the 21st century, based on five principles which are clear to the whole world and serve to bring the world together. Such an awareness of Kazakhstan's role is a key component of our national idea, 'Mangilik El'.

Number five, we have progressed along a complex but productive path of reforms. We have created a country that is dynamic and has strong prospects. Today, the example set by our country is setting the standard for many developing markets in Eurasia and the entire world. During the extremely difficult days of the global crisis, our economy maintained positive growth rates. Last year, Kazakhstan came fiftieth in the Global Competitiveness Index. We were forty ninth in the index measuring ease of doing business. By the end of 2013, Kazakhstan had seen GDP growth of 6% for the year. Unemployment was around 5%. The country's total international reserves amount to almost USD 100 billion.

Clear tasks for modernising Kazakhstan have been set and are currently being implemented. They include, first and foremost, the industrial development of our economy. Within the context of this programme, some 780 new plants were built in four years, and 160,000 jobs were created. This year, another 130 firms will begin operating. The implementation of the programme will enable us to create 950 companies in Kazakhstan, providing 250,000 new jobs worth a total of USD 70 billion. This plan is being implemented to the letter, and the necessary funds and resources are being provided. As a result, more than 250 different types of new product will emerge in Kazakhstan. Today, finished goods made in Kazakhstan are exported to 111 countries around the world.

Each year we are opening hundreds of new firms, including projects in the fields of electricity, energy-saving techniques and 'green technologies'. Kazakhstan was the first of the CIS countries to adopt a development strategy based on a 'green economy'. Innovative clusters are being developed, such as the deep processing of raw materials in oil and gas, the chemical industry, agricultural production, car and aeroplane construction and the manufacturing of locomotives and rail cars, electronics and many others. Currently, Kazakhstan has the greatest economic potential of all the Central Asian countries. Our economy is twice that of all our neighbours combined.

We are resurrecting the Great Silk Road. In 2015 we will complete the construction of the Kazakhstani section of the transport corridor between Western Europe and Western China. Over the last few years we have built, along with our neighbours, new main railway lines leading to China and South-East Asia, Iran and the Persian Gulf states. We are seeing rapid changes in education, and our task is to transform Kazakhstan into one of Eurasia's main centres of educational excellence. Operations involving heart transplants/transplants of other organs, and stem-cell treatment, are now commonplace in our country. Kazakhstan is one of the twenty states in the world in which such forms of treatment are possible. This all points to the fact that we have made a great start as we seek a place among the leading countries in the world.

Our concept for getting into the top thirty most developed countries in the world sets out specific tasks. Number one, the trend for industrialisation will be adjusted and strengthened. We will plan our industrial development on the basis of five-year plans. Each five-year period will result in new science-rich industries being created: the production of electronics, laser technologies, communication equipment and medical equipment, genetic engineering, the search for and discovery of new types of energy, and others. We are planning to introduce innovative incentives for the development of traditional sectors including the mining industries, the oil and gas industry and agricultural production. I have also set the challenge of joining the global market for geological prospecting.

Number two, we have drawn up a plan to increase labour productivity in agriculture. Our goal is to transform Kazakhstan into a reliable and powerful regional centre for the export of foodstuffs: meat and dairy products, grain, flour and flour products. State-of-the-art agricultural and innovation clusters will be created.

Number three, an important mechanism to create a science-rich economy is the development of research science. The amount we spend on science will reach 3% of GDP. We will create the most favourable possible conditions for attracting foreign investment, which we expect to bring with it an influx of new technologies and innovations. I call on businessmen from all countries and leading multi-national corporations to create service and assembly facilities in this country. Developing infrastructure and simplifying the tax system are among the challenges that we will tackle in a determined manner.

Number four, our plans to foster dynamic growth in our national infrastructure will include a host of important challenges. We will need to create major conglomerations in Astana and Almaty, and then in Shymkent and Aktobe. These will be urban centres of economic and socio-cultural growth. The modernisation and construction of new transport routes continues, at international level and elsewhere. It is in Kazkhastan's interests to create logistic centres in countries which are of interest to us as we seek to export our products to global markets.

We see the development of energy as linked to the creation of a fully-fledged nuclear energy sector. Our traditional energy sector is based on our coal, oil and gas resources. As far as nuclear energy is concerned, Kazakhstan is the world's biggest manufacturer of uranium ore, and is engaged in its partial enrichment; the introduction of a full-cycle production process is currently under discussion. In the long-term we plan to construct a nuclear power station. We will also build new oil refineries. This represents a great opportunity for mutually beneficial cooperation with your countries. Ahead of us is an event of global scale: our hosting of the international exhibition 'EXPO-2017' in Astana. I invite all interested countries to take part in building and decorating the national pavilions and the other sites at the exhibition.

Number five: the key link in the chain is the development of SMEs. The share of our national wealth that SMEs provide must reach 50%.

Number six: an important priority is the development of human capital. Our plans include the creation of a uniquely advanced education system, which will help us compete on equal terms at the regional level. Measures have been set out for the development of national healthcare, and to increase life expectancy among Kazakhstanis. For the first time, we have set ourselves multi-faceted tasks to improve the conditions for people with disabilities. The state benefits paid to these people will rise by a quarter. The state will draw up programmes for the social welfare of those with disabilities. All those who are in receipt of state aid will become participants in employment and social programmes. There are plans to draw up a long-term concept for cultural policy, and increase global awareness of Kazakhstan's cultural legacy.

Number seven, a host of specific measures have been planned to encourage an atmosphere of honest competition, justice, the rule of law, and an advanced legal culture in the country. The work done to reform the judicial system will be continued. I have ordered that a new anti-corruption strategy be drawn up. State bodies are focused on working actively with the non-government sector and administrative reforms will be developed, the powers of local agencies will be expanded, and their accountability to the people will be increased.

Taking the long-term objectives of the 'Kazakhstan-2050' Strategy into account, I have approved the new concept for Kazakhstan's foreign policy until 2020, which is open and accessible. It acknowledges global trends and is oriented towards effective interaction with our partners around the world. Today, some positive trends can be seen in the global economy. The forecasts all predict economic growth in Europe, the USA and other countries. It is essential, therefore, that we take two important international factors into account.

Number one. We must not forget the cyclical nature of the global economy. Periods of growth are always followed by downturns. This has been seen many times throughout history, and therefore Kazakhstan and the world in general must be ready for any economic twists and turns and, consequently, in international politics.

Number two. During periods of growth, security issues become increasingly important. The unresolved social problems in a host of countries in both the Old and New world, still pose a serious threat of domestic conflict. You can judge for yourselves. Whatever the experts may say today about the causes of the current complex situation in the Ukraine, the key reasons are nonetheless to be found in the social dialectic.

There are also some current forecasts which offer little solace, particularly regarding individual regional economies. The geopolitical situation remains complicated. The challenges of regional security in Central Asia are closely related to the political response to the situation in Afghanistan. This year is a very important one for Afghanistan: a presidential election will be held and coalition troops will be withdrawn. The international forces have played an historic role in stabilising the situation not only in Afghanistan but throughout the whole of Central Asia.

We particularly value the contribution made by the United States, Germany, the UK and many other countries. In my view, a period of economic rebirth has now arrived for Afghanistan. I think that we all have a vested interest in Afghanistan being at peace and enjoying stable development. We are prepared to continue our efforts to normalise the situation in the country, along with the rest of the international community. Kazakhstan will be playing an active role in these efforts to help us preserve stability in the region.

Kazakhstan welcomes the Geneva negotiations aimed at restoring some order to the situation in Syria and is hopeful that they will be a success. In Almaty, Kazakhstan hosted two rounds of multilateral talks aimed at resolving the problem of Iran's nuclear programme. By so doing we made a contribution to the task of achieving a 'Geneva breakthrough', which we most certainly welcome and support.

My attendance at the inauguration ceremony for Iran's new President and at the negotiations which took place at the time was also intended as a peaceful step towards resolving a significant problem. Kazakhstan, which voluntarily rejected the use of nuclear weapons and thereby earned acclaim and acknowledgement from the whole global community, is a positive example and a 'beacon' by which countries such as Iran can be guided. The negotiations between six states were an important milestone for the regional centre for the UN which was created in Almaty. We will continue this work.

Today, it is crucial that all geopolitical centres recognise that in the 21st century, far greater resources are required to ensure our security. I am talking about financial resources, the provision of personnel, new approaches in the way we react, including fresh collective approaches on an international basis. This makes Kazakhstan's initiative on adopting a Global Anti-Crisis Strategy more pertinent than ever.

We remain true to our core foreign policy principles: pragmatism, consistency and balance. We will expand our country's involvement in international affairs. In recent years, Kazakhstan's cooperation with other states in multilateral formats has increased, too. Last year alone, Kazakhstan received visits from the leaders of Russia, China, the European Commission, the UK, Indonesia, Spain, Belarus, Kyrgyzstan, Turkmenistan, Finland and Latvia.

One of the priority areas in our joint work with the Caspian Sea states has been to determine the Caspian Sea's legal status. Kazakhstan organised the World Anti-Crisis Conference which was backed by the UN and took place within the context of the Astana Economic Forum.

An important task is to develop our friendship and cooperation with the Russian Federation, China, our neighbouring states in Central Asia, the USA and the countries of the European Union. Kazakhstan has expanded its cooperation with countries in the Western Hemisphere, South-East Asia and Africa. Kazakhstani Embassies have opened in Vietnam and South Africa. This year, we will open Embassies in Ethiopia, Mexico and Kuwait.

Kazakhstan is involved in multilateral efforts to strengthen global peace and security. Our Parliament approved the deployment of twenty Kazakhstani military observers on UN peacekeeping missions to Haiti, the Western Sahara, the Ivory Coast and Liberia. Kazakhstan has always been at the forefront of global efforts to strengthen the non-proliferation of nuclear weapons. Our position on this remains unchanged: we are for a world free from nuclear weapons! A summit is to be held in The Hague on issues of nuclear security, with Kazakhstan in attendance.

As you know, Kazakhstan has officially started its campaign to be elected as a non-permanent member of the UN Security Council for the period 2017-2018. I would like to take this opportunity to appeal to you and your governments and call on you to support our country's candidacy.

For us, as a state situated in the middle of Eurasia, it is vitally important that we take part in international processes. This year will mark twenty years since I put forward the idea of creating a Eurasian Economic Union. It is symbolic that it is in this year that an agreement will be signed between Kazakhstan, Russia and Belarus on the Eurasian Economic Union. A number of other states have also expressed their interest in joining this process. The Eurasian Economic Union is a common market. It will be a fundamentally new association for the 21st century, operating on principles of equal rights and mutual benefit and taking into account the interests of all those taking part. According to forecasts, by 2030, the three countries stand to gain a 25% boost in additional GDP growth, or USD 600 billion.

The members of the future Eurasian Economic Union are not hiding from the world, but rather continuing to cooperate actively with all their partners. In this regard, we support the proposal by the Russian President on the future formation of a free-trade zone between the Eurasian Economic Union and the EU. We have heard all manner of opinions being voiced by experts about the Eurasian Economic Union and I think that it is essential to recognise that this is not a political organisation. As things stand, it is purely about economic cooperation, which is dictated by the needs of our countries. I think that the time has come to move from a critical and distrustful view of our union to a careful study of it, so as to understand its essence, and to search for ways of developing mutual cooperation.

Kazakhstan feels that the price of successful development of the whole Central Asian region is the active promotion of integration within different regions. Our country also sets great store by all aspects of the cultural and humanitarian dimensions of foreign policy. This includes the provision of official development aid as part of international cooperation.

Diplomacy has always been, remains and will always be a patriotic art form, in the highest sense. I would like to express my deep gratitude to all the ambassadors, heads of diplomatic missions and representatives of international organisations for the worthy and noble mission you are pursuing in the Republic of Kazakhstan. For our part, we will create all the essential conditions required to ensure that you can go about your activities and lead your lives in comfort, and enjoy your leisure pursuits. We will be putting the practices into effect used in other countries for further development of our economy, our politics and other areas.

I wish you success in your work and happiness and prosperity to your families!

Speech at the Meeting for the heads of foreign
diplomatic missions accredited to Kazakhstan
Astana, 5th February 2014

TWENTY-SEVEN

A UNIFIED PEOPLE

At the 21ˢᵗ session of the Assembly of the People of Kazakhstan,
Nursultan Nazarbayev emphasised the role of a united Kazah people
as a key factor in implementing the Strategy "Kazakhstan-2050"
and building a united and harmonious state.

Gathered here today are representatives of all regions of our vast homeland! Our forum is attended by Kazakhstanis of various ages, generations and professions, who, together, through honest toil, created and are developing our country! I would particularly like to welcome all our veterans, who, through their hard work and toil, protected our friendship in outstanding fashion and forever bound us together in friendship. I am grateful to all those who, together with me, created the Assembly of the People of Kazakhstan, and are committed to this idea. In their day-to-day work, they protect and develop the great principles of peace and harmony.

There are many young people present today, including many who are the same age as our independence itself. I see this as a good sign which tells us that the ideas of tolerance, friendship and brotherhood have been adopted by new generations of Kazakhstanis, and will be adopted forever. This goes to show that our work is not in vain! This shows, far more than any words, that our Assembly has firm foundations in terms of safeguarding peace and harmony!

Since our very first days as an independent nation, thousands of meetings have taken place here and in our regions, cities, districts and towns. Almost two decades ago, when we established the Assembly, we went further than all known models around the world. We found the only true mechanism to bring people together on a shared, patriotic platform. The essence of this platform is understood by all and helps to provide elementary human needs: jobs, prosperity for our families, a good education for our children, good healthcare, housing, security and leisure.

In our society, no one ethnicity is given preferential treatment, and all are equal before the law. All Kazakhstani citizens are the children of the same native land. All of us are the children – diverse, yet equal – of the same Kazakhstani people. We all share one concern: the prosperity of the entire Kazakhstani people. We all share one goal: that our common homeland should flourish. This is our shared success, our shared pride. This is the policy to which I have always adhered, the one I am implementing now and the one I intend to stick to as head of state! Stability and harmony are the goals of the work done each day by every Akim, every company director, every citizen!

The Assembly is always in step with the times. Its support has been the decisive factor at every vital stage in our history as an independent country. I will never tire of saying that unity and togetherness are the key values of our society. Thanks to this, we have stimulated our economy, strengthened our citizens' wealth and shown the way forward for our country. We have managed to implement the 'Kazakhstan-2030' Strategy ahead of schedule.

Today, our unity is the key factor in implementing our new 'Kazakhstan-2030' Strategy. Becoming one of the top thirty most developed states in the world is our key objective and the shared destiny of all Kazakhstanis. The Strategy reflects the wisdom of our great, multi-ethnic people. It is based on the lofty principles of our unique culture of peace and spiritual harmony.

Number one. The idea that all Kazakhstanis are equal, regardless of creed, language, religion or social status. All forms of discrimination are completely unacceptable and will be punished severely under our laws, as will any attacks on peace and harmony.

Number two. Joint responsibility for the development of our economy and for improving the people's prosperity. Kazakhstanis of all creeds are actively taking part in the process of industrialisation and the development of SMEs, science, education, healthcare and sport. In our economy, no-one is divided into categories based on ethnicity. Our people work together in multicultural workforces, enjoying amicable relations.

Number three. In Kazakhstan we have resolved the issue of the state language, the official status of Russian and the development along equal lines of the languages of all ethnicities and cultures. This year marks the 25th anniversary of the first law we passed on languages. In the future, all our citizens will speak the state language, and this will only make us more equal and strengthen our unity. For a quarter of a century we have been steering a clear course in our language policy: we have gradually developed the state language and created the conditions needed to develop the languages spoken by all ethnicities. There are few countries in the world today in which the majority of the population is able to speak and think in at least two languages. Kazakhstan is one such country, and this is one of the things that makes our nation so rich. We are introducing a programme for developing trilingualism. In our country, sixty media publications are available in fifteen languages; these include thirty four newspapers and twenty six websites for ethnic cultural centres.

Number four: one can measure our state's enlightenment by the respect it shows for the great spiritual legacy of all religions worshiped in Kazakhstan, and on the basis that everyone enjoys freedom of choice. This atmosphere of inter-faith tolerance is probably not found anywhere else in the world. At the same time, our country is a secular one, and religion is detached from the state. We also renounce extremism under religious slogans, attempts to politicise religious teachings from within, and attempts to impose on our people religious views and ideas that are alien to us.

Number five. The formation of a society of universal labour is the main condition for employment among Kazakhs, and quality of life for all our workers. Hard work, responsibility and discipline: only in this way will it be possible for the whole of Kazakhstan to develop.

Number six. A nationwide Kazakhstani culture is forming thanks to close cultural cooperation among all of the country's ethnic groups. Kazakhstani art and traditions are developing in our country, and at the same time we are developing the cultural legacy of all ethnicities. We are proud of Kazakhstan's growing contribution to world art, literature and sport, by people of all creeds among our fellow countrymen.

Number seven. The Assembly of the People of Kazakhstan is both the foundation and the guiding principle in our culture of peace and spiritual harmony. The Assembly is an innovative model for the nationwide representation of all citizens' interests, and a successful tool for our fledgling democracy. It is consolidating the activities of 820 ethnic and cultural associations throughout the country. These associations include some 70,000 activists and over three million people are engaged in this work.

The Assembly has become a consolidating, supra-political body for national sovereignty. It says much that the deputy group in the Assembly contains twenty one Majilis members, representing all the parliamentary parties. The Assembly is ensuring productive dialogue between the state agencies and the population, and solving pressing issues affecting the lives of people of all ethnicities. Last year alone, the Assembly organised 10,000 events, with more than 3.5 million people taking part. In most of the regions, Houses of friendship have been established and are in operation, attracting more than 720,000 visitors each year. The concept for the development of our Assembly until the year 2020 is being implemented. 97.5% of Kazakhstanis who were surveyed believe that our Assembly represents the interests of our entire nation. This is a very good sign.

These are the seven basic principles behind Kazakhstan's culture of peace and spiritual harmony. Now, this is our shared cultural legacy, which we are passing on to our descendants, as our nation's treasure.

The 'Kazakhstan-2050' Strategy ensures that we remain focused on the serious, hard work in the complex conditions of the 21st century. We have an open country. And we are not shut off from the rest of the world. We are bound to the outside world by thousands of economic and political ties and links between ordinary people. We must face up to many challenges of a global and regional nature in the years to come. I have said this openly and honestly in my messages to the people.

To be quite frank, strengthening peace and harmony is the key criterion in terms of implementing the Strategy-2050. The events which we see taking place in world politics indicate the global complexity in the current century. One cannot read the news reports from Ukraine without being pained to the very core. The country is one of our close partners in the CIS. We are bound to it, not only by decades of mutually beneficial cooperation, but also the common ground in our histories. In troubled times, Kazakhstan became a second home for hundreds of thousands of Ukrainians. Those who were forcibly deported to our country. Those who were evacuated during the Second World War. Those who felt a calling in their hearts to come here, and to build some of our industrial giants and work on our virgin soil.

This year, we are celebrating the sixtieth anniversary of the start of the virgin soil saga and remembering those who worked in order to create our country's grain breadbasket. I congratulate all those who, despite the harsh conditions, grew crops and built infrastructure on the barren steppes. Today, more than three hundred thousand of our citizens are Ukrainians. The Ukrainian land is carpeted with the sacred ash of many thousands of Kazakhstanis who heroically gave their lives to liberate it from fascism. Thousands of Kazakhstanis went to university in Ukraine. As you know, I am one of them. It was in Ukraine that I learned the art of metalwork. Therefore we, the Kazakhstani people, feel compassion for the Ukrainian people and wish to express the brotherly hope that stability and unity will soon be restored in Ukrainian society. We are convinced that the Ukrainian people should decide their internal problems, without outside interference, through peaceful negotiations involving all interested parties.

The 21st century has so far taught us five immutable truths.

Number one, a stable economy means a stable society, and a stable life for every person. In some countries, this truth is often relegated to the background to suit the political ambitions of various parties and groups. Yet here, development of the economy is the key part of our 'Strategy 2050', which we are resolving on a day-to-day basis. Number two, the independence of our state will remain inviolable only through full adherence to the Constitution and the laws, primarily on the part of the citizens of our country. Number three, relations between different ethnicities and issues of civil equality and language policy – none of these things should be the subject of political games. They must not be put off until a later time. And, even more importantly, they must not be ignored or cynically used as an argument in the struggle for power. This would be dangerous for the state, the people and each individual. Everyone must therefore understand that there is only a very fine line between chauvinism or nationalism and open neo-fascism – a line which can all too easily be crossed.

We must always remember the great sacrifices made by our people and the peoples of the whole of the CIS in the Second World War in the name of the Victory over the Nazis. This must always be a subject that is painstakingly instilled in each new generation: in the family, at school and at university, and among the workforces at our companies. It is important that our memory of the Victory over fascism should never be allowed to die! The ninth of May is therefore an important date for us all.

I have asked the Akim of Astana to look into the possibility of erecting a monument in honour of the legendary general Ivan Vasilievich Panfilov, and naming one of the capital's new streets after him. Recently, a central square in the town of Nevel, in the Pskov Region of Russia, was named after one of our compatriots, the famous cavalryman from Pavlodar, Abylkhair Baimuldin, who was buried in the square in January 1944. A bronze bust of him will be unveiled on his tomb during the celebrations marking Victory Day. We are grateful to the Russian people for honouring the memory of all war heroes, and for respecting them! We are all obliged to remember and pay our respects to all the Kazakhstani heroes who fought in the Second World War. A patriotic upbringing for our young people is something that should be promoted, as the Assembly's main area of work, particularly in the context of the celebrations next year marking the seventieth anniversary of the Victory over fascism.

Number four: I believe that for any country, the issue of integration is linked with the people's prosperity. Integration will only be successful and bear fruit if it is founded not on the political situation that happens to be in effect but on a sound economic paradigm. A form of integration that improves people's lives, creates decent conditions for their employment and business, and provides extensive opportunities to develop the economy. It is in precisely this context that Kazakhstan is establishing the Eurasian Economic Union together with Belarus and Russia. Here in Astana we plan to sign an historic agreement on the formation of this integrated association. It is symbolic that it will be signed in the year that marks the twentieth anniversary of the idea of a Eurasian Union, which I proposed at MSU in

1994. We are creating an economic union so that together we can make a technological leap forward in the 21st century. The three countries will be integrated so that they can help each other hold off global competition. That this competition will be ferocious is something I don't doubt for a minute. I firmly believe that in the 21st century, there is no other advantageous alternative to Eurasian integration.

The objective language of statistics demonstrates that the turnover of goods in Kazakhstan and the countries in the Customs Union has risen by 88% since it was created and now amounts to USD 24 billion. Our exports to these countries have risen by 63% and are now worth almost USD 6 billion. It is important at this stage that all the necessary steps towards integration are taken via 'national diplomacy' and broad public support, first and foremost on the part of the Assembly.

Number five: the world has entered a time of major change. International relations are undergoing a significant crisis. I am concerned by reports of a possible end to cooperation between some of the leading nuclear powers in the area of physical protection of nuclear materials. This could seriously undermine the entire process of global nuclear disarmament and wipe out all the successes achieved in this field in recent decades, including the progress made at the recent global summit in The Hague. As for our country, in a move in which the will of the people was on our side, we shut down the Semipalatinsk Test Site and acquired non-nuclear status. We, the people of Kazakhstan, remain true to the ideals of peace, free from the threat of nuclear self-destruction.

Today, we are witnessing an acute crisis in international politics. In these circumstances, I hereby declare that Kazakhstan and Russia are amicable neighbours, allies and strategic partners. Last year, we signed an Agreement on good neighbourly relations and union in the 21st century, and an Agreement on military and technical cooperation. In the foreseeable future, both countries will be taking all the necessary steps to ratify these agreements. Our relations with Russia are an important part of our foreign policy. I would like to emphasise once again: the countries of Central Asia, Russia and China are our neighbours, and therefore we have always had, have and will continue to have, a close friendship with them.

The current situation in global politics represents the dramatic playing out of a paradigm shift in the world order, towards multipolarity. I first spoke about this back in 2012, when proposing the G-Global initiative. I believe that the current challenges facing the world will be overcome if deep changes are made in international law, foreign policy practices and the methods used in inter-state relations. Our proposals on the principles of G-Global are thus of more use to the global community now than ever before. I am sure that they are capable of providing a more constructive path to global development, as opposed to the chaotic one we see today.

The Assembly boasts far-reaching international connections. I call on all of you to use your international contacts to promote the idea of G-Global. The Assembly must also have its own clear action plan for taking part in the preparations for such major international events as the worldwide exhibition, 'EXPO-2017', in Astana, and the Universiade-2017 in Almaty. At these events we must show the world our culture, the tolerance of our people for a multi-ethnic society, and the things we have achieved in circumstances of peace and harmony.

Stability and unity in our society are the most important factors as we seek to develop along the route to implementing our Strategy. It is therefore essential that we apply a number of new measures to promote the Kazakhstani model of tolerance and harmony further.

Number one. Next year will mark twenty years since the creation of the Assembly and the adoption of the country's Constitution via a referendum. These are two great events, which constitute a unifying thread running through our history books. It was the Assembly, in its first sessions, which backed the adoption of the Constitution in 1995. It was the first of all the public institutions to call on the people to vote for the Constitution in the referendum. I therefore propose that next year, 2015, be declared the Year of the Assembly of the People of Kazakhstan. I hereby order the Government, in conjunction with the Assembly, to draw up and implement a National Plan of measures related to the staging of the Year of the Assembly of the People of Kazakhstan and the twentieth anniversary of the Constitution. In connection with this, I propose that a Forum for the people of Kazakhstan be held next year in Astana.

Number two. Six weeks ago, on March 1ˢᵗ, a brand new phase commenced in the mega-project 'Roadmap for peace and harmony', which is dedicated to the twentieth anniversary of the Assembly. Special emphasis must be placed on the work done in each city, district centre, town and village. We must reach every home and every family! Today it is essential that we enhance the role played in the regions by the councils of social harmony, created under the auspices of the Assembly.

Number three: we must strengthen the structure of the Assembly at the regional level. We must adopt the concepts for the development of small assemblies in all regions and in the cities of Astana and Almaty, which were drawn up on my orders. I hereby task the Assembly's Secretariat with monitoring all issues related to the construction of Houses of Friendship in the Atyrau, West Kazakhstan, Karagandy, Kyzylorda and Mangystau Regions. As for our capital, Astana, first of all it must become a worthy example of tolerant relations between different communities. All the requirements set out in the Law on languages must be followed here to the letter. Specifically, the road infrastructure, public transport in the city, the streets and avenues and the other facilities in the city must have signs which fully comply with requirements of the legislation: they must be in both Kazakhstani and Russian. At the moment this is not the case in all parts of the city: the bus-stops are only announced in one language, and the same goes for the signs indicating the bus routes. Why does the small assembly of Astana not monitor this, and report it to the authorised bodies responsible for compliance with the law?! This is also important for all other cities and towns throughout the country. In the run-up to the Global exhibition 'EXPO-2017', we must also ensure that place names and signs in English are put up around the city. The same also applies to Almaty, which will be hosting the Universiade-2017. Secondly, the motto for the year 2015 in Astana should be: 'Astana – a city of peace and harmony', and all of the Republic's ethnic cultural associations should be encouraged to join in with this project.

Number four. Today, the issue of creating a mechanism for managing all of the Assembly's ongoing work has become more pressing than ever. I hereby task the Government, by the first of June 2014, with resolving all issues related to establishing a state institute for meeting the needs of the APK, to be located at the House of Friendship in Almaty, and also, in conjunction with the Akims for the regions, of regional institutions which can service the needs of the small assemblies.

Number five. The status of the deputy secretaries of the regional assemblies must be enhanced. I hereby order the Agency for matters of state service to re-categorise the position of deputy secretary of the APK in the regions and the cities of Astana and Almaty to category D2 in the Register of official positions for civil servants.

Number six. 22 April will be the 10th season of the republican headquarters for young working brigades 'Zhasil El' ('A green country'). This is another vivid embodiment of our young people's patriotism and hard work. More than 200,000 young people have already taken part in implementing this programme. They have planted more than 44 million trees and landscaped 111,000 hectares of land! I would like to pass on my sincere greetings to all the warriors in the working brigades and wish them productive work for the good of our homeland! It is essential that we bring in proposals, with a time-limit of one month, on the further development of 'Zhasil El'. Young people have complained to me on numerous occasions, saying that in some regions there have been slip-ups in this work.

All of these measures will serve to strengthen the role played by the Assembly in society, and enhance its responsibility for peace and harmony in our shared home of Kazakhstan.

Our outstanding female poet Fariza Ongarsynova, who, sadly, passed away recently, once made a wise observation during a conversation I had with her. She said that to create something is to be able to add, to that which is already known to everyone, a scintilla of one's own soul and personal experience. A culture of peace, spirituality and harmony is a living and breathing creation, on the part of all seventeen million of our citizens, who put their hearts and souls into the flourishing of our sacred land every single day. Each of the different ethnicities in our country is creating a decorative ornament for their own life, combining it with the patterns of other ethnic groups. And together we are creating the unique, multi-coloured, priceless canvas of our Great History, entitled 'Kazakhstan'.

Not long ago, in *Kazakhstanskaya pravda*, I read the thoughts of a man who hails from Karaganda, like me – the director of the Ukrainian cultural centre Nikolai Matiyashin, who said that today Kazakhstanis are able to 'bathe' and 'luxuriate' in an atmosphere of peace and harmony. What golden words these are! I am firmly convinced that in our society, in which people are living amicably with one another, soul to soul, the world will always be bright and spacious.

It so happens that our session today is taking place with Easter just around the corner: it will be celebrated in two days' time by all the Christians among our fellow countrymen. It is also a public holiday for all Kazakhstanis, regardless of their faith. We celebrate the Islamic public holidays and those of the other faiths in Kazakhstan in exactly the same way – together. This goes to show the broadness of soul that our people have. In these bright days of spring, I wish all Kazakhstanis peace, kindness, mutual understanding and prosperity!

Speech at the 21st session of the Assembly of the People of Kazakhstan:
'The 'Kazakhstan-2050' Strategy: a culture of peace, spirituality and harmony'
Astana, 18ᵗʰ April 2014

TWENTY-EIGHT

EURASIAN INTEGRATION

The idea of the Eurasian Economic Union was first proposed
by President Nursultan Nazarbayev in 1994 at the Lomonosov
Moscow State University. In this speech, the Head of State outlines
the principles and prospects of Eurasian integration.

I congratulate the university's staff on the colossal changes which have occurred at Moscow State University in recent decades. As an honorary professor of this university, I am delighted by your academic triumphs and by how you have consolidated your high standing in academic and educational circles around the world. It gives me great satisfaction to recall how, fourteen years ago, Vladimir Putin supported my idea to open a branch of the M.V. Lomonosov MSU in Astana. This year, the branch in Astana will be conferring its one thousandth degree. This is a landmark event! Graduates with degrees from MSU are currently working in economic, academic and other areas of life in Kazakhstan. I am therefore grateful to all those who took part in helping to make the Kazakhstani branch of MSU come into being.

Twenty years ago, here at MSU, I first proposed my idea of creating a new association for integration – the Eurasian Economic Union. The concept was based on a truth that is equally close to and comprehensible to all the citizens of our countries. Our shared history, mutual economic attraction to one another, the close inter-relationship between our cultures and the similarities between what our people strive for in life, give our peoples the opportunity to build multilateral ties between us of a new kind. I have been, and remain, a firm advocate of the idea that a successful Eurasian Union is only possible if based on principles of goodwill, equal rights and mutual benefit, and if we take into account the pragmatic interests of each member state. This initiative has become the starting point for a new historical process, which is currently referred to as Eurasian integration.

Firstly, my idea, which was incomprehensible and underestimated by most CIS politicians from that time, is today widely acclaimed by business circles, and at the public and humanitarian level. A huge number of joint forums have been established and are currently in operation, all of which are driving Eurasian integration. These include the Eurasian Development Bank, the Eurasian Business Council, the Eurasian Media-Forum, the Eurasian Association of Universities and many others.

Eighteen years ago, one of the first facilities which we opened in Astana was the Lev Nikolaevich Gumilev Eurasian National University. Today, it is the leading institute of higher education in Central Asia. Lev Nikolaevich Gumilev was one of the most perspicacious of Russia's intellectuals, who foresaw that the Russian state was destined to go down the Eurasian path. Works by the outstanding thinkers K.N. Leontiev, N.Y. Danilevsky and many others all testify to this. The history, geography, culture and economy of Russia all point to the same thing. Today, the concept of 'Eurasian integration' has become a brand which is used frequently by politicians, economists, journalists and social circles.

Secondly, I particularly want to emphasise that the modern Eurasian initiative has never been detached from reality. Above all, it always takes account of the fact that independence and political sovereignty are the priorities for all the states involved in the integration process. And at the same time, its essence, right from the start, has been the genuine concern for the interests of the ordinary citizens of Kazakhstan, Russia, Belarus and also the other states in the Eurasian land-mass. In 1998, I proposed a programme of 'ten simple steps to take us closer to ordinary people'. In the years since then, practically all of these steps have been implemented.

The shared borders between the states of the Customs Union have become transparent, so that the peoples of our countries can cross them unimpeded, as can goods, cargo, and currency. Since 2009, the turnover of goods for Kazakhstan and its partners in the Eurasian Economic Area and the Customs Union has risen by 88%, to USD 24.2 billion. Our exports to Russia and Belarus have increased by 63%, with the volume of processed goods that are imported doubling. We are establishing joint ventures with

Russian and Belarusian companies. Our countries also have agreements in effect on the mutual recognition of diplomas in higher, secondary and vocational education.

Every year, tens of thousands of citizens from Kazakhstan, Russia and Belarus, along with a host of other countries in the CIS have been using their equal rights to study at universities in our states, find work and receive emergency medical care. Opportunities are being expanded for citizens of one state to manage SMEs in other member states. Eurasian integration gives us a plethora of advantages for the productive development of our cultural and humanitarian ties, and tourism. All of this brings concrete benefits for millions of people. And it is already impossible to imagine that none of this might ever have happened.

Thirdly, the Eurasian initiative has altered the nature of the integration processes throughout the CIS and lent dynamism to them. The Organisation for the Agreement on Collective Security has been created. In 2000, the Eurasian Economic Community was established. On the whole, the activity of the Commonwealth of Independent States and its structural departments has become more concrete. There are almost forty inter-state sectors operating within it.

Fourthly, the Eurasian initiative, at the turn of the 20th and 21st centuries has had a serious impact on international relations, including beyond the borders of its initial geographic area. Basic Eurasian principles have been applied to the creation and activities of the Shanghai Cooperation Organisation. On the same pragmatic basis, the Conference for Interaction and Confidence-building Measures in Asia has been operating successfully for more than twenty years now. In 2010, at the Astana summit of the OSCE, I proposed that we start work on forming a common continental platform for security in Eurasia. Founded on principles of trust, equality and mutual benefit, it could include both a European and an Asian dimension. This position was reflected in the Astana Declaration of the OSCE, 'On the road to a community of security'.

Number five, the Eurasian idea is currently, in the middle of the second decade of the 21st century, assuming real geo-economic and geopolitical features. The Supreme Eurasian Economic Council and the Eurasian Economic Commission are operating successfully. Kazkahstan, Belarus and Russia are applying a Common Customs Code, and coordinating their macro-economic policy. It is symbolic that in the year of the twentieth anniversary of the idea of the Eurasian Economic Union in Astana, there are plans to sign an historic Agreement on the creation of this integration association. A host of other countries have also indicated that they are interested in joining. The economic potential of Eurasian integration is extremely high. The aggregate size of the three member states' economies is USD 2.2 trillion. The total volume of industrial products manufactured by the three states amounted to USD 1.5 trillion. The potential effect of integration, in the form of an increase in total GDP, could amount to around USD 900 billion by 2030.

Thus, Eurasian integration is providing a competitive edge to our strategy in the run-up to the third global industrial revolution. This industrial revolution is taking place in conditions in which we are seeing the drama of a paradigm shift in the world order, towards multipolarity. The current instability in the world is a crisis not only of economics but also of international law and global politics. The G8 and the G20 will not be able to cope with these problems. It is for precisely this reason that I put forward the G-Global initiative in 2012. 160 countries are getting actively involved in it. G-Global incorporates some of the fundamental principles for peace in the 21st century: evolutionary change; justice, equality, consensus; global tolerance and trust; global transparency; constructive multipolarity.

I believe that the global challenges we currently face will only be overcome if deep-seated changes are made to international law, foreign policy practices and the methods used in relations between states. Our proposals on the principles of G-Global are thus of great use to the world community now more than ever before. I am sure that they are capable of providing a constructive method for global development. On the whole, we are currently seeing the hugely positive role and specific results emanating from the Eurasian integration process. Further deepening of integration is not only about providing new opportunities, but it is what we owe current and future generations of our states' citizens.

Twenty years ago, I spoke about how Kazakhstan and Russia must be at the core of the integration process, leading to the creation of the Eurasian Economic Union. It is essential to underline the important role played by Vladimir Putin in ensuring that Eurasian integration was given a new boost in its development at the start of the 21st century. In 2010, it received backing from Dmitry Medvedev.

Relations between Kazakhstan and Russia have always been, and remain, a fine example of partnership. Last year was a breakthrough year for our countries. A unique Agreement on good neighbourly relations and union in the 21st century was signed in Yekaterinburg. Today, there are practically no fields in which our countries do not interact with one another, on the basis of mutual trust. A process of industrial cooperation is taking place, at the inter-regional level and elsewhere. We have seen successful development in our energy partnership and in our cooperation in the aerospace industry, and we have been expanding cooperation in the cultural and humanitarian field. Russia is Kazakhstan's biggest trade partner.

Last year, turnover of goods between our countries amounted to USD 24 billion according to 2013 statistics. This is a record figure in the entire history of our relations. It was achieved in many ways thanks to the Customs Union and the Single Economic Area. Last year was certainly not easy for our economies, however. At the end of last year we signed a bilateral Agreement on military and technical cooperation. A unified anti-aircraft defence system is in operation. On issues of regional security, we are working closely with Russia within the context of international organisations. Trust, equality before the law, mutually beneficial cooperation and unity – these are the shared values of Kazakhstanis and Russians, which we must hand down from generation to generation.

The global financial crisis, from which the world has still not properly recovered, has accelerated the process of regionalisation between the various corners of the planet. This process is taking place in North and South America, South-East Asia, the region below the Persian Gulf and the Arab-Islamic world, Australia and Oceania, and West Africa. We are seeing major regional systems being formed, with unified algorithms for economic and financial relations between states. It is self-evident that in the 21st century, regional integration is becoming an important factor in countering global risks. At present, in circumstances of universal globalisation, this is a fundamental issue for states' economic and civil development, and for ensuring their competitiveness in the world.

Today, when talking about the Eurasian Economic Union, some experts and politicians like to indulge in scaremongering about a supposed 'reincarnation' of the Soviet Union. I believe that such talk is far-removed from reality and completely baseless. Firstly, the kind of institutional base needed for reintegration along the Soviet model simply does not exist today. All of that has been consigned to history, once and for all and irreversibly. Secondly, the peoples of the post-Soviet area have built states of their own. Thirdly, the current system of property ownership, and the structure and economic way of life of our societies have moved far beyond the archaic world of the Soviet days.

In this regard we share the same view as the leaders of Russia and Belarus. Yet it is not hard to see that in the modern world, there are several regional integration projects that could be implemented. None of them, however, provokes such unambiguous assessments as the creation of the Eurasian Economic Union. Let me say quite frankly that in these negative responses, I see, on the one hand, attempts to camouflage concerns that the Eurasian Economic Union has the potential to become a fairly strong rival to other global economic powerhouses.

In essence, to put this in the language of rights, we are talking about methods of unfair competition being deployed on a global scale, just as our integration is in its early stages. Why are these detractors not discussing the massive potential for bringing together the European and Eurasian economic unions? After all, the benefits to all parties are self-evident.

On the other hand, the various absurdities that they are claiming only serves to underline the potential and prospects of the idea of Eurasian integration. Twenty years ago, when I proposed the Eurasian Union project, I foresaw that economic pragmatism would determine whether or not it was a success. I have always been, and remain, a genuine supporter of the well-known formula: "the economy first, politics later". This principle is all-pervading, and applies both to our country's domestic policy and its foreign policy. This approach has ensured that we have been consistent in all areas of Kazakhstan's development – from economic reforms to the establishment of pragmatic relations with our partners in the international arena.

Since our first day of independence, our country has been developing without straying from our trajectory or backing down, without social turbulence or internal conflicts. We have always remained a worthy partner, and we have not shifted our foreign policy priorities like a weather vane. Speaking frankly, many countries in the CIS proved unable to form such a complex policy as ours, and to achieve such stable development. Today, when the world is talking about Ukraine, I cannot pass over this issue. You will know that I studied in Ukraine, and I am not indifferent to the fate of the Ukrainian people.

I feel a pain in my heart when I see the turbulent events taking place in that country. Ukraine was the second largest country in the former Union in terms of its industrial potential and industrial base. It had far more opportunities for steady, independent growth than all the other republics. However, two decades of independence in that country have had little impact on the economy and on the prosperity of ordinary people, being far more concerned with politics. It is in this that I see the main cause of the current crisis in Ukraine. We wish our brother nation of Ukraine a rapid return to stability, harmony and unity. However Ukraine is aligned, good relations with us are in its best interest. This is something we must remember.

I am sure that the involvement of our states in integration is bound to serve as an incentive for the industrialisation of our national economies, the provision of jobs for our people, and the creation of favourable conditions for the development of business. The only kind of integration that will be successful will be one that ensures prosperity for our people, and provides new opportunities for honest and fair work, primarily in their home country, rather than far off in some distant foreign field. The issues of the economy and of the citizens' prosperity are priorities as far as Kazakhstan's participation in Eurasian integration is concerned. We see huge opportunities in the future of the Eurasian Economic Union for an innovative breakthrough and for accelerated development in our country.

As you know, a new Strategy for long-term development until 2050 is being implemented in Kazakhstan. We fulfilled the goals of the 'Kazakhstan-2030' Strategy ahead of schedule and have now set ourselves a new goal: becoming one of the thirty most developed countries in the world by the middle of the 21st century. We intend to achieve this goal as a sovereign and worthy partner of the common Eurasian geo-economic area. I propose that our partners in the Eurasian Economic Union set the bar high: by 2050 we should aim to be in the world's top three integrated zones. The role of the Russian economy is very important in this regard. The growth of our association must therefore be based on principles of economic pragmatism; responsibility; evolutionary change and the openness of the Eurasian Economic Union. Kazakhstan has commenced its journey towards new heights from a high starting-point.

Last year we were ranked fiftieth in the Global Competitiveness Index. We came fiftieth in the ratings for ease of doing business, and are improving in this regard. By the end of 2013, Kazakhstan's GDP growth stood at 6%. The country's combined international reserves amount to around USD 100 billion. Clear goals in our modernisation process have been set and are being implemented in Kazakhstan. These include, first and foremost, the enforced industrialisation of the economy. As part of this programme, we built 780 new plants in four years and established 250 new product lines.

Today, 111 countries around the world are buying ready goods made by Kazakhstani firms. Each year we are opening hundreds of new innovative companies, including projects in the fields of electricity, energy-saving techniques and 'green technologies'. We were the first country in the CIS to adopt a development strategy based on a 'green economy'. We are seeing the development of such innovative clusters as the deep processing of raw materials in oil and gas, oil-related chemicals, and tourism.

We have laid the foundations for new sectors in the economy, which have never previously existed in Kazakhstan: manufacturing cars and aeroplanes, freight trains and passenger trains, satellites, electronic goods and much else besides. The agricultural sector is growing rapidly, as one of the regional centres of food production.

In 2015 we will finish constructing the 'Western Europe – Western China' transport corridor: 2,700 km long, it will transverse our country, and parts of it are also being built in Russia and Belarus. Along with our neighbours, we have built new mainline railways leading to China and South-East Asia, and we are finalising construction work on a railway to Iran and the Persian Gulf states.

Important changes are also under way in education. Around 20,000 young Kazakhstanis are currently studying at leading universities around the world. 10,000 graduates from the world's best universities are already employed in our economy, in our civil service, in manufacturing, or at our schools, universities and hospitals.

In Astana, a new, world-class university has been opened, and schools have been built across all regions of the country. Heart transplants and transplants of other organs have become a reality in Kazakhstani medicine, as have stem-cell treatments and other innovative practices. Life expectancy among Kazakhstani citizens is on the rise. This is possible thanks to the serious state funding that was directed into this industry. As you know, I have always had a special respect for the scientific legacy of the 'Eurasian school', particularly for the original historical concept set out by Lev Gumilev. This area has left us with a great many ideas which were ahead of their time. In the 21st century, the profound study of these ideas has a special relevance. Yet the most valuable thing of all, for those of us living in conditions of universal globalisation, is the fact that Gumilev's works give all peoples the opportunity to take pride in their unique historical and cultural code, and the fact that we are all Eurasians! Eurasian integration represents a great opportunity which the objective course of historical progress has opened up to us at the threshold between two millennia.

The idea of the Eurasian Economic Union, which has widespread popular support among the academic community and elsewhere, is now a detailed programme of practical action. The EurAsEU, the area of free trade incorporating most of the countries of the CIS, the Customs Union and the Single Economic Area of Kazakhstan, Belarus and Russia – is the fruit of the work we have done together. In the 21st century we have witnessed the compression of historical time. It is one of the challenges which the whole world is having to confront. Many of the practical issues of Eurasian integration need to be solved within a severely truncated time-frame.

For the sake of comparison, the process of integration in Europe required eleven years to create a customs union, thirty four years to establish a common market, and forty years to create an economic and monetary union. In those days, the historical background was different, and there was a different system of risks and challenges. Eurasian integration does not currently have so much time on its hands. The Customs union began operating as recently as in 2011. We must act given the time pressure in the global economy – the consequences of large-scale technological changes on the horizon in the 21st century, and other challenges.

The Eurasian Union may have to confront crises in the world economy, such as the one the EU is currently experiencing. Crisis situations could also develop in our own economies. The background situation in Ukraine means that this is not the best of times for us. There are a fair number of people who would like to see our idea fail. Therefore we must take these challenges into account as we sign the agreement on the Eurasian Economic Union.

These factors must not engender any kind of 'illusory' approaches to our decisions. Regrettably, there is an acute 'lack of patience' among experts – frankly speaking – who want to see the future economic union thrown together as quickly as possible, according to a template. Naturally, this would be harmful to the content of the agreement. I am not an advocate of such simplistic approaches.

Everyone must be clear that we are not creating a gleaming snowflake, which might melt whenever there are fresh changes in geo-economic or geo-political circumstances. For the sake of objectivity, I would like to underline that 'quick decisions' were taken in the past, regarding other certain integration associations in the CIS. Before that, too, in the 1990s, agreements were signed in various formats on the creation of common monetary, customs and economic areas and so on. Where are those unions today, though? Who remembers them now? They are nothing more than unsuccessful attempts, which are not even recorded in the history books in our schools. In the case of the Eurasian Economic Union, we don't have the option to make such mistakes or make empty declarations. To be frank about it, any oversight or omission at this stage could prove fatal to the integration process, depriving it of the support of business circles and millions of people.

This conviction lies at the heart of a series of fundamental positions that Kazakhstan took during the negotiation process for the creation of the economic union. This year, we are crossing an historical threshold as we sign the Agreement on the Eurasian Economic Union. At the same time, we should look today towards the future, by defining our strategy for our further course of action, over a minimum fifteen to twenty year timeline.

First and foremost, it is important to understand that the main mission of the Eurasian Economic Union, in the first half of the 21st century, is summarised in two important aspects. Firstly, in becoming one of the key economic macro-regions in the world. According to experts' calculations, in the current century the global 'economic centre of gravity' will move towards the East, to Asia – among other places, it will incorporate the territory of our future economic union. We are located between the biggest production centres in the world – the EU and the Asia-Pacific region. This gives us a natural competitive edge, as a geo-economic bridge between East and West, Europe and Asia. At the same time, we cannot simply be middle-men in the transfer of goods and technologies from one area to another.

The Eurasian Economic Union must immediately establish itself as a new centre for global innovation and a magnet for multinational business. Secondly, an important component of the mission of Eurasian integration consists of ensuring that each member state becomes one of the most developed states in the world. The Eurasian Economic Union must be a blessing rather than a burden for the peoples of all its national economies. We must have a clearly defined system of indicators measuring the impact of Eurasian integration in terms of increasing living standards among the population, and the productivity and competitiveness of the economy. Only by being committed to such an approach will we ensure that the 'Eurasian option' is attractive, erasing any doubts that might arise about the goals of the Eurasian Economic Union, goals which will be key to determining our destiny.

The whole process of Eurasian integration must be functionally and practically subordinate to finding a solution to this crucial two-pronged civilising mission. Only then will it be possible to ensure continuing success in Eurasian integration and all-encompassing public support for its aims and objectives. In my view, for the strategic development of the Eurasian Economic Union over the next fifteen to twenty years the following priorities should be adopted.

Number one. The formation of the basic conditions required to accelerate the innovative technological breakthrough by national economies across the whole Eurasian integration area. I consider it important to draw up and adopt a programme for innovative and technological cooperation in Eurasia for the period leading up to 2025.

It is important to define, without sparing any resources or strength, the common points of economic growth and establish a host of industrial consortia in the sectors with the strongest prospects, for example, in the deep reprocessing of mineral resources, aerospace, the chemicals sectors, engineering, agricultural production, energy and transport. I consider it important to establish a Eurasian Innovation Council, which could analyse the issues relating to our cooperation in innovation, on an equal footing for all member states. We must create joint research and development clusters, on both a bilateral and multilateral basis. Specific projects must become the driving force in economic integration: they must create competitive products and jobs, and draw more money to the national coffers.

Number two. The territory of the Eurasian Economic Union must become an advanced link in continent-wide infrastructure, on the scale of the whole of Eurasia. Here it is important to draw up and implement a number of projects. For example, we must create a unified Eurasian network for telecommunications, build a high-speed railway line along the route 'Minsk-Moscow-Astana-Almaty', modernise the existing network of roads and railways, particularly those leading to Europe in the West or to the Chinese transport systems in the East, and also implement the project for a 'Eurasia' canal: 'The Caspian Sea to the Black Sea'. Of key significance for the future Eurasian economy is the creation of a Unified internal gas transportation network, which could supply gas to all the national economies at identical, approved rates. We must draw up and adopt the joint programme, 'Eurasian energy', as a roadmap for deep-rooted integration of our energy complex. We have also proposed that Russia takes part in building a nuclear power plant in our country.

Number three. It is abundantly clear to me that the core of the Eurasian economy must be formed by SMEs. This is a hugely important issue in terms of ensuring that there is a flexible reaction to all possible global economic challenges. Institutes for financial or service support may be created on the basis of the existing Eurasian Development Bank. We must create an information and analytical infrastructure and scientific and practical infrastructure for Eurasian integration.

The creation of these mechanisms for the Eurasian Economic Union must become a focal point for top experts and academics in our countries, and a forum for agreeing and implementing our mutually beneficial strategies. It would make sense to establish a Eurasian agricultural academy, which can incorporate the scientific and practical potential of the national agricultural sectors. Cooperation in the agricultural sector will give a powerful boost to exports of foodstuffs, without creating competition between our agricultural producers.

Number four. The goals of the Eurasian Economic Union place particular demands on its legal and administrative mechanisms. These must form an instrument which is founded on firm principles, but at the same time is sufficiently flexible to react promptly to any changes. It is obvious that the structure and methods by which the bodies of the Eurasian Economic Union are managed cannot simply be copied from other integration structures. We need to seek innovative models for management, which satisfy our association's unique mission. This will protect them from bureaucracy and prevent civil servants in the national government bodies creating sinecures.

As you know, I have proposed that supra-national agencies for the Eurasian Economic Union be housed in Astana, which is located right at the heart of the Eurasian continent.

This was not a proposal born of ambition. It would represent a huge workload for our country. I based this proposal primarily on the need to have a balanced system for regulating the whole economic area. Secondly, it is based on the importance of removing all external suspicions with regard to Eurasian integration, from those who would claim that Russia is 'taking control of everything'. As another alternative, I would remind you that twenty years ago I called for a city which is at the crossroads between Europe and Asia to be made the centre of a union. I believe that it would be worth considering the Kazakhstani cities of Atyrau and Aktobe or the Russian city of Yekaterinburg as candidates. Astana would be better equipped for this role, however. Today, I would support the arguments for the creation of a new Eurasian conglomeration, a new centre of growth in the middle of the territory of Eurasian integration. It could be the cement that holds all the regulatory threads together, by dint of the fact that we would have roughly the same distance between the administrative centre of the Eurasian Economic Union and all the farthest corners of the common economic area.

Number five. I am firmly convinced that economic integration will take effect and will lead to deeper cultural and humanitarian ties between our nations. The 21st century is, without doubt, making the cultural sector the most important component of our national economies, producing a sizeable percentage in GDP growth. This includes tourism, including historical and cultural tourism, eco-tourism and medical tourism. It includes educational services, which are particularly important for our industrial and innovative development and our systems of governance. It includes the entertainment sector, sport and the information industry. At the same time, it is important that the process of cultural and humanitarian integration does not erode the spiritual and cultural diversity of the Eurasian area through the dominance of any one particular segment. I consider it unacceptable for there to be an erosion of the national component of any of our countries' cultures. It is therefore important that we encourage the study, in our schools and universities, of the history, literature, cultural legacy and languages of each other's states.

I consider it important that any Eurasian broadcasting corporations which are formed in our countries in the future use the state languages of all the countries involved in the process of integration. This will draw us closer together and lead to greater trust. I also propose that we declare the day of the signing of the Agreement on the creation of the Eurasian Economic Union to be the Day of Eurasian Integration.

This, on the whole, is my vision of the strategic path which Eurasian integration must follow in the 21st century. The construction of our economic union is not some sort of outdated dogma. We face the task of confronting many complex challenges in our times. The decision to pursue integration is not a 'magic wand', and no miracles are guaranteed. Time can persuade people that a decision is correct that few other phenomena can match. The experience of the past two decades since I published the idea of Eurasian integration only goes to confirm this. I sincerely hope that my approach and my vision for this important stage in the creation of the Eurasian Economic Union will receive backing in academic circles and among the public in Russia. I am deeply convinced that the 21st century will be a century of great flourishing for Eurasia.

Speech at the M.V. Lomonosov Moscow State University
"From the concept of the Eurasian Union to new prospects for Eurasian integration"
Moscow, Russian Federation, 28th April 2014

TWENTY-NINE

GLOBAL CHALLENGES AND SOLUTIONS

*At the 2014 Astana Economic Forum, the President of
Kazakhstan outlined the global challenges facing humanity and
shared his views on possible solutions to these issues.*

I am delighted to welcome you to our capital, which symbolises how independent Kazakhstan has grown in recent years. Our forum has been transformed from a regional forum for debate into a significant occasion in international economic life. The proposals and ideas put forward by the forum were presented during Kazakhstan's participation in the G20 summit in September 2013. The virtual platform for global debate, G-Global, is successfully operating and now has more than 4 million users engaging in discussions. The current forum is notable for the large number of people present: some 10,000 delegates from 150 countries. With the support of the UN, the second global anti-crisis conference took place during the Astana Forum.

The global situation is continuing to hold countries in a state of tension. We must be prepared for various scenarios in which global trends may develop. Alongside the reverberations caused by the global financial and debt crisis, which are refusing to subside, social tension in the Eurozone and the outbreaks of social unrest in Arab countries, we are also facing new threats today.

First of all, against the backdrop of the economic recovery in developed countries, there has been reduced competitiveness in developing economies. Experts are predicting a strengthening of the flow of capital, which, in negative scenarios, could lead to a reduction in investment in developing countries of 50% or more.

Secondly, income inequality is growing steadily, and is widening the disparity in quality of life between the rich and the poor, thereby fuelling social tension. International studies have shown that poverty and the growing gulf between the rich and the poor were the third most important global problem in a list compiled in 2014. This is not just a problem that affects poor countries. It is affecting people in Western Europe: Germany, Austria, Spain and France all cited the gulf between the rich and the poor as the number one cause of concern. According to data from the International Labour Organisation, the number of people out of work last year rose by a further five million.

Thirdly, against this backdrop of social tension, economic, social and political conflicts are becoming more frequent, sometimes assuming the proportions of military operations resulting in real economic consequences. The world has once again plunged into a phase of escalating tension and the expansion of military capabilities. Yet the principle of 'social' Darwinism, when only those who are strong are seen to be right, is destructive, because it leads to the destruction of everything that has been created over entire generations. We are paying too high a price today for conflicts which will not lead to solutions, but will merely make matters worse. A multitude of new issues are arising, which require solutions. Yet we have still not found solutions to the old questions about the role of the state in these new conditions, the architecture of the world's financial and economic relations, bipolarity and the Bretton Woods agreements.

We must be prepared that, in the medium-term, economic growth will be weakened considerably. Whereas, in the period from 2000-2007, the global economy rose at an average rate of 4%, in the years ahead it is set to fall to a level of 2.5%. In the real economic sectors of countries in Europe, the situation is likely to worsen rather than improve. GDP growth in the Eurozone in the first quarter proved to be twice as low as expected. Problems are also being experienced in the US economy, even though it was considered to have confidently seen off the effects of the crisis. The data for April shows that GDP in the US has grown by just 0.1%, and a number of banks believe that this adjustment will be followed by a downturn. The US imports more than it exports and consumes more than it produces.

A huge backward step in the current balance of trade is also characteristic of a number of other G7 countries, and also for many small and medium-sized countries. Risks for the world economy come in the form of speculative raw materials 'bubbles', traces of which are visible in a number of key sectors of the global raw materials market. The creation of 'bubbles' enables a large volume of cheap liquidity. The US, Japan, the UK and the Eurozone alone have poured more than USD 5.5 trillion into the economy. This action is, naturally, having an impact on developing markets.

In these circumstances, we must not allow ordinary people's social well-being to worsen. Today, almost 1.5 billion people live on little more than a dollar a day. Almost 2.5 billion people have an income of less than two dollars a day. That is nearly 40% of the Earth's population. More than 200 million people in the world are unemployed. 1.5 billion people are self-employed or do temporary work.

Many countries in Africa and Asia exist in the so-called 'poverty trap', whereby their extreme poverty engenders even greater poverty. The mindset that they are "too poor to develop", and the perception that has taken root in people's minds that poverty is the norm, are leading to dependency and marginalising countries and regions to the fringes of global development. At the same time, the poorest regions in the world are also the most dynamic in terms of demographics. In the period leading up to 2030, around 90% of world population increase will take place in two regions: Africa and Asia, where poverty averages 30%.

This will lead to a rise in global inequality in the distribution of wealth. According to assessments by the research institute at Credit Suisse, we have a current situation where approximately 40% of the world's wealth is in the hands of just 1% of its population. Meanwhile, around 70% of the Earth's population possesses just 3% of the world's wealth. Taking the demographic trends into account, this trend can only become stronger. Such a state of affairs could significantly undermine global development and provoke colossal social conflicts in the future. Instead of a post-industrial world, human civilisation will return to a time which experts are describing as the 'new Dark Ages'.

Ever since Kazakhstan gained its independence, the country has positioned itself as one that is taking measures to reconstruct the existing architecture of global development. We set a precedent by voluntarily deciding to decommission our nuclear arsenal. In 1992, during my first speech as head of an independent state at the UN, I put forward the idea of convening a Conference on Interaction and Confidence-building measures in Asia. The fourth CICA summit took place just a few days ago in Shanghai, indicating just how successfully this idea has been implemented. CICA's twenty six member states backed China's initiative for a new concept for development in Asia. An Asian bank for investment in infrastructure has been established for the development of those countries which are resurrecting the Great Silk Road.

We have risen from being a newly independent state, emerging from the ruins of the Soviet Union, to become a country that has held the chairmanship of the OSCE. At the historic OSCE summit in Astana, the Astana Declaration was adopted. Kazakhstan is geographically and historically situated between two geopolitical titans – Russia and China. Our great strength today, however, is that we have a balanced, multi-faceted political course. Against all expectations, we have preserved peace and harmony in a multi-faith, multi-cultural society.

It is essential that we all concentrate on our key task: reducing inequality and rooting out poverty. In a global world, it is impossible to live in harmonious sustainability when there are such serious problems in the world – particularly when they affect our near neighbours. The fire of the conflicts they create could spread to any country. In my view, if we are to solve these tasks, we must make progress in two areas.

Firstly, we must make maximum use of the potential of economic development, and not allow any significant new economic turbulence. Secondly, we must draw up a "roadmap for eradicating poverty", incorporating large-scale instruments for developing human capital in the poorest countries in Asia and Africa. It is important to depoliticise economic relations as much as possible. We must all avoid setting countries or regions against one another in an artificial manner, and refrain from using the rhetoric of conflict.

Kazakhstan has always followed the principle of "the economy above all". It is thanks to this that we are actively developing today. Kazakhstan has become one of the top-five fastest growing countries in the last fifteen years. We have now adopted the 'Kazakhstan-2050' Strategy and are completing tasks designed to provide all-encompassing modernisation. We are striving become one of the thirty most developed countries in the world. And we intend to achieve these goals through close integration with our neighbours.

We are not indifferent to what is occurring in our region. Any growth that comes at the cost of breaking away from our neighbours, of allowing them to descend into chaos and disorder, will ultimately make us all weaker – both the region and the world as a whole. It is essential that we have a new, more effective and just architecture for global economic integration. We are advocating the idea that the integrated associations and economic unions that have been created, or could be created, should not be set off against one another. On the contrary, they must cooperate with one another in a constructive and fruitful way.

Today, the work that has been done to form the Eurasian Economic Union is coming to its conclusion. We see in this union one of the competitive associations of countries, to rank alongside the two hundred or so other regional associations of countries around the world. In a few days' time, on May 29th, the Agreement on the Eurasian Economic Union will be signed in Astana. An important component of the Agreement is the task of establishing a common market for financial services.

In this regard, a national agency will be created in Almaty to regulate the financial market. Factors, including a favourable investment climate, further development of Islamic financing, and shared borders between countries in Central Asia, gives Almaty the opportunity to establish itself as the financial centre of the New Silk Road.

Another significant factor is the strengthening of the role of international institutions. In order to minimise political risks, it is essential that we devise an effective international inventory to guarantee investments and the performance of contractual obligations. In addition to a stable economic situation, we also require wide-ranging measures to ensure a sharp increase in economic activity in the poorest nations. This must become the main purpose and significance of the 'roadmap for eradicating poverty' that we are proposing. I see its key tools as investment in the individual and the development of entrepreneurship and infrastructure.

Kazakhstan has considerable positive experience in this field. At the start of the 2000s, when a period of dynamic growth in our economy began, we faced a choice: how to transform this growth into prosperity for our citizens? On the one hand, we had an opportunity to expand the reach and quantity of social support. This would have had an instantaneous effect, and people's prosperity would have started to rise. However, the choice we made was to invest in the individual. This is a choice which does not have a rapid effect, but leads slowly but surely to qualitative changes in people's living standards.

We began the implementation of the 'Bolashak' programme, thanks to which 10,000 young people, mostly from deprived families, received or are currently receiving a world-class education paid for by the state. We are investing heavily in the education and healthcare systems and into social infrastructure. Life expectancy in Kazakhstan has risen by 4.5 years over the last seven years. In a phenomenally short space of time we have managed to cut the level of poverty among the population by a factor of thirteen. We also managed to avoid any real divisions in society on the basis of incomes.

Today, we are prepared to share our experiences with other countries in the region. In particular, we can provide special programmes of grants, so that talented young people from all countries of Central Asia and other states can study at Nazarbayev University. In conjunction with the UN, the World Bank and other international organisations, we are willing to create a platform for the development of this complex 'roadmap for eradicating poverty'. A persistent battle to reduce poverty has been, is, and always will be my central objective for Kazakhstan. In 2004-2005, our country achieved the targets for the millennium set by the UN in terms of reducing poverty, ahead of time. In 2007, the Government of the republic set itself higher goals for development: 'TRT plus'. We committed to cut poverty among the rural population by 2015. In 2012, we undertook national consultations on the formation of a new global agenda for wold development after 2015. We believe that one of the main objectives for 'post-2015' global development is inclusive, social and just economic development.

In the 21st century, all countries and all politicians must learn to live in a G-Global world. To live on the basis of its principles of evolutionary change, trust, openness, tolerance and dialogue. Globalisation has undoubtedly brought the whole world much closer together and made it more transparent and accessible for everyone. Yet now, the world, having barely made it through the most difficult financial and economic crisis of our times, might once again sink into a state of recession and downturn. Attempts to balance the system of international relations on the knife-edge of curtailing global dialogue is a dangerous approach.

Firstly, Kazakhstan is particularly concerned that dialogue between leading states on issues of global nuclear security could come to a halt. This could undermine all that has been accomplished over the last few decades in terms of reducing the nuclear threat.

Secondly, we cannot but be concerned by the signs of the apparent powerlessness of the Organisation for Security and Cooperation in Europe in bringing an end to the conflict in Ukraine. One of the reasons for this is the lack of political will to reform this organisation, shown by its directors even after the historic Astana Summit of the OSCE in 2010.

Thirdly, Kazakhstan is deeply disappointed by the fact that some countries are currently replicating the worst legacies of the last century, lapsing into a lack of restraint and seeking to justify the use of force to resolve disputes. This is creating dangerous precedents for the rest of the world, effectively encouraging subjectivity in resolving inter-state disputes.

Fourthly, Kazakhstan wishes to express concern over the use of sanctions which effectively undermine the principles of free trade and a free market on a global scale. I wish to point out that such a practice has never been effective in international relations. It is one which restricts global economic growth, creating barriers to the formation of a just global energy system.

The fall in the level of trust in global politics is a dangerous process. For in the 21st century, global trust is closely linked with economics. The greater the level of trust, the greater the chance of restoring substantial growth in the world economy.

The start of the 21st century, in spite of great hopes for an improvement in the world order, has proved to be full of threats and new challenges. The global crisis which began six years ago is going nowhere fast. It is only expanding with each passing year. Humanity is thirsting for a radical new strategy for global development. I talked about this back in 2009, in my articles 'The keys to the crisis' and 'The fifth way'. Time has shown us that this is a crisis founded on archaic global growth models, from which a new world must be born. We are currently standing in the cradle of this new world.

In the current circumstances, it is essential that we give the G-Global project dynamism and application, and create a unified intellectual underpinning, and combine all the ideas and opinions expressed by the Astana Economic Forum over the years, with those that have been submitted to its portal. Beyond that, it is important that we should categorise the knowledge that has been gleaned by subject, year and author and analyse it to evaluate how this information can be disseminated through mass media, on social networks and in scientific works. We must also draw up a list of proposals to submit via the UN to other economic and political forums. I hope that this forum will make a contribution to the international debate about development and the creation of the conditions required for global inclusive growth. Those attending it will play a key role in setting the UN's Agenda in the field of development after 2015 and the achievement of new goals in sustainable development.

Speech at the 7th Astana Economic Forum
Astana, 23th May 2014

THIRTY

THE EURASIAN ECONOMIC UNION

*During the ceremony held at the Palace of Independence of the
Republic of Kazakhstan, three Heads of State – the Presidents
of Belarus, Kazakhstan and the Russian Federation signed an
historic document to establish the Eurasian Economic Union.*

I congratulate the peoples of our countries on the signing of the Agreement
on the creation of the Eurasian Economic Union!

We are combining our economic potential in the interests of the flourishing
of our peoples. The Union is an economic one first and foremost, and does not
touch upon issues related to the independence or political sovereignty of the
states involved. It is symbolic that this historic decree on the creation of the
Eurasian Economic Union has today been signed in Astana. Astana is located
right at the heart of Eurasia. It is the youngest capital in the modern world.
Many exciting chapters concerning international events have already been
written into Astana's history. The city has hosted congresses for the leaders of
global and traditional religions, summits for OSCE (Organisation for Security
and Co-operation in Europe), the Shanghai Cooperation Organisation, the
Organisation for Islamic Cooperation and other international organisations.
We are currently preparing to host the Global exhibition 'EXPO-2017'.

Kazakhstan has made an historic contribution to promoting ideas of Eurasian
integration. It was here, at the turn of the century, that the Eurasian Economic
Community was created and a host of important decisions were taken, which
have determined the course of, and the dynamics of, our integration process.
It is therefore entirely appropriate that Astana is the birthplace of the Eurasian
Economic Union. I have no doubt whatsoever that this will represent the
continuation of the great chronicle of friendship, good neighbourly relations
and mutual support between the peoples of Kazakhstan, Belarus and Russia. In
the 21st century, we must realise the potential of Eurasian integration together.

I first made public my initiative concerning the creation of a Eurasian Economic Union at the M.V. Lomonosov Moscow State University twenty years ago. Time has an exceptional ability to persuade – one that few other things can match. The experience of the last two decades in the history of the new Eurasia confirms this view. The idea of Eurasian integration received support from the President of Russia, Vladimir Putin, and the President of Belarus, Alexander Lukashenko. It was this support that enabled us to reach the point we are at today – the signing of this agreement. Together, we have commenced the practical implementation of this noble idea.

In the last five years alone, commodity circulation between Kazakhstan and the member states of the Customs Union has risen by 88%, reaching USD 24 billion. Our exports to partner states which are in the process of Eurasian integration have increased by 63% and now amounts to USD 6 billion. These are not merely abstract figures. Behind these statistics lie hundreds of companies and firms, and new areas of cooperation between partners from Kazakhstan, Belarus and Russia. This will mean thousands of new jobs. It will mean stability and an increase in the profits made by Kazakhstani business, as it opens up new sales markets for itself.

Armenia and Kyrgyzstan are currently taking specific steps towards acceding to the agreement. The deepening of Eurasian integration is in the interests of all our countries and peoples. One of the key goals is to bring together the capabilities of each member country for joint modernisation and more competitive economies. It is important that we learn from the experience of other integration projects – primarily the EU. What I mean by this is that none of the member states must be allowed to find itself at risk of a process of de-industrialisation. And there must be no decline in traditional industrial sectors or in agriculture. This is precisely what the recession in the European economy has taught us. Past experience throughout the world tells us that integration is first and foremost about providing long-term, stable conditions for economic growth and new opportunities for promoting the prosperity of our citizens.

We see the Eurasian Economic Union as an open economic community which is harmoniously woven into global networks, acting as a bridge between Europe and a resurgent Asia. As we surge ahead with Eurasian integration, we are moving carefully through all the phases one would logically expect: an area of free trade, a customs union, a single economic area.

Today, as we sign the Agreement on the EAEU, the largest integration association in the modern world has been enshrined into law. Its population – some 170 million people – is the seventh biggest. It is one of the largest consumer markets on the planet. Its member states account for around a quarter of all the valuable minerals, with a total value of some USD 40 trillion in today's prices. Our integration association is the world's largest exporter of energy resources, and, in recent years, of wheat for human consumption, as well. Member countries are self-sufficient in food and energy and have the communications infrastructure required both inside the common market and also with other countries. We are self-sufficient in the key resources which guarantee the member states' independence.

Thus, a new geo-economic reality for the 21st century has been born today. It was created through a massive effort. Let me be quite frank: the birth of the Eurasian Economic Union has been hard-won. Ahead of us lies the far from simple challenge of getting it going and developing it against a backdrop of global instability. Integration does not guarantee us an ideal life in and of itself. There will be new challenges and new tasks for us to resolve. We must be ready to solve them together and overcome all crises through our combined efforts.

We are creating a fundamentally new model of good neighbourliness and cooperation between the peoples of the great expanse of Eurasia. Its foundation will be high levels of trust, strong friendship and mutual support between our states – all of these virtues have passed the test of time and proven their worth. The Eurasian Economic Union is about new opportunities, first and foremost for millions of citizens living in our countries. Favourable conditions are being created for the growth of SMEs in all the member states. The labour markets of our states are being united, which is an important factor in increasing people's professional level and increasing labour productivity. Equal conditions are being provided to citizens for access to education services and social infrastructure in every state in the Eurasian Economic Union. The removal of internal barriers has already had a positive impact in strengthening our cultural and humanitarian ties increasing tourism between our countries. All of these benefits are abundantly clear to our citizens. And this is leading to broad support for the process of our integration among the people.

I would particularly like to address the young people of our countries. The Eurasian Economic Union is being created for you. It gives you the benefit of being able to secure a high-quality education and professional skills in any of the member states. Today's event is opening up new opportunities for the future of our countries, and, above all, for new generations.

It is for us to show the whole world that these decisions were the right ones and that our integration with one another is viable. I would particularly like to thank the heads of government and of the most important ministries in our countries for implementing the agreements which have been reached in such excellent fashion. I would like to highlight the contribution that has been made to the compilation of the draft Agreement by members of the Eurasian Economic Commission, and by countless experts from all three countries. A colossal amount of work has been done, and many difficult issues concerning the future activity of the Eurasian Economic Union have been resolved. A huge thank to you all! The new document must now be subjected to thorough examination and ratification by our countries' parliaments.

Today is a remarkable day for the peoples of Kazakhstan, Belarus and Russia. The Eurasian Economic Union is a new, durable mechanism for eternal friendship, cooperation and good neighbourly relations between our peoples. I believe that the twenty ninth of May is a day that deserves to be added to the list of significant dates for our countries, to be marked as the Day of Eurasian Integration. Once again I congratulate the peoples of our countries and all the participants and guests at the ceremony on the signing of the Agreement on the Eurasian Economic Union! Let the journey begin for our economic union!

Speech at the ceremony marking the signing of
the Agreement on the Eurasian Economic Union
Astana, 29th May 2014

THIRTY-ONE

FOREIGN DIRECT INVESTMENT

The 2015 Council of Foreign Investors focused on the participation of foreign companies in the second stage of the industrial and innovative development programme of the Republic of Kazakhstan.
At the meeting, the President of Kazakhstan announced a visa-free regime for citizens from the ten developed countries with the largest investments in Kazakhstan, to attract further international investment and capital.

Over the years, these meetings of ours have become something of a tradition, whilst the Council itself has become an open forum for debate on some of the most important topics both for investors and for Kazakhstan. On the May 29th this year, Kazakhstan, Russia and Belarus signed an Agreement on the creation of the Eurasian Economic Union. For Kazakhstan, a country which does not have a direct access to one of the world's oceans, the provision of free access to the markets of Russia and our other neighbouring states is of crucial significance. The building of effective economic ties between our countries is enabling amicable, benevolent neighbourly relations to be established in the region. At a time when there is instability in a number of countries and the investment climate is worsening, in Kazakhstan, this economic union is creating new opportunities for foreign investors. The aggregate size of the economies of the three states amounts to USD 2.5 trillion. It is a common market containing 170 million people, which operates on the basis of common rules and is creating the conditions necessary to provide free circulation of goods, manpower, services and capital. All of this is opening up new horizons for investing in Kazakhstan. The unique conditions that have been created for investors, the extremely low tax rates and the stability in relations between investors and the state, means that Kazakhstan is able to position itself as the best gateway for access to the vast market of the Eurasian Economic Union.

The subject of our assembly today is: 'Issues concerning the participation of foreign investors in bringing about the Republic of Kazakhstan's industrial and innovative five-year-plan'. The first five-year-plan for industrialisation began under difficult circumstances: at the time of the global economic crisis when there was high volatility in the major markets for the goods we produce. Nonetheless, we managed to safeguard jobs and create new ones, and attract investors to our manufacturing sectors. Within four years, 651 projects were carried out as part of our map of industrialisation, with a total value of around KZT 2.4 trillion, and approximately 70,000 jobs were created. One in seven of these projects was implemented with the help of foreign direct investment.

By way of example, the company 'Alstom' organised the manufacturing of locomotives in the city of Astana. In cooperation with Renault S.A., Nissan Motor Company and AvtoVAZ, a full-cycle plant is being built for the manufacture of automobile components. The pharmaceuticals factory AO Khimfarm, in the city of Shymkent, has undergone refurbishment with the help of the Polish company Polpharma S.A. In the Kostanay region, production of off-road vehicles has commenced, with the participation of the Toyota Motor Corporation.

The implementation of these projects and the attraction of investment are taking place in spite of the unstable economic climate in the world. The global flows of foreign direct investment are shrinking. Whereas in 2007, at the height of the previous economic boom, FDI was worth some USD 2 trillion, in 2013 it was down to USD 1.4 trillion.

In spite of these circumstances, Kazakhstan remains a stable and reliable partner for foreign investors. Our economy maintains its resilience and dynamism, in spite of the global crises. We are doing all we can to support investors and are constantly seeking to improve our support packages.

It was with this in mind that the second programme of industrial and innovative development was devised. The implementation of this programme will be a magnet for investors, and Kazakhstan must be one of the leading industrial, logistical and financial hubs on the two-way path between Europe and Asia. All the component parts of our economic policy will be tied to the objectives of industrialisation: monetary and credit policy, fiscal policy, rate policy and others. Such a transformation cannot be made without the support of foreign investors. In this connection, I would like to familiarise you with the founding principles incorporated into our partnership.

Number one. A stable macro-economic climate. For more than a decade, Kazakhstan has gradually built up a stable macro-economic environment. For this indicator, we are already in the top thirty countries in the global competitiveness index, achieving twenty third place in 2013. There are few countries in Central Asia and the former Soviet bloc that can boast a stable credit rating, a low level of state debt, inflation and unemployment, a high level of international reserves and, no less importantly, a proven ability to resist global crises. The government is systematically introducing a host of coherent measures aimed at creating the best possible conditions for conducting business. We have a progressive legislative base. In accordance with my directive dated the first of January 2015, scheduled inspections of entrepreneurs' activity will be abolished. Inspections will only be scheduled on the basis of a finely tuned system of risk assessment. An exhaustive list of permits and notifications will be drawn up and clearly defined, along with issuing procedures. In order to engage in an effective dialogue with foreign investors, we have established platforms for dialogue at the very highest level: the Council of foreign investors under the President and the Council for improving the investment climate, chaired by the Prime Minister. Forty eight inter-governmental agreements have been drawn up to encourage mutual protection of investments; conventions have been signed with forty six countries on the avoidance of double taxation; ten special economic zones have been created.

As I have mentioned, businesses operating in Kazakhstan will have access to the markets for goods, services and manpower in Russia and Belarus. In the near future we intend to accede to the World Trade Organisation. This will also create additional favourable conditions for foreign investors. Universally recognised international rules in the field of trade, investment, the protection of intellectual property and other areas will be applied in Kazakhstan. We are setting great store on our cooperation with the EU, increasing the two-way trade and investment each year. Joint work is already taking place on the development of a new 'Agreement on the expansion of cooperation between Kazakhstan and the European Union'. By 2015, a set of measures designed to move Kazakhstan into the thirty most advanced countries, based on the conditions for conducting business, will be drawn up.

Number two. Financial support for investors. All programmes, if they are to be implemented successfully, are dependent on provision of appropriate financial support. The implementation of the new programme of industrialisation and investor support will be given all the funding required. To this end, approximately KZT 600 billion will be set aside in the state budget over five years. We have also decided to earmark KZT 1 trillion from the National Fund. In addition, we have already signed framework agreements with the World Bank, the European Bank for Reconstruction and Development, the Asian Development Bank and the Islamic Development Bank. Under these agreements, at least KZT 1.3 trillion will be invested in Kazakhstan over the next three years.

In order to implement these plans, we have already created the Coordination Council, under the direction of the Prime Minister, whose members include members of Government and representatives of the international financial institutes which I have listed. Special sub-groups have been set up within the Council. They are drawing up development programmes on a variety of different areas within the economy. On the basis of these programmes, a concrete list of projects will be drawn up which will be implemented with full, all-round support from the Government.

Number three. A visa-free regime for investors. In order to increase the amount of business contact and international cooperation among businessmen, it is essential that we remove the barriers associated with visas. Today, we are announcing the unilateral establishment of a visa-free regime for the citizens of the ten states which have demonstrated the highest levels of investment activity in Kazakhstan. This list includes the USA, the Netherlands, the UK, France, Germany, Italy, Malaysia, the UAE, South Korea and Japan.

Number four. Laying the foundations for an innovative economy and training the workforce. Through our combined efforts, we will achieve huge successes in the strategically important area of Kazakhstan's innovative development. We are inviting investors to get actively involved in the implementation of our plans. I call on you to create corporate scientific and research centres and development centres, and to establish them within the grounds of the Science Park at Nazarbayev University, the 'Astana Business Campus'. I am aware that companies such as BG Group, Total S.A. and Chevron Corporation are already collaborating with the University. Among other partners that the University acquired more recently are Samsung Group, Hewlett-Packard, the Microsoft Corporation, Royal Philips and General Electric Company; these companies are all keen to establish R&D centres at the site.

At present, we are modernising our system for staff training. As a positive example of this I would like to highlight the initiative by the French company Eurocopter Group with the creation of a summer Academy. I want to ask other foreign companies to follow their example. In connection with this, I am ordering the Government to encourage foreign investors to get involved in partnering with our colleges and higher education institutions.

Number five. Public-private partnership. The Government must put into practice the principles of public-private partnership, using all existing mechanisms and new ones. It is essential that we concede to the private sector educational organisations, healthcare organisations, water supply organisations and organisations from other sectors which were traditionally the domain of the state. I also invite foreign investors to play an active part in the planned privatisation of at least 700 companies. Furthermore, I call on foreign investors to review their approach to purchasing goods and services in Kazakhstan. For example, by providing information at least two years before the planned acquisitions and entering into contracts for an equivalent period, you can give local companies the opportunity to be properly prepared, so that they can get involved in providing services to your firms. Some encouraging work has been done in this area by the company Tengizshevrooil, but it is important that we consolidate this work with all foreign investors. In addition to the measures I have listed, the

Government must resolve a host of issues which are obstacles to business. It is essential that by 2015 we have moved to a system of so-called 'Eurocodes'. Functions related to expert assessment in the field of construction must be transferred to a specific body. By 2020, the proportion of non-state expert assessment projects being conducted in Kazakhstan must reach 90%.

By the end of the year we must radically simplify the procedures for distributing plots of land for construction and increase the duration of leases for land plots intended for agricultural use. We must review the system for protecting intellectual property and effect a transition towards OECD standards in this field.

Number six. A new set of incentives for investment. The sectors which we are proposing to you for investment under the programme of industrialisation are specific areas with strong prospects:
• the traditional (raw materials) sectors, which provide a platform for economic growth and stable employment;
• the manufacturing industries, which are the biggest drivers of high-quality growth and diversification;
• innovation sectors, which will lay the foundations for a 'knowledge economy' and provide an opportunity for sustainable development in the long-term.

We will also continue to develop the service sector (tourism, SMEs, services), which is capable of providing mass employment. In order to make these priority areas more attractive, the Government has devised a large-scale set of incentives and state support based on global practices.

Number one, investors in priority sectors of industrialisation will be exempted from corporate income tax and land tax for a period of ten years, and from property tax for a period of eight years.

Number two, the state will reimburse up to 30% of capital expenditure once the facilities have been put into operation.

Number three, there will be no quotas or permits whatsoever as regards the importing of manpower for the duration of an investment project's implementation, and for one year after the facility has been put into operation.

Number four, investors will be given a guarantee of the stability of legislation as regards increases to the tax rates and fees, with the exception of VAT and excise duty.

Number five, a 'one-stop shop' principle will be introduced for investors working with state institutions.

Number six, the institute of an 'investment ombudsman' will be established, to protect investors' rights and interests.

Number seven, investors working in priority sectors will be given assistance in the form of guaranteed orders.

All of these exemptions will be set in stone under the investment contract between the Government and the investor. I have made allowance for the measures listed above in the amended version of the Law 'On investment'. This draft law was drawn up by the Government and approved by Parliament just a few days ago. Today I shall be signing the draft law in your presence, and it will thus be passed into law.

We are anticipating reciprocal measures from your side, and look forward to our collaboration with you, it will be in Kazakhstan's interests to do business as it will lead to further economic development.

Speech at the 27th plenary session of the Council of Foreign Investors
Burabay, Akmola Region, 12ᵗʰ June 2014

THIRTY-TWO

KEY ROLE OF THE FAMILY

The National Contest "Happy Family" was established in 2013 and has become an important aspect of state policy to strengthen the institution of marriage and support a family-centric, moral and ethical education for young Kazakhstanis.

I congratulate you on the conclusion of the first national competition, 'Mereili Otbasi' – 'Happy Family'! This is a triumphant occasion for all seventeen million Kazakhstani citizens! Our country is like one big home of peace and harmony, which we are building together as a single family. We have done this for evermore, so that there may be security, prosperity and wealth in this country for our children, our grandchildren and all future generations. So that everyone always has a roof over their head, the ability to study, to improve their health, to secure gainful employment and be able to put bread on the table. This is the most cherished thing that a people can have!

There is a profound meaning to today's celebrations. Firstly, the chronology of civilisation on the planet is a great story that shows how the human family forms the foundation of any society. Secondly, the family is the greatest possible asset. Throughout centuries and millennia and from generation to generation, the family has been the keeper of the moral fabric and the national traditions of every society. Thirdly, the family is an unquenchable source of love for one's people, its culture and daily life. It is the core of our patriotism and of our eternal concern for the flourishing of our homeland, seen through the prism of the happiness of our parents, children and grandchildren. It is the interconnectedness between the generations, which goes back centuries. Fourthly, in the 21st century, the era of globalisation means that the family and the values of a happy marriage have become important conditions for progress. This is confirmed by the experience of all successful countries in the modern world.

In the 'Kazakhstan-2050' Strategy, we have set out a lofty objective:

becoming one of the thirty most developed countries in the world. It is more than just an action plan. We are showing the way ahead for the future of our country, the future of our family. In the middle of the 21st century, the most developed states will be those in which a clear majority of families will be enjoying peace and prosperity. They will be those which raise their children properly, give them a high-quality education, genuinely care for their senior citizens and lead a healthy lifestyle.

As we created and strengthened Kazakhstan, we accomplished a vast amount of work in a short space of time. We transformed the country, and today a completely new generation is emerging, with new opinions and an eagerness to look to the future.

In the years of independence, in spite of all the complexity and global crises, the incomes of Kazakhstan's citizens have risen more than sixteen fold. The state's expenditure on education and healthcare has risen ten fold. We are carrying out an industrialisation process and building new companies, so that Kazakhstanis are able to have steady jobs and decent salaries. Through our support for SMEs, we are opening up new opportunities for hundreds of thousands of Kazakhstani families. We are implementing residential construction programmes. At present, around six million square metres of residential housing is being built every year in Kazakhstan.

These are very telling figures. All the more so given that in the 21st century, the world is becoming more complicated than ever. Just look at what is happening in the world! In many countries, people don't have the luxury of being able to think about economics and culture! For they are currently lacking the most important thing of all – peace, harmony and security!

According to UN estimates, there are more than 100 million homeless people in the world. There are 12 million children without a roof over their heads. 1.5 billion people are living in improvised housing with no electricity, water supply or proper sewage systems. Yet in our country, hundreds of thousands of families have seen their housing conditions improve in recent years. All of this represents extremely convincing evidence that we chose the right course and are doing all the right things, thinking only of our people's prosperity. We will continue this work. Our formula for successful forward movement is contained in one simple truth: prosperity for every family represents the flourishing and success of the whole of Kazakhstan.

Today, we need a more effective policy on strengthening the family, protecting new mothers and children and providing people with decent pensions in their old age. The society of universal labour that we are creating must also be a society of universal social responsibility. We cannot relax on the basis that many indicators for social welfare show that the situation in Kazakhstan is far better than in other countries – even in some of the most developed countries in the world.

We must not lose sight of the fact that regrettably there are still some unfavourable things happening in society. I am referring to the fact that each year, around 1,500 Kazakhstani children are orphaned. Many them are orphaned despite the fact that their parents are alive and well. At present there are around 34,000 orphaned children and children with no guardian in Kazakhstan. Almost 149,000 children have development disabilities and are in need of our support. More than 7,000 elderly people are living in care homes, even though many of them have able-bodied and successful children. Society must look on the abandonment of people's own children or parents as a shameful phenomenon.

We have to be concerned by the high level of drug and alcohol addiction among the population, and by the number of people infected with HIV. The problems associated with instilling moral and spiritual values in young people are very topical today. Often, even children and teenagers from wealthy families become subject to the influence of dubious, pseudo-religious movements. These are the challenges of our time, and they therefore require systematic measures to be taken by both the state and society.

Number one. A national plan of measures should be drawn up to strengthen family relations, morality and ethics as well as the spiritual and moral values in the Republic of Kazakhstan between 2015 and 2020. It must stipulate a whole range of measures involving charitable associations and the media. I am ordering the President's Administration and the Government to come up with proposals within two months.

Number two. The principle nerve centre and spiritual home of this crucial work must be the National Commission on Women's Affairs and Family and Demographic Policy, overseen by the President. We must strengthen the team working for the Commission, bringing in respected figures from civil society to participate in its work. I am ordering the President's Administration to take further action on this issue.

Number three. The further development of legislation on family and marital relations, children's rights, encouraging parents to take a greater responsibility for their children's upbringing, and looking after children whose parents are in old age by the time they reach the age of maturity. We must explore the introduction of legislative mechanisms for the protection of the elderly when they are attempting to find work, and from other forms of age-related discrimination. It is essential that we strengthen the favourable legal environment for citizens who adopt and bring up orphaned children. Such families must be given help from all quarters, with both the state and charities playing a role. It is pleasing to see that with each passing year, the number of people adopting children from children's homes is rising. We must strengthen the legislative foundations for expanding the practice of fostering and guardianship within families. In many countries there is a practice of 'host families', with whom children who have been left without a guardian are able to live, on a temporary basis. We must see what we can learn from such practices.

Number four. The systematic development of infrastructure for supporting families, young mothers and children, and worthy pensions for people in their twilight years. First and foremost, I am ordering that the idea of instituting a Commissioner for Children's Rights, using public funds, be examined.

We must form a unified, national database of orphaned children and children left without a guardian. A network of institutes should be developed which operate on a public-private partnership basis, providing all-round support to young families, single mothers, children and the elderly. We already have past experience of creating a network of crisis centres in Kazakhstan for mothers with new-born babies, 'Analar Oui'– 'The Home of the Mother'. This undertaking must be supported. Of particular concern is developing institutions for children with disabilities. I am giving the Government and the regional Akims the task of ensuring that in 2015, 100% of our special schools for children are equipped with the internet, multimedia teaching resources and interactive whiteboards.

Number five. We must strengthen awareness of work on family and moral values. It is important that we maintain societal intolerance for negative phenomena such as drunkenness and alcoholism, smoking and drug addiction, an irresponsible attitude to family obligations, and a lack of respect for the elderly. I call on all the media platforms to actively involve themselves in this work, by showing examples of families which are genuinely close-knit and loving to a wide audience.

Today, the state is creating the best possible environment for honest and worthy toil. Hard work is at the core of family stability. We have one of the highest levels of employment of any country in the world. At the heart of the 'Kazakhstan-2050' Strategy is the working individual. Those who dedicate their working lives to a specific profession – whether it be farming, building homes, assembling cars, teaching children, treating the sick or harvesting crops – are considerably more content with their lives than other people. They save for the future only what they have earned through the fruit of their labours. This approach has been proven both scientifically and by life itself. I am certain that the future lies in patriots who are committed to their work, in innovation and in industrialisation.

We have a vast land-mass and a population that is eager to interact and communicate with others. A people that loves visiting new places, engaging in trade, and finding new work. This is why we are building new roads. We have laid down more than 40,000 km of roads and over 2,500 km of railways. This work will continue. Never before have we built as much as we are building now! All this is being done so that Kazakhstanis can be brought closer to one another, for closer interaction and the ability to travel and engage in trade. It is being done so that not a single one of our regions may be deemed to be too remote from our capital, and so that Kazakhstan and every corner of it can forever be a comfortable, cherished home for every family and every citizen.

We gathered together today for the final of the first national contest, 'Mereili otbasi'. The contest has given us the gift of a huge number of beautiful, life-affirming stories about a great love and about caring for one's nearest and dearest, about overcoming life's hardships, about honest toil and about holding the family's honour dear. Fifteen different ethnicities were represented among the families which took part, whilst thirty four families contained more than one nationality. The entrants came from all manner of professions: there were teachers, doctors, firemen, athletes, policemen, scientists, farmers, people from the energy sector, oil workers, railway workers, and people from the arts. The stories of each family, taken together, add up to a great encyclopaedia of Kazakhstani life! The most worthy and deserving families are the winners of the regional contests. The stories of each family were so compelling that they could quite easily form the plot of a novel or a movie.

Speech at the awards ceremony for the winners of the national contest 'Mereili otbasi'
Astana, 19th September 2014

THIRTY-THREE

NATIONAL COMPETITIVENESS

The National Welfare Fund "Samruk-Kazyna" was founded in 2008 to manage state assets and increase competition and sustainability in the national economy. At the Forum, the Head of State set "Samruk-Kazyna" the objective of becoming one of the world's leading sovereign wealth funds.

The Fund for the prosperity of the nation, 'Samruk-Kazyna', includes some of the state's key assets: railways, oil and gas resources, hydrocarbon pipelines, telecommunications, energy facilities, the nuclear industry and an international airlines with over sixty routes to nineteen countries around the world.

The combined value of the Fund's assets is equal to half of Kazakhstan's GDP. In the last 3 years, the companies in the Fund have paid more than KZT 2.5 trillion to the state budget. 'Samruk-Kazyna' is one of the biggest employers in the country, employing some 350,000 people. The 'Samruk-Kazyna' Fund is effectively a second National Fund. It is the wealth of our nation, and contains the source of our present and future prosperity. The programme for transforming the Fund is based on change programmes implemented by some of the world's leading funds. It stipulates a number of objectives.

Firstly, to increase the value of the companies in the Fund; secondly, to increase the efficiency with which the portfolio is managed; thirdly, a clear delineation of responsibilities between the Government, the Board of Directors of the Fund, and the Fund and the companies in its portfolio. I wish to emphasise that we are about to commence work on solving an extremely complex task. The countries which have made progress in this area are enjoying impressive results.

The National Fund of Singapore, for example, Temasek Holdings, increased the capital of its companies more than three fold as a result of a transformation in 2004, from USD 54 billion to USD 176 billion. Temasek Holdings is in effect a private company, which manages state assets. The senior directors are appointed by the government; however, the state does not give Temasek Holdings any exemptions or preferential treatment whatsoever. 21% of the total capitalisation of the Singapore fund exchange consists of the assets of Temasek Holdings companies.

Successful transformation and the implementation of a new strategy have also worked at the Malaysian state investment fund, Khazanah Nasional, and the Fund of the United Arab Emirates, 'Mubadala'. Traditionally, the state has been considered less effective at management in comparison with private owners. But if state companies are managed on corporate and market principles, this problem can be successfully resolved. The most eye-catching example as far as we are concerned is provided by state companies in China. These are examples by which we can be guided, as we attempt to fulfil the colossal task we have set ourselves. It is essential that we create world leading companies.

The Samruk-Kazyna Fund must deal with these challenges which are of national significance. Within the context of the transformation, efforts must be directed primarily towards creating additional value for the companies in the Fund, so that in five years, total assets double and reach a value of USD 200 billion. Growth must be achieved by the creation of added value by companies in the portfolio. This can be achieved by increasing productivity and investing in highly efficient and profitable projects.

Furthermore, in five years' time, at least three of the companies in the Fund must be in the Fortune-500 list of the largest global companies. At present, this list consists mainly of Western companies with revenues of between US$5 billion and US$500 billion. Nonetheless, the number of Asian companies in the list has risen markedly in recent years. Between 2003 and 2014, the number of Chinese companies in the Fortune-500 rose from eight to ninety five, whilst the state oil corporation, CNPC (China National Petroleum Company), made it into the top five. There are also eight Russian companies in the list.

The key criteria for inclusion in the Fortune-500 list are the size of a company's revenue and the transparency of its financial reports. In terms of the size of revenue, at least two of the companies in the Fund – KazMunaiGaz and Kazakhstan Temir Zholy are already capable of making it into the list. Today, the companies held by Samruk-Kazyna have practically no competitors at all within the country – competition consists of multinational and state corporations from around the world.

At present, only Air Astana, which has brought in a strategic foreign partner, is providing real competition in the global market. And only Air Astana is managing to use capital more efficiently than its rival companies around the world. Kazatomprom and Kazakhstan Temir Zholy are also producing fairly good results in terms of capital efficiency. Yet the other companies in the Fund, unfortunately, are unable to boast such successes. Kazpochta and KEGOC are still local companies with a low level of efficiency, and cannot currently compete with equivalent companies from around the world.

For our companies to join the ranks of the biggest global players, the Fund must do the following: Number one; efficiency and productivity must be increased significantly. Rates of growth must not remain at two to three per cent: a jump of 30-40% is required over the next five years. To do this, we must actively engage strategic partners and investors, who offer technological production facilities, management expertise, and expert market knowledge. As a result, the companies in the Fund should be able to enter foreign markets and be competitive – primarily markets in the Customs Union and other states.

Number two; the Fund must develop its science and technology potential. A science and research centre for the Fund has been created at Nazarbayev University – this is just the first step. We need to create research labs within companies themselves, and recruit leading academics and scientific figures.

The amounts spent on R&D by Fund companies must increase ten-fold in the medium-term. Unless the Fund creates its own innovations, technologies and new products, it will never be able to raise productivity and break into global markets.

Number three; we must continue to implement the National IPO programme. We must involve as many Kazakhstani citizens as possible in the programme, so that each person can feel the growth of the economy as their own wealth increases. We must set clear rules, so that shares will end up in the hands of the people, not in the hands of a small number of quick-off-the-mark investors. It is essential that we have complete transparency in all procedures and full access to information.

Number four; the Samruk-Kazyna Fund must enable the development of the private sector in our country. Temasek Holdings once set itself the goal of not only managing state assets, but also creating new firms and sectors which would strengthen the country's economy. Thus, in the late 1960s, Temasek Holdings founded a small dockyard called Keppel Singmarine and turned it into one of the largest shipbuilding companies in the world. Temasek now holds 20% of the corporation's assets. Another example is South Korea: in the past it was a small and predominantly agricultural country, yet it has succeeded in building private industrial corporations from companies that were once small firms trading in fabrics, rice and car parts. Today, companies such as Hyundai, Samsung and LG are leaders in new technologies and manufacturing. The Samsung Group's assets alone are equivalent to 17% of the entire South Korean economy.

Samruk-Kazyna can also grow new industries and companies, and create and strengthen manufacturing processes. Once it achieves a certain level, the Fund could then leave these sectors, thereby contributing to the development of the country's private sector. It is in this capacity that Samruk-Kazyna should show its leadership ability.

Number five; another national task is to develop SMEs. By 2050, the contribution by SMEs to our GDP must reach 50%. Samruk-Kazyna must not be left on the sidelines. The Fund must create the conditions required to develop SMEs around each of its companies. The transformation is about creating the conditions required for the implementation of this objective, as only targeted businesses must remain in the Fund. Supplementary functions can be completed by SMEs.

There is also a requirement to ensure the involvement of senior representatives of government in the process of transformation, starting with the head of state. I believe this is one of the key conditions for the successful industrialisation of the country and to ensure Kazakhstan becomes one of the top thirty most developed states in the world. I will therefore be personally looking into this issue. Another important factor is recruiting young people to the Fund who want to work for the good of the state. It is essential that we promote such employees on the basis of their knowledge and experience, rather than on any other criteria. We must have a precise plan which incorporates clear deadlines. I am ordering the Prime Minister to organise independent monitoring, so that I can personally be aware of the areas in which the process is stalling, and take appropriate measures. Today is an important day for us all: we are launching the transformation and are determined to implement it. We have all the capabilities required to do so.

Speech at the Forum for the transformation of the
Fund for the prosperity of the nation, 'Samruk-Kazyna'
Astana, 6th October 2014

THIRTY-FOUR

ASIA-EUROPE COOPERATION

At the 2014 Asia-Europe Meeting, Nursultan Nazarbayev delivered a speech at the plenary session entitled "Promoting Financial and Economic Cooperation through Enhanced Connectivity between Europe and Asia." According to the President, one of the most important elements in strengthening relations between the two continents is to promote the potential for integration in the Eurasian region.

Thank you for bestowing on our country the honour of becoming a fully-fledged member of the ASEM (Asia-Europe Meeting). The task of searching for joint responses to the challenges and threats of the modern world means that the countries of Europe and Asia have a united agenda. I am convinced that the most effective method of overcoming the crisis must be to realise our continent's potential for integration. Today, countries in Asia and Europe account for more than 50% of global production. Two thirds of the Earth's population live in these two continents. In the decades to come, cooperation between Europe and Asia will determine global trends in development. I would like to share my vision of the prospects for cooperation on the Eurasian continent.

Number one: globalisation and the growing interdependency between the world's economies means that the world requires a paradigm shift in international cooperation. We must shift towards practical action on matters such as removing protectionist barriers, opening up new markets and increasing mutual trade. Kazakhstan has adopted a set of new incentives for market access for foreign investors. Investors have been given a ten year exemption from corporate income tax and land tax. The burden placed on business on the part of the licensing and permit bodies has been reduced. Stability has been guaranteed in the tax legislation. The Government is providing compensation of up to 30% of capital expenditure on investment projects. Kazakhstan has unilaterally lifted the visa requirements for the citizens of a whole host of countries. In the coming years, our country intends to accede to the World Trade Organisation. We are counting on the support of the ASEM's member states.

Number two: global financial architecture is still in need of transformation, which I have proposed to the global community on numerous occasions. The financial sector must not develop in a way that is detached from actual levels of production, at the global or national level. We need strong political will and a set of decisive measures designed to overcome the imbalances in the financial sector. There is a pressing need to create an effective model for regulating the international movement of capital. The speed and uninterrupted nature of financial operations means that new financial bridges are required to provide financial cohesion.

The regional financial hub of Almaty has great potential in terms of servicing financial flows in Europe and Asia. This would be of benefit to all and create strong prospects.

Number three: the development of transport and transit infrastructure is a key area; Europe requires a rapid, secure route to Asia. The Great Silk Road represents an excellent foundation. In 2015, Kazakhstan will launch its section of the 'Western Europe to Western China' motorway. This route will cut the time for deliveries of goods between Asia and Europe by two and a half times. We have completed the construction of main-line railways to China and South-East Asia. In the near future we will open a railway line to Iran and the countries of the Persian Gulf.

Number four: one of the pressing tasks we face is to provide access to modern technology and energy resources. By 2020, more than a third of the world's population will be experiencing a shortage of energy resources. Kazakhstan, as a reliable supplier of energy resources to both Europe and Asia, is further diversifying its energy routes. Today's priorities include such issues as the development of alternative sources of energy and the creation of environmentally clean technologies. In 2017, the International exhibition 'EXPO-2017' will take place in Astana. The theme for the exhibition will be 'The Energy of the Future'. We invite the member states of the ASEM to get actively involved in this exhibition.

Number five: together with Russia and Belarus, we have signed an Agreement on a Eurasian Economic Union. The EAEU will become a key link in the infrastructure chain, on the scale of the whole of the Eurasian continent. I would like to emphasise once again that the EAEU is an organisation that is strictly economic in nature. It would be wrong to look at it through the prism of the past. The EAEU provides unique opportunities and broad horizons for effective implementation of cooperation between Asia and Europe.

Number six: as a fully-fledged member of the 'Asia-Europe' forum, Kazakhstan is willing to provide full-scale support for the development of dialogue, mutual understanding and cooperation within our continent. A key forum for debate is the Astana Economic Forum, which attracts world-renowned experts, Nobel prize-winners, politicians and economists every year. I have also initiated the G-Global project, as a platform for approving international actions and producing a global anti-crisis plan.

In the 13th century, the great Italian explorer Marco Polo discovered Asia for his fellow Europeans. Today, Asia and Europe must discover one another all over again, and establish a radically new foundation for cooperation. I am deeply convinced that through our combined efforts, the 21st century will be a golden age for our great continent.

Speech at the 10th summit of the 'Asia-Europe' Meeting
Milan, Italy, 16ᵗʰ October 2014

THIRTY-FIVE

ISLAM AND DEVELOPMENT

In this speech, the President of Kazakhstan shares his views on the prospects for the development of Islamic countries in the context of global socio-economic challenges including poverty, population growth and environmental degradation.

'Information partnership for economic growth', is an important current topic. Against the backdrop of the global financial and economic crisis, economic growth remains an important factor for the stability of states and the development of their economies. The members of the Organisation of Islamic Cooperation currently control 70% of the world's energy resources and export 40% of raw mineral materials. Yet the countries in the organisation only account for 7% of global GDP and just 11.25% of the total volume of global trade turnover. There is a need for decisive cooperation and the adoption of initiatives to meet and overcome the global challenges we face. The Muslim world is currently facing such problems as rising population numbers, poverty, the gradual depletion of natural resources and the worsening state of the environment.

During Kazakhstan's chairmanship of the Organisation for Islamic Cooperation, the Astana Declaration was adopted, to promote modernisation and reform as the foundations for the Islamic world's development in the 21st century. Kazakhstan remains a firm advocate of further strengthening and development of the Islamic world on precisely this platform. As you know, we have now been an independent nation for twenty two years. After the break-up of the Soviet Union, a new country appeared on the world map: Kazakhstan. In this short space of time, we have completed a long journey, growing our economy sixteen-fold and increasing GDP per capital from USD 500 to USD 13,500.

We are a multi-ethnic country which respects all religions, languages and cultures. The stability of Kazakhstan, which is home to representatives of more than 100 ethnicities and forty six religions, sets a fine example of the development of a modern society. Kazakhstan has been slowly but surely implementing the priorities it set itself in creating an alternative, innovative-industrial economy. We are striving to create a system of mutual assistance in food production, and policies for supporting SMEs.

As part of our new innovative-industrial programme, we are working closely with our partners: the United Arab Emirates, Iran, Turkey and Malaysia. The volume of investment from these countries is currently in excess of USD 3 billion, and we are working on more than fifteen potential projects worth a total of USD 2.5 billion.

Kazakhstan is creating all the necessary conditions to attract investors. We have built transport and logistics infrastructure, we have built or renovated more than 10,000 roads and 2,500 railway lines. The distance between China and the Persian Gulf has been reduced to 1,200 kilometres.

As a land-locked state, we are striving to build amicable relations with our eastern neighbours – the People's Republic of China, with whom we share a border that stretches for 1,700 km, and with our northern neighbour – Russia, with which we share a 7,000 km long border. The city of Almaty will be the key link in the global project to restore the Silk Road, which will connect the Pacific Ocean with Western Europe via China.

Kazakhstan could become a global centre for food security. The total land area set aside for agricultural purposes in our country amounts to ninety million hectares, of which twenty five million hectares are arable and sixty one million hectares are suitable for grazing. At present, we export up to ten million tonnes of wheat. A further increase in agricultural sector investment would lead to a three-fold increase in the amount of food we produce.

The work we do with the Islamic Development Bank is extremely important to us. Kazakhstan was the first of all the former states of the Soviet Union to draw up a partnership programme with this bank. The bank is taking part in a new programme of cooperation with international financial organisations for 2015-2017, worth a total of USD 13.5 billion. The bank is committing more than USD 1.5 billion to the programme. In addition to attracting funds, the institutions in the Islamic development bank group are providing significant advisory support for the development of Islamic banking in Kazakhstan. In 2007, the President of the UAE, Sheikh Khalifa bin Zayed bin Sultan Al Nahyan, and I took the joint decision to open the first Islamic bank, Al-Khilal, in Kazakhstan, with capital of USD 500 million. We are positioning our biggest city, Almaty, as a regional hub for Islamic financing for the countries of the CIS and Eastern Europe. The relevant laws have been passed and the Islamic financial instruments are in operation.

Kazakhstan's active participation in introducing and growing Islamic financing has resulted in our receiving an international award as a 'Global leader in the field of Islamic finances'.

Speech at the 10th International Islamic Economic Forum
Dubai, UAE, 28th October 2014

THIRTY-SIX

CHALLENGES AND ACHIEVEMENTS

In this chapter, Nursultan Nazarbayev highlights
Kazakhstan's main achievements over the years since independence
and outlines the key challenges facing the country.

Today we are confidently achieving yet another milestone in our great history. The passage of time is pushing us further away from that day, on December 16th, 1991, when the Republic of Kazakhstan first declared itself to be an independent state. And with each passing year we are becoming more deeply aware of the everlasting, historic strength of the choice which our people have made. The decision to live in a free, sovereign state, in peace and harmony, trusting one another. The decision to determine our own fate and build our own future.

The great spirit of independence unites us all, making us stronger and surer of ourselves. It is embodied in every new-born babe born into the world under the bright and sunny skies of Kazakhstan. It is within every citizen of the country and in every Kazakhstani family, in every newly built house and every town, village or city. It is strengthened as our economy grows, as each new industrial project is unfurled, as each new highway is laid down across the vast expanses of our Motherland, with each tonne of golden wheat that is harvested from our fields.

Independence was hard-won through the efforts of many generations of our forefathers, who gave their blood and the sweat of their brow to defend our sacred land. Independence represents the unwavering determination of every citizen to defend Kazakhstan until the last drop of blood is let, as our heroic ancestors willed us to do.

The domestic and foreign policy that we have implemented stems from the wisdom of our people. The wisdom of the friendship, support and unity of all Kazakhstanis. The wisdom of our 'Kazakhstan-2050' Strategy, and of all the decisions on which so much depends, the wisdom and the dignity of our people, the hospitality and magnanimity we show to our friends and partners around the world.

Independence is about the efforts that each and every one of us puts in. It is about the efforts made by schoolchildren and students as they make sense of science. It is about the efforts of all the professions which serve to enhance our national wealth. It is about the efforts of all Kazakhstanis, as they bring up each new generation in boundless dedication to our Motherland.

Independence is the great unity of our people, with its unique state language, history and culture, and respect for the ethnic languages of all Kazakhstanis. All of this represents the philosophy of independence – embodied in life. By adhering to this destiny strictly, we will forever hold aloft the heavenly banner of our Motherland, proudly lifting it to ever newer heights of development in Kazakhstan. May it be ever thus!

Our worthy response to the global challenges we face was the new economic policy, 'Nurly Zhol' ('Bright Path'). First of all, it involves placing our bets on infrastructural development against the backdrop of global volatility – this is a characteristic common to successful nations in today's world.

Secondly, by building high-quality roads and lines of communication, we are deepening our cooperation on regional and global economic ties.

Thirdly, our grand projects concerning the construction of infrastructure hold the key to stability in foreign investment. They will ensure that we are able to enjoy sustained economic growth.

Fourthly, it is a strong guarantee of employment, an increase in labour productivity and the prosperity of the nation.

Fifthly, 'Nurly Zhol' represents new opportunities for all the regions.

The new economic policy, 'Nurly Zhol', would be impossible without the National Fund. Thirteen years ago, we created it as an important mechanism for ensuring economic security. It has played an important role in helping us overcome the after-effects of the global crisis of 2007-2009. Even now, the National Fund is rescuing the economy as prices tumble in global markets. We are investing in infrastructure and manufacturing and helping business, SMEs first and foremost. At the same time, the National Fund, far from growing smaller, has risen almost four-fold over the last five years! The new, one-off investment in the economy will include new mechanisms for growth.

There are difficult times ahead. The crisis and the sanctions introduced in world politics increase the risks to the global economy. All countries are finding it hard going at present. The global markets in hydrocarbons, metals and the other products that we export are falling. We are going to have a tough time, too. And we must take this into consideration. We will therefore need to take steps to reduce expenditure in the budget that has already been approved. This will not affect social expenditure, however. As you know, I have already ordered the Government to fulfil all its social obligations to the people.

Today, the Government and the National Bank face two more important tasks. Firstly, the 'de-dollarisation' of the economy. Secondly, the transition towards targeted inflation. These must be the component parts of the new economic policy, 'Nurly Zhol'.

Crises never last very long. This one, too, will eventually pass. We will revert to the plans we introduced and we will overtake our previous rate of growth in all areas.

The great, historic feats of the current generation deserve a special place in our history. We have completed a magnificent journey. This journey saw the birth of the Assembly of the People of Kazakhstan in March 1995. It saw the adoption by the nation of our Constitution, on 30th August 1995. It saw Astana declared the capital of our homeland in 1998. Our main city has become a truly sacred place to all Kazakhstanis, the symbol of our common love for the Motherland.

We, the modern generation of Kazakhstanis, as a united people, have identified an 'axial age' in our country's modern history, the direction we must take in the future. We have also altered the course of the country's historical development and made it more dynamic. For the first time in our history, we have not followed the course of events, but have instead overtaken events, by proposing first the 'Kazakhstan-2030' Strategy and now the 'Kazakhstan-2050' Strategy. Every single year of the 21st century will go down in history as a time of growing success for our country. We, the modern generation of Kazakhstanis, have the genuine creators of the great chronicle of the new Kazakhstan. We have created a new country and given our people a new destiny!

In a few days, we will turn over the first page of the New Year, 2015. First of all, events will be held to mark the Year of the Assembly of the People of Kazakhstan and the twentieth anniversary of the adoption, by the whole nation, of our Constitution. These are the main foundations of our statehood.

Secondly, we will celebrate an important date in our national history and culture: the 550th anniversary of the formation of the Kazakh Khanate.

Thirdly, along with the other countries of the CIS and the rest of the world, we will celebrate the seventieth anniversary of the victory over fascism in the Second World War. The memory of the achievements of the generation which fought in the war is something that we will cherish for all time.

We are a people who have, for all time, related to our past with gratitude and forgiveness. Our interpretation of our past history has always been one that is fully rounded and positive. It must unite all Kazakhstanis, rather than divide them.

We have, for centuries, shared the same historical path as Russia. At present, our shared history represents a firm foundation for integration in the context of the Eurasian Economic Union. This idea, which I put forward twenty years ago, has now been enshrined in law. It will become reality as of 1st January 2015, when the EAEU starts operating. At the moment it incorporates Kazakhstan, Belarus, Russia and Armenia. The new economic union is open to other countries as well.

The chronology of time links us to the history of China, over several millennia. With each passing year, the friendship and strategic partnership between us and the People's Republic of China grows stronger. Today, we are restoring the Great Silk Road, thereby transforming the region covered by the Shanghai cooperation organisation into a transport and trade bridge with Eurasia.

Our historical spiritual and cultural ties with the countries of Asia are enriched by the successful work by the Conference for Interaction and

Confidence-building measures in Asia. This year, we proposed that an Organisation for security and development in Asia be created within it. In nearly two and a half decades of independence, we have established cooperation with the United States, the EU and many other countries. They are our friends and our strategic partners, with whom we are working together in the name of peace and stability. This work takes the form of congresses for the leaders of global and traditional religions, the creation of a Central Asian zone free from nuclear weapons, the Astana summit for the OSCE, the 'Partnership for peace' programme and dozens of joint economic and cultural projects.

This year, we completed the preparations for a draft agreement on a long-term partnership between Kazakhstan and the EU. The process of Kazakhstan's accession to the WTO (World Trade Organisation) has entered the finishing straight. Ahead of us there still lies the task of writing a 'golden chapter' of world history, about the forthcoming international exhibition 'EXPO-2017' in Astana.

Kazakhstan's national history must always be founded on the principles of uniting our society, in friendship and mutual understanding with our neighbouring states. It is with this in mind that Kazakhstani history books should be written, scientific research should be undertaken, and the educational process in our schools and universities be developed. The whole history of the Kazakhstani people, the whole history of independent Kazakhstan, is a history of unity and togetherness. Nurturing this unity is the highest good we can do. In the 21st century, only those countries which achieve strength through unity, joy through hard work, and friendship through their people, will survive. We, the people of Kazakhstan, have taken this idea to our hearts. In the years since independence, we have become inured to difficulties and strong in spirit.

We are one of the 193 member states of the UN. Each of us has our own particular plans and our vision for the future. Human life-spans are limited to just 'three score years and ten'. The life of a people grows longer with each new generation. There can therefore be no greater dream than the dream of a people that endures for all time. 'Mangilik El' ('Eternal Country') is an idea which opens up tomorrow to us, expressing our faith in the future; it is a symbol of irreversible, durable stability.

The 'Kazakhstan-2050' Strategy is a path designed for millions, along which many generations of our descendants will be destined to travel, until that historic date which we have earmarked, thirty six years from now. In 2050, the generation born at the time of independence, in 1991, will become the older generation, for the young Kazakhstanis just entering adulthood at that time. They, the children of independence, will be around sixty years old. They will become a generation of elders.

There is an old Kazakhstani saying: *"Elu zhylda – el zhana"* (*"The world becomes new every 50 years"*) These words were spoken back in the days when there was no scientific or technological progress, nor any innovative technologies. Our era is a time of great acceleration in so many walks of life. In the 21st century, society changes radically every five years or so. There are therefore two key rules which determine the fate of a nation. Number one. The succession of generations and the passing on of values. Number two. The nation's dynamism and the innovation shown by its young people.

We must bravely take charge of our history. We will grow even stronger if we are always united. This is the key to the thousand-year meaning of our shared national idea of 'Mangilik El'

Speech at the assembly celebrating Independence Day of the Republic of Kazakhstan
Astana, 15th December 2014

THIRTY-SEVEN

FIVE INSTITUTIONAL REFORMS

At the 2015 Congress of "Nur Otan", the party nominated Nursultan Nazarbayev to compete in the early presidential elections held on April 26, 2015. In this speech, Nursultan Nazarbayev presented his election platform consisting of five institutional reforms.

We have completed a great journey since we first obtained our independence. Our country has become one of the fifty most competitive countries in the world. Our GDP has risen twenty-fold and in 2014 stood at USD 13,000 per capita. Today, we are working to achieve the main goal contained in the 'Kazakhstan-2050' Strategy: to become one of the thirty most developed countries in the world.

Over the last four years, all the tasks that I spoke about during the campaign in 2011 have been completed. Firstly, GDP has risen by 5.7% on average each year. The first five year plan for enforced industrial and innovative development has been completed. Secondly, the agricultural sector has been given a powerful boost in its development. Thirdly, big changes have been made in our infrastructural sectors. Fourthly, SMEs are growing. And fifthly, Kazakhstan is now steering a course of social modernisation. Since 2010, the people's income has risen by 43%, and average monthly salaries have risen by 64%, nearing KZT 130,000. The social welfare payments made by the state have risen 1.4 fold, and the minimum pension has risen by a factor of 1.8.

Number six: in four years, large-scale administrative reforms have been introduced. The state apparatus has been reformed. 60% of the functions of the Government have been put into the hands of the ministries and Akims. The number of ministries has been streamlined, reduced from seventeen to twelve. Nine agencies have been made smaller and joined ministries as committees. Elections have been introduced for the Akims of cities of district significance, and also for Akims in the countryside. Deep-seated reforms are underway to the law enforcement agencies and the judicial system. A fierce campaign is being waged against corruption. The secular nature of the state has been strengthened, as the basic foundation for our multi-faith harmony and peace.

Number seven: the authority enjoyed by the country on the international stage is set to grow stronger.

On the whole, everything that we have planned has been accomplished! A gigantic step forward has been taken! This is a victory march for us all! At present, the global situation is growing ever more complex. The collapse of prices for energy resources and metals in the world's markets has led to a dramatic rise in economic risks. Almost all countries are facing serious geo-political and economic challenges.

Kazakhstan's response to the economic risks has been its new economic policy, 'Nurly Zhol' ('Bright Path'). It includes, firstly, measures to counteract the economic turbulence within the context of state programmes for infrastructural development, and secondly it stipulates that the course of industrialisation will be continued in the second five-year period. Our social policy has also been clearly defined. The tough policy with regard to the budget and savings will not affect the state's social obligations.

At the same time, the global challenges and risks are so deep that they raise questions about the durability and success of each and every state. We therefore face new challenges. First of all, we must not allow a scenario to unfold, whereby negative external factors affect state development. Secondly, we must preserve the rate of growth that we have attained. Thirdly, we must prepare the necessary conditions for long-term development. Fourthly, we must continue to push towards the top thirty most developed countries in the world.

We need an extraordinary, powerful response to the global challenges facing our state faces. We must not stand still. On the basis of the successes we have achieved, we must move forward to strengthen our statehood. I am therefore proposing five institutional reforms.

Number one: the formation of a modern, professional and autonomous state apparatus, which ensures that economic programmes are delivered and state services provided in a high-quality manner.

Nowadays, one cannot help but note that the administrative services of the state are dependent on the political stratum. This politicises decision-making even in cases where professional governance without politics is required. In the state apparatus, teams are formed around a particular benefactor. Such patronage creates ripe conditions for corruption, nepotism and reduces the potential of the workforce. Simultaneously the civil service remains fairly unattractive given the low salaries on offer. Civil servants have no clearly defined career prospects, and promotions are dependent on the notorious benefactors I mentioned before. I am aware that important state programmes and projects are suffering due to the incompetence of particular civil servants at various levels.

An important task we face therefore is to make the body of civil servants professional and autonomous. Elections, and replacement of the ministers, Akims and other senior figures must not affect the work done by the administrative civil service. We must move from the current system, whereby people are appointed to positions, to a career-based model for the civil service. Every director must start at the bottom and move up through the various managerial levels.

We must bring in a new system for salaries of civil servants based on their performance and contribution to the managerial process. Every year, we should consider if bonuses should be paid to political civil servants, and awards to administrative civil servants, based on the results and successes they have achieved in the economy. If they have done a good job, they will stand to receive a bonus. If they have not done a good job, and there is no growth in the economy or in their results – their pay will fall.

The time has now come to open up new channels in the search for talented civil service candidates, including in the private sector. It makes sense to bring in foreign managers for certain roles. The fact that such people might hold a different citizenship or not speak our language, should not be an obstacle here. This is how many successful countries do things.

The qualification requirements for acceptance to the civil service must be toughened. We must bring in full testing of civil servants at all levels. It is important that we arrange systematic work to protect the principles of meritocracy and a zero tolerance for corruption. To this end we should organise, within the structure of the Agency for the affairs of the civil service, a separate, independent department to counter corruption.

Meritocracy must become the overriding principle not only for the state apparatus but also for the entire civil sector, including our courts, law enforcement agencies, national companies and holding companies. We must draw up a new law on the civil service and make amendments to the law on the fight against corruption.

Service to the state must be the basis for strengthening unity in our society. The civil service should become a prototype for a just Kazakhstani society, in which everyone is given equal opportunities for self-fulfilment based on meritocratic principles, regardless of ethnicity.

Number two: we must ensure the rule of law, guaranteeing rights to property and creating the conditions needed for entrepreneurial activity, and protect contractual obligations, which, ultimately, will become a basis for economic growth. Today, the weakest link in the judicial system is the recruitment of judges and their qualification requirements are ineffective, which often results in corruption among them. Judges must not be a corporation which is divorced from society and beyond public criticism. Openness is a cure for the corruption we have noted among our judiciary.

The work of the agencies of the interior ministry also is opaque as far as society is concerned. The police must work to raise the level of confidence society has in it. Citizens currently find it hard to believe that an officer in the transport police would be prepared to fine an Akim or a minister for breaking the rules of the road. I could cite a recent example involving the US Secretary of State, John Kerry. He was fined for failing to clear away the snow outside his house.

It is thus essential that we raise the status of police officers and make them more accountable to citizens. We must draw up a set of measures to ensure transparency in the law enforcement agencies, develop information technology and provide video recorders to those on patrol. It is important that we bring in a new system of professional and psychological recruitment testing for the police, to ensure that police officers regularly improve and build on their qualifications.

We must tighten the qualification requirements for judges. Candidates aspiring to a position as a judge must have at least five years' experience of working within the legal system, and not merely as a notary public, police officer or at a legal college or university. Candidates must undergo a tough examination session as a condition of their practical judicial experience, held in the courts, and lasting at least a year. All judges in senior courts must spend time working in the courts of first instance. It is also important that we introduce, for those of our judges who are just starting out, a trial period of at least a year. Upon successful completion of this period, they may be recruited as judges.

Foreign and Kazakhstani investors must be convinced that Kazakhstani justice is dispensed in a fair and just way. In order to increase the level of public confidence in the justice system, foreign judges must be brought in to examine disputes concerning investment, and must try these cases in line with the best standards used in foreign and international courts.

Of particular importance is the issue of modernising the country's Armed Forces. They must be modern, mobile and professional. The army's battle-readiness should be enhanced by increasing professionalism and provision of advanced equipment and machinery.

Number three: industrialisation and economic growth, founded on diversification. A professional civil service and rule of law will create the conditions needed to implement the economic reforms designed to accelerate the formation of a middle class. In order to achieve qualitative growth and diversification in the economy, we are implementing a programme of industrialisation. It is a modern programme and an essential measure. Industrialisation is not only a tool for the economy, but also an important factor in the state's development and the formation of the middle class. However, industrialisation and the manufacturing sector have not yet become real drivers of economic growth. The Government must solve this problem.

There are imbalances within the system of state support for agriculture. Colossal sums are being allocated to the agricultural sector in the form of subsidies for production of goods with low added value. Yet agricultural producers are hardly paying any taxes. Today, it is important that we develop the sector for reprocessing agricultural raw materials on the basis of a new, complex programme. In this regard, we must set about implementing around ten major projects involving multinational companies in the reprocessing sector. Industrialisation must create jobs via SMEs and develop the country's export potential.

Customs procedures are currently very time-consuming, rates policy is complex and muddled, and the non-rate barriers run counter to current international practices. We must undertake large-scale work to simplify the rates policy in the context of the Eurasian Economic Union. A key task, in the long-term, is to ensure dynamism in our economic development. The outcome of the work we do must be the emergence of three or four new export products, via economic diversification.

A key area is the development of small and medium-sized service firms in the service sector. We must adopt a new programme to develop tourism. This is an important factor in absorbing excess labour resources in rural areas. We have poor levels of urbanisation. 43% of the population live in rural areas.

In previous years, during the course of Kazakhstan's integration policy, extremely important mechanisms were established to expand our economy's involvement in global economic networks. The process of creating a financial centre in Almaty must move forward more rapidly. In this regard we must enshrine Almaty's special status using the legislation.

Number four: a nation with a shared future. We have achieved notable successes in the development of our own model of stability and harmony. The Constitution of Kazakhstan guarantees that all citizens have equal rights, regardless of creed, ethnicity, religious beliefs and social status. At the same time, it is essential that we continue to strengthen Kazakhstan's identity. This must be founded on the principle of citizenship. All citizens must be able to call on the same rights, bear the same burden of responsibility and have equal access to opportunities.

Our unifying values, centred on the idea of 'Mangilik El' ('Eternal Country'), are civil equality, hard work, honesty, the cult of learning and education, and a secular country – a country of tolerance. In this case, citizenship will be the most reliable foundation for a sustainable and successful state.

The development of a triad of languages – Kazakh, Russian and English – is the cost of uniting our society and making it more competitive. We must ensure that we have effective social mobility for all the citizens of Kazakhstan, with no discrimination whatsoever based on differences or disabilities.

Our main goal is that Kazakhstanis should set the new national values – the rule of law and state traditions – above their own ethnic behavioural models. The Eurasian idea is one that unites all Kazakhstanis, given that in the Kazakhstani people there is a genuine synthesis of the best qualities of Asians and Europeans.

The middle class must be seen as the foundation of the Kazakhstani nation, a source for a professional state apparatus. It is the driving force with the largest vested interest in the rule of law, the state's accountability before the people and stability in the country. A broad middle class is thus the key to our national identity. Our common value system for all citizens must be the idea of 'Mangilik El', a state document which was drawn up at a critical time. In our schools we must bring in a programme of study to teach the values of the all-Kazakhstani idea of 'Mangilik El'.

In our country, seventeen different faiths live side by side in peace and harmony. The biggest of these are Islam, Orthodox and the Protestant faith. Khanafit Islam, which has historically existed on the land of Kazakhstan, is notable for the importance it places on moderation and patience, and a wise interpretation of the Islamic values. Orthodoxy, the faith to which most of the Slavic population in Kazakhstan adheres, sets great store by matters of conscience, on the individual's moral choice, and on kindness and compassion. In recent years, there has been a significant increase in the congregations of Protestant churches in Kazakhstan. The Protestant faith places successful and productive labour at the centre of the individual life, along with such values as frugality and benevolence. Thus each religion has its own merits. Our religions must always unite Kazakhstanis, serving the interests of peace and harmony, helping to develop our society and economy and strengthen our state.

Number five: a transparent and accountable state. Kazakhstani society is gradually adapting to the changes that have been taking place. This is an important factor which enables us to avoid intensification of our internal disputes, and strengthen our political stability.

The past experiences of many countries show that violating the principle of "a strong state and the economy first, politics later" leads to catastrophe, and the break-up of society. In some of these countries political regimes are destroyed, while in others, we see the collapse of the economy, or the eruption of conflicts or even civil wars. We are well aware of this possibility given the history of various countries, and today we are seeing this situation before our very eyes in many states. The series of civil wars and bloody conflicts in recent times, in various parts of the world, has shown that ill-thought-through, enforced democratisation does not guarantee a state's stability and does not ensure successful economic modernisation.

The five institutional reforms are five steps which the country must take, in precisely the order I have set out. Only if this is done will our reforms be effective, and society and the state remain united and stable. This is precisely the route that all successful states have taken.

Firstly, we must expand the practice whereby the directors of state bodies make regular reports. Secondly, we must ensure transparency in decision-making. Via the mechanism of 'open governance', the citizens must actively get involved in the process of decision-making by state bodies at all levels. The basis for this will be the new law on access to public information, which we must draw up and adopt. It is important to enhance the role of the social councils attached to the state agencies and Akims. Thirdly, we must introduce civil budgeting. I am referring to the participation of representatives of civil society in the allocation of budget resources in the regions. Fourthly, we must strengthen the system for making appeals. In the legislation, we must expand citizens' powers to appeal against the actions of civil servants. Fifthly, we must ensure that self-regulation is widely introduced in society. We must gradually reduce the areas of responsibility of state bodies, transferring powers regarding the provision of socially important state services to the institutions of civil society as and when they are prepared.

If we achieve positive results in these five areas, we will be able to solve the issue of the new system for electing local executive bodies. Constitutional reform must be gradually introduced, involving the devolution of executive powers from the President, to the Parliament and Government, taking our traditions into account.

Together, these five reforms will create the necessary conditions to strengthen our statehood and help us move into the top thirty most developed countries in the world. This is our path towards implementing the 'Strategy-2050'.

Each of the five institutional reforms represents a huge challenge and a massive amount of work for our country. The success of these reforms can only be guaranteed by the firm will of the executive and the people. As experiences around the world show us, to create a strong state, and a developed and liberal society, forty to fifty years of stable progress is required. The measures proposed here will radically change the relationships in society. To ensure their implementation, I propose that a national commission on modernisation be established, under the President. This commission will coordinate the entire set of reforms. Thus our central task over the coming years is to initiate and gradually accomplish all five of these institutional reforms.

In just a few days, I have received a huge number of letters and messages from citizens, workforces, educational institutions and charities in our country expressing support for our decision to call an early election and asking me to stand as a candidate in the election. A huge thank you to all of you for being so favourable in your assessment of the work I have done for the good of Kazakhstan and the Kazakhstani people! There can be no greater reward than to enjoy such trust on the part of one's people. I am sincerely grateful to all those who have had warm things to say to me.

I hereby declare that I am willing to stand as a candidate for President on behalf of the Nur Otan party in the forthcoming elections. I call on you, my peers and fellow party members, and on all Kazakhstanis to come together once again and be victorious! Our shared spiritual strength and supreme goal is 'Mangilik El'! It will fill our progress with energy as we continue to develop in the 21st century.

Speech at the 16th Congress of the Nur Otan party
'A modern state for all: five institutional reforms'
Astana, 11th March 2015

THIRTY-EIGHT

20TH ANNIVERSARY OF THE ASSEMBLY

The 2015 Forum was dedicated to the 20th anniversary of the
Assembly of People of Kazakhstan.

It is symbolic that the forum 'My country's destiny is my own destiny' is taking place in the Akmolinsk region. Here, people with over 100 ethnic backgrounds live together in peace and harmony. There are 266 Councils for social harmony. That is more than anywhere else in the republic!

This year, within the context of the Year of the Assembly of the People of Kazakhstan, more than 500 events will take place in the Akmolinsk region. Within three years, the indicators for agricultural goods production in the region have doubled. The programme of industrial and innovative development is operating successfully. Last year alone, ten new projects were launched and KZT 17 billion was made. This year there are plans to introduce another twenty five projects to the map of industrialisation, with 2000 new jobs created.

Entrepreneurship is being developed successfully. There are 53,000 SMEs operating in the region, producing goods worth more than KZT 250 billion. The state is supporting growth in the agricultural sector, in the hope that it will yield high returns.

The region has one of the highest levels of children with access to nursery education, at around 90%. This year, another four nurseries and seven schools will be built. Eleven new healthcare facilities will be constructed.

You are well aware that the world is currently undergoing a new wave of global crisis. We must take measures to resist the problems presented by the crisis. We have everything we need to make this possible. At the sixteenth congress of the Nur Otan party, therefore, I initiated five national reforms for the development of Kazakhstan. The first of these is the formation a professional state apparatus. The second is the supremacy of the law. The third is industrialisation and economic growth. The fourth is a nation with a united future. The fifth is a transparent and accountable state.

These are new priorities which will help us overcome the negative consequences of the impact from within, strengthen the country and build a modern Kazakhstan for everyone.

The state's main task consists of ensuring that working people have jobs and a stable income, housing and confidence in the future. We are working on all key areas of the everyday needs of our citizens: a just system of law and order, security for people, an accountable state, an effective civil service, ensuring equal rights for all Kazakhstanis.

These five reforms are what the country needs and what ordinary people need. We will continue the process of industrialisation and increase labour productivity. The state will assist SMEs and farmers.

Today, a strong social policy is being implemented. We are taking care of young people, pensioners, and also everyone who is in need of state support. We will continue to build schools and hospitals and other social infrastructure.

To achieve the goals we have set, the country must preserve its commitment to the ideas of the Assembly of the People of Kazakhstan, stability, friendship, tolerance and prosperity.

In Kazakhstan, all the necessary conditions are in place for all-round development and the provision of high-quality education. Young people are now given the ability to store knowledge which will stay with them throughout their lives. If you waste time, you can never get it back – it's crucial to make proper use of it. I call on you to love our Motherland and serve it faithfully. You can do this through assiduous study, which will enable you to become professionals worthy of respect and provide for your family.

Speech at the forum of the Assembly of the People of Kazakhstan,
'The destiny of the country is my destiny'
Akmolinsk region, Kokshetau, 16ᵗʰ March 2015

THIRTY-NINE

ELECTION VICTORY

President Nursultan Nazarbayev notes the unity and solidarity of the people of Kazakhstan. He underlines that despite the global economic crisis, Kazakhstan continues to reform, with the objective of becoming one of the top thirty most developed nations in the world..

In accordance with the country's constitution, I swore my oath of allegiance to my people! Today, I uttered this oath on the eve of the most well-intentioned and joyful celebration of all – the day of the unity of the people. The power of the unity of our society has been clearly shown by the presidential election that has taken place. I am grateful to all our people!

We have shown the whole world the power of unity and fierce togetherness among people. The election that has just been held will go down in history as the biggest ever in terms of voter participation. The Kazakhstani people have placed great trust in me, by once again calling on me to serve our homeland. We have been on a complex journey together: we backed ourselves, attained independence, built our state, discovered a new Kazakhstan for the world, and found ourselves as a united and great nation. The trust you have given me has always inspired me and given me confidence in my own strength. And now I wish to say, taking responsibility for my words, that just as in previous years I will faithfully serve the people, protect the country and the prosperity of all our citizens, and defend our highest national interests.

The election on 26 April 2015 confirmed that the people of Kazakhstan are together, and are focused on the future. We are one family, and we have one homeland. The fate of each of us is wrapped up in the fate of Kazakhstan. Together, we have completed a journey from chaos to enlightenment. We have succeeded, without any excesses or cataclysms, in undergoing a complex 'triple journey': from the Soviet system to a market economy, democracy and new harmony between ethnicities. By adopting the first long-term Strategy, 'Kazakhstan-2030', we made a sure-footed start on the road toward sustainable development. Our country overcame the 'Asian crisis' of 1997-1998. And despite the challenges, we began building our new capital, Astana, the pride of all Kazakhstanis.

The effectiveness of our state-building process was proved by how we successfully overcame the global economic crisis of 2007-2009. Unlike other states, Kazakhstan maintained its economic growth and did not experience a fall in the living standards of our citizens. By 2012, Kazakhstan had made it into the top fifty most competitive economies in the world. We have become a country with a medium-sized level of income among the population. We are among the fifty biggest economies in the world. The 'Kazakhstan 2030' Strategy worked. The key objectives which I set in 1997 were completed in just fifteen years.

I have identified the important landmarks which give us a clear idea about the price of our statehood. The older generation remembers all this very well. But the younger generations must also understand and remember the price that was paid for the prosperity currently enjoyed by the country. It was during those difficult years that the best character traits of our people made themselves known: a constructive approach, balanced views and pragmatism. By being true to these values we will make our dream about 'Mangilik El' ('Eternal Country') a reality – and build a powerful and effective state that will last for centuries.

The Strategy-2050 has set a new, ambitious task for the nation: to become one of the top thirty most developed states in the world. At the start of the second decade, the global situation enabled us to accelerate our development. Today, however, the globalised world is developing in line with a scenario that is not ideal. Before our very eyes, all corners of the world are beset by crises and conflicts. The number of failed states, whose citizens are suffering in a state of extreme poverty or dying in military conflicts, is increasing. Instability has made its way right up to the borders of Central Asia.

Over the last two to three years, as I have looked on at the problems facing the world, I have thought about how to strengthen our beloved Kazakhstan and safeguard it, and avoid being knocked off course as we seek to join the thirty most successful countries in the world. I have discussed the situation with the leaders of other states. I wish to warn the nation, fully aware of the responsibility I must take for my words. Our further development continues to be threatened by five new external challenges.

Number one. The crisis in the world order and the rise in general uncertainty. The world security system is enduring a test of strength caused by a new type of conflict. New players from outside the system are appearing in the global arena, using extremism and violence.

The second challenge is the continuing turbulence in the world economy. The sanctions and the 'currency' and trade wars are exacerbating these problems in all countries.

Number three. The process of climate change is currently leading to unpredictable consequences and disasters of various kinds.

Number four. Central Asia could be affected by new fault lines around the world, which will also represent a challenge to the entire region.

Challenge number five: the crisis in the world order and instability in the world economy are putting international coordination efforts in the battle against these challenges in doubt.

In response to the turbulence in the world economy, we drew up a new economic policy, 'Nurly Zhol' ('Bright Path'). It contains bold and rapid actions with the main goal of creating new jobs and shoring up the foundations for economic growth. It is important to realise, however, that the external threats are growing. In order to cope with these external threats, we must become stronger from within. It is a huge mistake to think that the outstanding successes and prosperity we have achieved over the years are not subject to change.

As I see it, there are five large-scale internal challenges facing the country. Firstly, we must increase the size of the middle class, as a mainstay of our stability, develop business and help the country become a state in which the vast majority of people are on middle incomes. Secondly, we are a huge country. We must therefore develop a unified internal market and have balanced development in all the regions. Thirdly, the battle against corruption is one of the key priorities in our work. Number four, we must create new jobs; to this end our industrialisation programme is being implemented and we are developing the business sector. Number five, we must strengthen unity in our nation in this new phase of our history. All these things are the challenges facing our state in the 21st century.

This period of global change means that each state faces a choice: either reform or degradation. Only those who are able to renew themselves, by introducing reforms, will survive this era of change unscathed. We face an epic task of fundamental importance: ensuring our ship of state is unsinkable. Our task in the years to come is: to strengthen Kazakhstan, and, in spite of this period of global storms, steadily rise to become one of the thirty leading states in the future.

I put forward five institutional reforms which formed my campaign platform. I see the result of the election on 26th April as a direct mandate from the people to bring in these reforms immediately. And I intend to show all of my will and determination, and focus the whole of the state apparatus and consolidate society's efforts into seeing these reforms through. In the very near future, a national commission on modernisation, under the President of the country, will be established. Its mission will be to manage the gradual introduction of the five reforms and coordinate activities of the state bodies, the business sector and civil society.

Operating in conjunction with the national commission will be the international consultation board, whose members will include respected foreign and Kazakhstani experts. This will enable us to make use of the best possible international experience. At the first meeting of the commission, I will present the National Plan – '100 specific steps for further state-building', which will explain what we intend to do in connection with the five reforms. '100 steps' is our response to the global and domestic challenges, and at the same time it is also a plan that will help us become one of the top thirty most developed states in the new historical conditions. Introducing the reforms is a top-priority national task over the next ten to fifteen years.

I decided to call the plan of reforms 'the national plan' because the reforms require the direct participation of every single Kazakhstani citizen. Reforms are a matter for the people, not just for the state machine. The essence of the reforms is the modernisation of the nation. The quality of the nation, the strength of spirit of the nation, its ability to accept the challenges of our times and keep moving forwards, are precisely the things that have been, and will continue to be, decisive in determining the success of our state.

As I see it, there is a strict order in which the reforms must be carried out.

Number one. The forthcoming reforms to the civil service system will create a transparent and effective model, whereby civil servants will respect the rights of citizens and serve their legal interests. Our civil service will become a prototype for a just Kazakhstani society, in which all citizens, without exception, are given equal opportunities for self-fulfilment based on meritocratic principles.

Number two. Reform of our legal system, to make it completely impartial. A fair and just court will be available to investors and the business community. The right to own private property will be inviolable. An investment judiciary and an international arbitration centre based on the example of the best international practices must make the business climate in the country among the most attractive in the world.

Number three. The term 'Kazakhstan's economic miracle' is already in common parlance. We have indeed achieved a huge amount in a short space of time. Today, Kazkahstan is an economic leader in Central Asia. But we mustn't stop at that. The reforms will make our national economy an advanced one, founded on knowledge. The key task is to improve the lives of Kazkhs. It is of fundamental importance that we create a large middle class. In order to provide economic growth founded on industrialisation, we will bring in radical structural reforms. Education and healthcare will be brought in line with the standards of the member states of the OECD (Organisation for Economic Co-operation and Development). In order to diversify our economy we will bring in multinational companies in the manufacturing sector, thereby ensuring that Kazakhstan is able to access the global market. Our country will become a transport and logistics centre in Eurasia. Using the high-tech infrastructure created for the 'EXPO-2017', the 'Astana' financial centre will be created, with a special status.

Number four. The diversity in our society is a strength, not a weakness.

All our citizens must enjoy the same number of rights, bear the same burden of responsibility and have access to equal opportunities. Our society has historically been formed from a multitude of languages and cultures, thereby becoming stronger and more united. Today, we are united by the values of 'Mangilik El': civil equality, hard work, honesty, the cult of learning, tolerance, honesty, loyalty and patriotism. And these are not mere empty words. Our ancestors used to say: "If you are looking one year ahead, grow some grain; if you are looking a hundred years ahead, plant a tree; if you are looking into all eternity – educate Man". The values of 'Mangilik El' are serving to inform our future prosperity. And we must continue to strengthen our shared civil identity for the sake of our country's unity and togetherness.

Number five. The reforms will make the work of the civil apparatus transparent and accountable to the citizens. The state must become compact and more powers must be delegated to the private sector. The plan of reforms which I am giving to the nation will enable us, firstly, to provide our citizens with security in a troubled world, and secondly, to introduce inclusive, all-encompassing modernisation.

In the first few years after obtaining independence we built the foundations for a sovereign state. This was the first stage in our process of state-building. Thereafter, once we became stronger, we set out a path towards becoming a fully-fledged state. That was the second stage. Now, as we launch these great reforms, we are laying a path towards 'Mangilik El'. This will be the third stage of our process of state-building.

The successful fulfilment of 'the national plan' demands a favourable international climate. We will continue to cooperate with our strategic partners: Russia, China, the USA, the EU and the Muslim world. We will work actively in international organisations. As a leader in Central Asia, Kazakhstan will support the shared architecture for security and the economic development in our region. We will have special ties with our closest partners in the Eurasian Economic Union – Russia, Belarus, Kyrgyzstan and Armenia. Kazakhstani diplomacy will step up its efforts to achieve peaceful resolutions to acute regional conflicts in the Muslim world and in the former Soviet bloc.

We currently face a series of new challenges. Our response is to strengthen our state and modernise the nation. As the wise Kazakhstani saying puts it: *"Asu bermes askar zhok"* (*"no peak is inaccessible"*). Kazakhstan's journey has brought our nation together, giving us a single goal and a common dream. The election showed that each Kazakhstani citizen is aware of the debt he owes to himself and to the country. And this is the source of my confidence in the success of the reforms, and in the success of my people and the state. I call on the nation to play as broad a role as possible in the reforms I have announced. The word 'Republic' comes from the Latin term 'Res publica', which translates literally as 'The common matter'. The modernisation of Kazakhstan is well and truly our common interest. Whatever challenges might lie ahead, we will cope with them, relying on the strength of our state and the wisdom of the people.

At this triumphal moment, I would like to pass on a few words from a prize-winning essay by a fifth-former at the school and lycee No. 7, from Aktau, Karina Danilova, which touched me to the very bottom of my soul: *"I would really like it if I could always live in a prosperous and peaceful country,"* she wrote. *"If we never had any wars, such as there were in Chechnya or Tadjikistan, from where my great-grandmother and great-grandfather – veterans of the Second World War – were forced to flee."* A peaceful sky above our heads: that is the most important thing for us all.

We, a nation that has come of age, are making a decisive step into a new era. May the eternal land of Kazakhstan ever be blessed! May our united nation ever be strong!

Speech made by the Leader of the Nation, Nursultan Nazarbayev at the ceremony inaugurating him as the President of the Republic of Kazakhstan Astana, 29th April 2015

FORTY

NEW WORLD ORDER

Nursultan Nazerbayev underlines the key global challenges which threaten the future of humanity. He proposes the creation of a unified Eurasian economic zone to help provide direction for the entire continent. The meeting, entitled 'Infrastructure – the driver of sustainable economic growth', was attended by some 3,000 business and government leaders, and other specialists, from over 90 countries.

Welcome to the latest edition of the Astana Economic Forum, which has today brought together leading politicians, economists, representatives of the business community and academia, international organisations and representatives of the media. Thank you. Welcome to Kazakhstan!

The AEF came into being as a response to the global financial and economic crisis of 2008. It was a crisis that affected 80% of the world's economy. And for seven years now, the economy has been unable to return to full health and regain the rates of growth it enjoyed in the past. Some fundamental problems remain, such as the high level of unemployment and the growing levels of debt. Many experts are currently talking about a gradual recovery, but the signs of growth are fragmented. And many countries still find themselves unable to escape the stagnation into which they sank. Other economists suggest that the global crisis of 2008 was a systemic one, that it was acyclical and that it will only end when the key cause of it – the deep inequality that had gradually been formed – is addressed; first and foremost, in the currency and trade markets. These economists believe that what most people took to be turbulence is in fact a hidden, latent characteristic of the next stage of the global crisis. And it is already moving from the financial sector into currency wars, economic wars in the form of illegal sanctions and socio-political wars which have shaken many countries throughout the world. It is this that has led to a growing stand-off between East and West, with Russia and China on the one hand,

and the US and NATO on the other.

What if, in the short-term, the global crisis moves from its latent phase to an open phase, in the form of a hyper-crisis? An answer to this question could be given by economic science, or global academic thought. This is precisely why we hold forums every year, including our Astana Economic Forum. And we work alongside the leading representatives of global academic thought to find a way in which to safeguard our countries and peoples from the looming threat of disaster. In order to expand the search for such responses, we created the worldwide network of experts and analysts, G-Global. Yet it would appear that this was not sufficient.

Today, the following challenges are taking shape and growing on a global scale, posing major threats to our future. First of all, the fragmentation of the world order. We are witnessing the break-up of the former checks and balances around the world, a loss of trust between the leaders of great states and the corrosion of international law. The international institutes cannot guarantee peace and stability. Secondly, there are the 'natural' factors: climate change and pandemics. Climate change is taking place more quickly than expected. This is seen in the acute nature of the consequences of natural disasters. Number three. The shortage in foodstuffs is continuing to grow. Under pressure from three parallel processes – growth in population, income and urbanisation, a doubling of the amount of food production will be required in the next thirty years. And this needs to be done at a time when the Earth's resources are wearing thin.

Kazakhstan is attempting to respond to these challenges in all possible ways. Speaking out for peace and stability in the region, we were the first to reject nuclear weapons, decisively and voluntarily. We are consistently seeking to strengthen relations with our partner countries, and are active members of the OSCE (Organisation for Security and Co-operation in Europe); we also initiated CICA (Conference on Interaction and Confidence Building Measures in Asia).

As a country of many different creeds and faiths, we are promoting tolerance and harmony between ethnicities. Congresses for the leaders of world religions are regularly held in Astana. Kazakhstan was the first CIS country to be recognised as a state with a market economy. Over the years since we became independent we have created a new economy almost from scratch. The country's GDP has risen twenty four-fold, and GDP per capita has reached USD 13,000, the level seen in countries with medium-sized income among the population. We have achieved most of the goals for development in the millennium set by the UN, reduced poverty twenty fold, from 60% to 2.9%, and built hundreds of schools and hospitals. Our country has become the leader in the CIS for attracting direct foreign investment – more than USD 200 billion. In just fifteen years, a new capital, Astana, was built on the naked steppes. The city has become the pride of all Kazakhstanis and the driver of growth in the nation's economy.

Here in Kazkahstan, we too are looking for answers to global problems. This is why we drew up the strategic programmes 'Kazakhstan-2030' and 'Kazakhstan-2050'. My articles, 'The keys to the crisis' and 'The fifth way' were dedicated to this subject. Our practical response to the crisis in the world economy was an all-encompassing state programme of industrial and innovative development and the programme 'Nurly Zhol' ('Bright Path') – Five steps towards the future. Our programme, 'Nurly Zhol', was aimed at securing Kazakhstan's place among the world's top fifty states which are leaders in terms of the quality of the infrastructure.

Kazakhstan is the ninth largest country in terms of area in the world. The construction of infrastructure requires large amounts of investment, but has a significance that lasts for centuries, as the legacy for future generations. In the next three years alone, USD 14 billion will be spent on the construction of new roads, electricity networks and communications. More than a third of this sum will come from our partners in international financial institutions. We will build a network of roads based on the beam principle, fanning out from the capital to the regions, and build railways, bridges, power lines, schools, hospitals, utilities facilities and housing. This will enable us to achieve balanced development in all regions, reducing the imbalance between them, both in terms of economic development and the socio-demographic situation.

The implementation of the 'Nurly Zhol' programme will enable us to achieve a number of significant outcomes. By 2019, we will cut the time it takes to move between our major cities, providing a route into our neighbouring countries. A unified energy system will be created, meeting all our electricity needs. At the same time, the programme will create half a million new jobs. The same thing happened in the USA and in South Korea. As a result of our industrial and innovative programme, and of 'Nurly Zhol', a new economy will be built in the country, along with a new infrastructural framework.

Our country has set itself some ambitious goals. Yet I am confident that they will be achieved. We realise that to achieve sustainable growth and move Kazakhstan into the category of developed states, we need deeper reforms, which will improve the institutional environment. To this end, I put forward five areas for reform in my campaign manifesto. These were: perfecting the system of state governance, ensuring the rule of law, stimulating economic growth, strengthening Kazakhstani identity and, lastly, increasing transparency and accountability in the state. In order to implement these reforms, a plan has already been adopted and published, outlining 100 specific steps that are to be taken and entitled 'A modern state for all'. As part of our reforms, leading-edge structures will be introduced and we will push forward the standards for state governance as seen in the most developed countries. To this end we signed a country-specific programme with the OECD.

In addition to this, I have signed a directive to create an international financial centre, 'Astana', at the forum that will be provided by the 'EXPO-2017' exhibition. We have held talks with representatives of the Dubai centre and agreed that we will embed their practices into Kazakhstan. Thus, our centre will be founded on principles of English law, with a system of tax breaks and an independent financial court. We are confident that the 'Astana' financial centre will become the core of Kazakhstan's financial infrastructure, and that in the future it will also be a financial hub for the whole of the Central Asian region. Meanwhile Almaty, where most of Kazakhstan's financial institutes are located, will continue to be a focal point for financial services and financial agencies within the country. All these measures are designed to ensure that we enjoy sustainable development in the long-term.

Investment in infrastructure is at the top of the economic agenda for many countries, regardless of their development. Great hopes have been placed on the Asian Infrastructure Investment Bank. More than fifty countries, including countries in Western Europe, have expressed a desire to take part in the Bank's activities. Kazakhstan has become one of the first founder members of this project.

The existing sea trade routes cannot satisfy the growing demands of international trade. The volume of trade between China and the EU already amounts to almost USD 600 billion and, according to forecasts, will rise to USD 800 billion by 2020. The development of the route to Europe over dry land is therefore of huge significance to a growing Asia. It is here that we see some new opportunities for ourselves.

Of particular importance is the initiative by the Chinese Premier, 'An economic belt for the Silk Road', which was first announced in Astana. We were among the first to back this initiative and we are already contributing to it. Our first major project is the construction of the Kazakhstan section of the arterial route 'Western Europe – Western China', which is 2,700 km long. Work on this route will be completed this year. It is anticipated that the flow of goods along the Kazakhstan section will amount to 30 million tonnes a year. The route will not only link China, Kazakhstan, Russia and Europe. Other countries in Central Asia will also have access to it: Kyrgyzstan, Uzbekistan, Tajikistan.

At the same time, we are constructing railways and new logistical capabilities. We recently opened a Kazakhstani port in the Yellow Sea, Lianyungang. Shipments of containers to this terminal have already begun. It provides a direct route out of Europe via Russia and Central Europe to the Asia-Pacific region and back by rail. In the first year of its operations, the amount of cargo sent from China to Europe rose by 80%. These were cargoes from eastern and central parts of China. Construction work has been completed on the railway from Zhezkazgan to Beineu, which connects China to the Caspian Sea ports via Kazakhstan. This makes it possible for goods to be transported through Kazakhstan, the Caucasus and Europe. This same railway line has been connected to the existing route from Kazakhstan to Turkmenistan to Iran, and on to the Persian Gulf port of Banderabas. This will enable us to access the West coast of India and the south of Pakistan. This road gives us access to the Middle East for our goods and products. This year, Kazakhstan could see a five fold increase in the amount of grain it supplies to Iran alone. The volume of cargo transported along this route will reach 10 million tonnes over the next ten years.

All these projects are aimed at increasing transit potential, both in our country and in the entire Eurasian Economic Union. This will be the new Silk Road. Forty countries have expressed an interest in free trade with the EEU. We must not stop at that, however. I am proposing that we create a new high-speed, multi-modal transport route, the 'Eurasian transcontinental corridor'. This route will stretch right across the territory of our country and enable us to provide unimpeded transit of goods from Asia to Europe and back. This will be a considerably shorter distance than going via the ocean. This transport artery will give a huge boost to the development of manufacturing.

Our joint initiatives in the field of transport are an excellent platform for cooperation. This platform must become the start of deep forms of cooperation and integration between countries and also between regional associations. I propose that a United Eurasian Economic area be created. It is important that we adopt unified rules which will take into account the national interests of all member states and at the same time be aimed at removing barriers and increasing mutually beneficial integration. The rules must concern, first and foremost, trade, transportation and the movement of resources. The creation of an economic belt around the Silk Road is something that, in essence, incorporates this principle. Within the context of the United Eurasian area we must create an ongoing forum, at which proposals will be drawn up and discussed as to the future areas of development for the continent, and promoting greater integration between its members. The Astana Economic Forum could become just such a platform.

I am sure that the outcomes of the work done by this Forum, and other new ideas, projects and initiatives, will enable us to increase the prosperity of all the citizens of the states in the region. They will create the conditions that will guarantee economic, political and social stability and predictability. We must strive to ensure that every state in our continent becomes part of the new flourishing of Eurasia, which will have a positive impact for the good of the whole world.

Speech made by the President of Kazakhstan, Nursultan Nazarbayev, at the eighth Astana Economic Forum Astana, 22nd May 2015

FORTY-ONE

PEACE AND HARMONY

Nursultan Nazerbayev underlines that since independence, Kazakhstan has created a successful model of inter-faith co-existence. He notes that there are 3,312 mosques, churches, chapels, synagogues and other places of worship in Kazakhstan. Nursultan Nazarbayev emphasises the importance of inclusive dialogue to develop a new security paradigm based on equality, mutual respect, cooperation, tolerance and understanding.

If something happens in the world on a one-off basis, it is usually seen as an historical accident. If it happens two or three times, it starts to be viewed as a developing pattern. But if it happens more frequently than that, then it becomes a great story! Astana is delighted to welcome the delegates and guests of the Congress for the leaders of global and traditional religions for the fifth time!

As we gather together beneath the dome of the only Palace of Peace and Harmony in the world, which was built following a decision at the first Congress, we are creating a great story of tolerance and global dialogue between cultures and religions. We are writing that story, one page after another, even in these complicated times. And all of us – politicians and religious ministers alike – are united by a single, shared sense of responsibility for the fate of people and nations, and for peace and tranquillity throughout the whole of our unique planet, created by the Almighty.

For the first time ever, the Secretary General of the UN, Mr Ban Ki-Moon, is attending our Congress. I extend a heartfelt welcome to you, Mr Secretary General! Your presence here underlines the importance that the entire world community places on dialogue between spiritual leaders in Astana.

The noble ideas put forward by the Congress of world and traditional religions have received widespread support from the global community, in both religious and political circles. These ideas give the world a chance to overcome the stereotypes which have become entrenched over the centuries regarding relations between religions, and provide an effective formula for global tolerance and mutual understanding in the 21ˢᵗ century. I am sure that the work done by the Fifth Congress for the leaders of world and traditional religions will help to make an important step towards this goal.

The central issue facing the Fifth Congress concerns the important role and responsibility of religious and political leaders for the safe and harmonious development of the modern world. In the 21ˢᵗ century, the world continues to be a place in which the majority are deeply religious.

According to data from a Gallup poll in a recent report on the global barometer of hope and despair, more than half the population of the planet – around 60% – see themselves as religious people. One in five people profess themselves not to be religious.

The phenomenon whereby religious teachings maintain their durability and retain their impact in an era of technological revolution was explained very precisely by the Italian author Cesare Pavese in the 20ᵗʰ century. "Religion," he wrote, "is the conviction that everything that happens to us is unusually important. For this reason, it will always exist." But does this mean that mankind's development will inevitably be accompanied by religious disputes, enmity, conflicts and wars between different faiths? I don't agree that this should be so.

Firstly, as Mahatma Gandhi once said, "God has no religion." In the 19ᵗʰ century, the Orthodox philosopher, Metropolitan Platon Gorodetsky, wrote the following: "The walls of our churches do not rise as high as Heaven." Throughout their thousand-year history, theological discussions have remained nothing more than verbal disputes, until politicians turn them into wars and conflicts.

Secondly, all the world's religions call for restraint and patience, non-violence and harmony. The Holy Koran contains the following words: "If anyone should kill one man, this shall be tantamount to the murder of the whole of Mankind." The New Testament in the Christian religion tells us: "Take care to do good before all people...Be at peace with all people." These words from one of the ancient Hindu texts, the Upanashads, call on people to take responsibility for their actions: "When a blade of grass is cut down, the whole Universe winces." The only true faith is that which prompts people towards love, compassion and kindness. This truth is eternal and everlasting.

Thirdly, modern history contains several examples of societies which are tolerant towards religion. Here in Kazakhstan, for example, we have created a successful model for the coexistence of eighteen different faiths, living in peace, harmony and mutual understanding with one another. Our laws on religious associations are founded on the principle of equality and freedom of conscience. In nearly a quarter of a century since we achieved Independence, Kazakhstan has lived through an era of the rebirth of spirituality. In Soviet times, in Kazakhstan as elsewhere, atheism was the official state policy. But our people never lost their faith in God. There are now 3312 mosques, temples, prayer houses, synagogues and other religious facilities in the country. We have forty seven religious publications regularly appearing in our country and have almost 500 foreign missionaries in our country. The key dates in the Islamic and Christian calendars are celebrations which are shared by all Kazakhstanis. The congregations of all the religions that have a presence in our country are all members of the great family of Kazakhstan. Together, we are creating a new country, in which there is no place for discord and infighting.

We are all united by a common goal: to build a flourishing state which, by the middle of the 21st century, will be among the thirty most developed nations in the world. We have set ourselves the goal of ensuring that all Kazakhstanis become a nation with a common future. The main foundation of this future is civil equality and tolerance, openness and law and order, unity of thought and unity in our practical undertakings to create decent living standards for every citizen. Its centuries-old significance is based on the values of peace and harmony being passed down from one generation to the next and from one epoch to the next.

This year, we are celebrating the twentieth anniversary of a unique organisation – the Assembly of the People of Kazakhstan. It has become a fundamental value and dependable mechanism for promoting harmony and tolerance among all citizens, of all creeds and faiths. We have shown the whole world that conflicts between religions and cultures are avoidable, even within the limits of one society. Conflicts can therefore be avoided at any other level of international politics as well. We have demonstrated that tolerant relations within society must be recognised as the responsibility of the state, religious associations, and ordinary citizens. The fact that Congresses for the leaders of world and traditional religions have been held in Astana serves as global acknowledgement of the success of our way of doing things.

The distinctive feature of our forum is that we discuss matters concerning mutual relations between religious and cultures, from the perspective of peace and stability on the planet. The relevance of such discussions is made stronger by the worrying course of events. Currently, the world is suspended in a state of dangerous uncertainty.

Firstly, there has been a drastic weakening of the global security regime. And this process, it would appear, has not yet reached its nadir. The international system of checks and balances is not functioning. It is regrettable that the atmosphere of trust between the leading states which was established in the decades following the Second World War has been lost. The pressure exerted through mutual sanctions is further complicating the situation in the global economy. It has only made the chances of overcoming the after-effects of the recent global economic crisis that much more remote. This distrust is having a negative effect not only on economic relations between countries and peoples, but also on humanitarian relations. Tourism between nations is decreasing, along with the level of cultural exchange, and cyber attacks are being made by some countries against others. This is a result of instability, distrust, and localised wars and confrontations.

Secondly, the number of military and domestic conflicts around the world has risen sharply. The conflict in Eastern Ukraine has significantly reduced the level of security in Europe and across the globe. An entire region, from West Africa to Afghanistan is in the grip of armed conflict.

Thirdly, the threat of international terrorism has increased due to the so-called 'Islamic State'. Using its global recruiting network, young people from various countries around the world have joined its ranks. Under cover of pseudo-religious calls to arms, its fighters have carried out shocking mass executions of followers of other religions, journalists and volunteers. I believe that we must join forces and underline our shared view that we are opposed to such an approach, and against the use of religion as a front for such atrocities. They are deliberately destroying a centuries-old cultural legacy in Iraq and Syria. There can be no other way of describing this activity than as crimes against humanity.

Fourthly, the number of people suffering from destitution or famine in the modern world has not diminished. At present, according to UN data, there are some 700 million children and teenagers living below the poverty line. There are 150 million abandoned children. 100 million children cannot get an education due to the lack of schools. 10 million children are suffering from a lack of medicine. There you have it – the initial environment that breeds social disorder, and which later leads to crime, social hatred, terrorism and extremism.

Fifthly, one would have to be blind not to see the global problem of diminishing spiritual and moral values. Via the media and online social networks, foul-mouthed sneers and jeers against people's spiritual beliefs are published, along with criminal examples of amoral behaviour and an 'anything goes' attitude, and vulgar examples of so-called 'mass culture'. The flows of so-called 'pseudo-culture' are leaving particularly painful wounds in the vulnerable souls of young people, undermining family traditions and destroying the ties that bind the generations together. All of these things represent critical challenges to the modern world order, security, and the spiritual mainstays and values of civilisation.

Today, it is important that we establish a wide-ranging debate on how to draw up a new paradigm for security and development. At its heart must be principles of equality, mutual respect, the acknowledgement of one another's interests, cooperation, tolerance and mutual understanding. In the 21st century, there is simply no alternative to dialogue in all areas – whether political, economic, cultural or spiritual. Today, mankind has at its disposal huge material, scientific and technical, and intellectual capabilities. There will be no progress unless people learn to live in peace and spiritual harmony with one another. Mankind is designed in such a way that the ethnic, linguistic, religious and cultural differences between us will always be there, for as far as it is possible to see into the future. Yet these must not be differences that divide us, but rather a unifying foundation.

I agree entirely with Pope Francis, who has said: *"That which unites us is much greater than that which divides us."* I am certain that conflicts between different ethnicities and faiths are born of incorrect policies. It is a policy that is fatal for countries, people and societies. Even today, we can see this in various parts of the world. But a far more long-lasting phenomenon has always been, and remains, mutual attraction between peoples, mutual knowledge of languages, cultures and the spiritual world, the development of trade ties and good neighbourly relations. This trend for amicable relations between peoples has become particularly strong in the 21st century, under the influence of globalisation. The spiritual and political focus can make mankind's world more morally acceptable and more tolerant.

The Fifth Congress of world and traditional religions must now adopt its closing declaration. I propose that it include a number of important appeals which reflect the pain and hope experienced by billions of people all over the world.

Number one. All military conflicts must be stopped and a truce declared. All parties involved in conflict must sit round the negotiating table and thrash out agreements on the cessation of violence, the protection of innocent civilians and a peaceful resolution to all conflicts.

Number two. In all countries and interstate relations, the resolution of political differences by armed force must be rejected once and for all.

Number three. It is important to call on political leaders of all the leading states to halt the growing gulf of mistrust in the modern world. We must bring to an end the sanctions against one another, which have caused more harm to the 'third world' and ordinary people than anyone else. It is important that we warn the world about the danger of resurrecting Cold War stereotypes, particularly any kind of 'bloc'-based mentality. Today, we must use all mechanisms within the UN and other international security structures to regulate differences and bring wars and conflicts to an end.

Number four. We must call on everyone to see reason and stop the use of the media, including the internet as a medium to incite inter-faith hatred between people. In this context, we must enhance the moral accountability of media owners and publishers, and all those who would describe themselves as part of the 'fourth estate'.

Number five. It is vitally important that states and societies join forces to tackle the problems of poverty, famine, epidemics, unemployment, and the battle against the aftermath of natural disasters and man-made disasters. This must form part of the new architecture for a secure and harmonious world.

The events of the modern era mean that our Congresses for the leaders of world and traditional religions are a crucial element of global 'spiritual diplomacy'. I call on the heads of all delegations to pass on, to the ministers and all those who adhere to your religions, the call to increase inter-faith dialogue. I call on all politicians and public figures to use their influence and abilities to bring an end to wars and conflicts and restore confidence in global politics.

Speech by the President of the Republic of Kazakhstan, Nursultan Nazarbayev, at the opening of the Fifth Congress for the Leaders of World and Traditional Religions Astana, 10ᵗʰ June 2015

INDEX